The Livable City

Revitalizing Urban Communities

The Livable City

Revitalizing Urban Communities

Partners for Livable Communities

McGraw-Hill, Inc.

New York   St. Louis   San Francisco   Auckland   Bogotá
Caracas   Lisbon   London   Madrid   Mexico   Milan
Montreal   New Delhi   Paris   San Juan   São Paulo
Singapore   Sydney   Tokyo   Toronto

McGraw-Hill

A Division of The McGraw·Hill Companies

1 2 3 4 5 6 7 8 9 0 K G P / K G P   0 6 5 4 3 2 1 0
ISBN 0-07-135913-3

The sponsoring editor for this book was Wendy Lochner.

Printed and bound by Quebecor/Kingsport. This book was printed and bound on acid-free paper.

McGraw-Hill books are available at special quantity discounts to use as premiums and sales promotions, or for use in corporate training programs. For more information, please write to Director of Special Sales, Professional Publishing, McGraw-Hill, Two Penn Plaza, New York, NY 10121-2298 or contact your local bookstore.

Partners for Livable Communities is a nonprofit organization working to improve the livability of communities by promoting quality of life, economic development, and social equity. Since its founding in 1977, Partners has helped communities set a common vision for the future, discover and use new resources for community and economic development, and build public/private coalitions to further their goals.

Partners for Livable Communities
1429 21st Street, N.W.
Washington, D.C. 20036
202.887.5990
202.466.4845 fax
partners@livable.com
www.livable.com

The editor for this book was Paula Park, and the production editor was Penelope Cuff. It was designed by The Watermark Design Office.

Contents

Acknowledgements

I would like to thank the many individuals who contributed to this report. First and foremost is Paula Park who served as editor as well as writer. Other writers and contributors who gave us their expertise include Bill Fulton and his team of Jonathan Walters, Morris Newman, John Krist, and Alicia Harrison; Bruce Katz and Jennifer Bradley; and Bonnie Cain, Libby Howland, and Donald Garfield. I am also indebted to Sue Coppa of Partners' staff who researched and wrote best practices along with her associates, Meg Cederoth and Rachel Kelson. Hannah Roberts was particularly helpful with proof reading and suggestions. Ching Han Wong collected the majority of background materials on the best practices, and Sara McKernnan contributed to the photo research. Other members of Partners' staff who have contributed to this work include John Bledsoe and Syeeda Hughes.

I also want to remember staff members Phil Walsh, Kathy Booth, Nick Pierpan, Chris Benner, and Liam O'Connor who helped us get the Community Futures and Quality of Life Initiative up and keep it running. This work in twenty communities, from 1995 through 1999, provided the working relationship to examine the issue of livability in America.

Many individuals and organizations gave generous support to Partners, particularly Mary Fenelon, Vickie Tassan, the Fannie Mae Foundation, Bank of America, and McGraw-Hill. In addition, individuals in livable cities across the country shared photographs and contributed their time through interviews. Lynne Komai of Watermark is the creative spirit behind the design of this book. And most certainly this book would never have been produced without the leadership of Penelope Cuff, senior program officer, and Ruth Kelliher, executive vice president, at Partners.

Robert McNulty

Contributing Writers

The following individuals were members of the writing team who crafted this report.

Robert H. McNulty is founder and president of Partners for Livable Communities. He has been a frequent writer, editor, and lecturer on urban strategies over the past twenty years. Among his titles are *Return of the Livable City, Entrepreneurial American City,* and *Economics of Amenity: Community Futures and Quality of Life.* He has also written for the *Washington Post, Atlanta Magazine,* and the *Christian Science Monitor.*

Paula Park has written on urban planning, education, justice, and growth and development issues as well as the environment for *The Sarasota Herald Tribune,* the *Miami Daily Business Review,* and *Miami News Time*s. A former editor at Brookings Institution, she has been an adjunct instructor at the Columbia University Graduate School of Journalism and School of International Public Affairs.

William Fulton is editor and publisher of *California Planning & Development Report* and economic development columnist for *Governing* magazine. Trained as both a journalist and an urban planner, Mr. Fulton has written three books, including *The Reluctant Metropolis: The Politics of Urban Growth in Los Angeles,* which was a *Los Angeles Times* best-seller.

Jennifer Bradley is a senior communications analyst on policy, strategy, and communications for the Center on Urban and Metropolitan Policy at Brookings Institution. Before joining Brookings, she was a journalist for *Role Call* newspaper and *The New Republic Magazine.* She has also written for *The American Prospect,* the *Los Angeles Times Book Review* and *The Atlantic Monthly.*

Bonnie Cain is president of the Bulletin Board Corporation, an editing and publishing enterprise. She also publishes *City Desk,* a community newspaper and Web site, and has managed teams of consultants working in adult literacy, project management and evaluation, and human resource development in Latin America and Africa. She has also written for the *Washington Post* and *Washington City Paper.*

Donald Garfield is a freelance writer, editor, and tourism/community development consultant. With advanced degrees in classical Greek and art history, he taught art history at the University of Arizona, before becoming senior editor of *Museum News,* the magazine of the American Association of Museums. He has published a number of articles and reports on cultural tourism and community development for Partners for Livable Communities, the World Bank's *Urban Age* magazine, and AAM.

Alicia Harrison is a research associate at *California Planning & Development Report.* She holds a master's degree in urban planning from the University of California, Irvine, and a bachelor's degree in geography and environmental studies from the University of California, Santa Barbara. She previously worked for Santa Barbara County and EDAW Inc.

Libby Howland is a writer and editor specializing in urban issues and real estate development. For many years she was the editor of *Urban Land* magazine, a monthly publication of the Urban Land Institute, a nonprofit research and education association concerned with land use and development issues.

Bruce Katz is a senior fellow at the Brookings Institution and director of its Center on Urban and Metropolitan Policy. His expertise includes urban policy, community reinvestment, government reform, and social policy. His many articles and papers include "Divided We Sprawl," with Jennifer Bradley for *The Atlantic Monthly.*

John Krist is the assistant opinion-editorial editor of the *Ventura County Star* in California. His weekly essays on environmental and land-use issues are distributed throughout the West, and he is the author of three books on national parks and wilderness areas in California. As the recipient of the Society of Professional Journalists' 1997 Eugene C. Pulliam Editorial Writing Fellowship, he wrote "Seeking Common Ground," a national report on alternatives to confrontation in the struggle to balance economic need with environmental protection.

Morris Newman is a well-known writer on architecture, urban design, and real estate development. His work appears regularly in *The New York Times, The Los Angeles Times,* and *California Planning & Development Report.* He has also written for *Planning* and *Governing* magazines. He holds a degree in architecture from UCLA.

Jonathan Walters is a staff correspondent for *Governing* and a public policy researcher based in Albany, N.Y. In addition to his *Governing* work, he has conducted public policy research for a wide variety of institutions including the National Academy of Public Administration and the Nelson Rockefeller Institute. His most recent book is *Measuring Up: Governing's Guide to Performance Measurement for Geniuses (And Other Public Managers).*

Foreword

In the 1960s, I was a young officer at North Carolina National Bank, a Bank of America predecessor. Charlotte was either a big exciting town, or a small unremarkable city, depending on where you came from and what you wanted to believe.

We worked in the old American Commercial building on South Tryon Street. Some days around noon, my boss and I would walk across the street to a little restaurant for a sandwich and few games of pool. The district north of the square offered little. What is now the historic Fourth Ward neighborhood was a wasteland.

When we were building the Plaza offices on the square in 1970, I'd go downtown with my kids after work, and we'd watch the wrecking balls and cranes as old buildings came down and a new one went up.

Picture that. It was a fair summer evening in downtown Charlotte in 1970. The most interesting activity for a man and his family was watching a tired old building come down. The streets were so quiet you could sit on the curb with your children and not worry about getting run over.

Today, downtown Charlotte is a much different place. We have bustling activity in the Center City seven nights a week. We have sporting and cultural events. We have bars and restaurants. We have residents moving into new apartments, town homes, and condominiums. We have business people, conventioneers, and tourists.

Today, Charlotte is a better city, a better community, and a better place to live than it has been at any point in its history –and not just in the Center City. Business opportunities have fueled our economy, from the skyscrapers and townhouses downtown to the new homes and shopping centers in outlying communities like Pineville, Matthews, and Cornelius. In-fill development has transformed scores of neighborhoods in between. We have improved the quality of life and created a very special place.

The question in my mind is, can it last?

Unfortunately, the storm clouds already are on the horizon. Traffic fills our roads and highways to capacity. The quality of our air, rivers, and streams has declined considerably. We find ourselves arguing over issues like transportation, land use, zoning, tax incentives, and environmental protection.

Like cities all over the country, Charlotte has enjoyed the benefits of growth for a long time without having to be too concerned about the cumulative effects of that growth. Unfortunately, I think those days are over, as they are in cities all over the country.

As the effects of unplanned, unchecked growth spread over the American landscape, citizens across the country are debating ideas to help us create more livable communities for the future. A broad approach to this debate that my company has embraced is *Smart Growth*. In a nutshell, *Smart Growth* simply means creating balanced growth solutions that take into account all the competing needs of our communities.

Smart Growth is pro-growth. The goal is not to limit growth, but to use incentives to channel it to areas where infrastructure allows it to be sustained over the long term.

Smart Growth is about choices. Many of us enjoy living in suburbs, while others prefer to live in the city. The point of *Smart Growth* is to build livable communities in urban, suburban, and rural areas that give citizens a choice.

Smart Growth is about protecting our environment. This means protecting the environmental quality and biological diversity of our farmlands, wetlands, and open spaces. It also means finding sound ways to reuse brownfields and pursuing design innovations that make all our developments easier on the environment.

Smart Growth is about using our resources wisely. This means encouraging developers to build dense residential corridors that will make public transit viable. *Smart Growth* means working together to rebuild our inner cities, instead of using our land, a limited natural gift, as a disposable product.

Smart Growth is about regionalism. This means encouraging community and business leaders to make decisions based on a clear understanding of regional growth needs and projections.

Smart Growth is about working together. One of the fundamental tenets of *Smart Growth* is that everybody gets a seat at the table. Developers, businesspeople, public officials, environmental advocates, and ordinary citizens all have an opportunity to participate and be heard on land use and development decisions.

Smart Growth is about families and communities. It's about thinking and acting to create neighborhoods with housing, employment, schools, houses of worship, parks, services, and shopping centers located so close together our kids can ride bikes wherever they need to go, without asking us for a ride every ten minutes.

A long time ago, on a fair summer evening in Charlotte's Center City, I brought my kids downtown to sit on a curb and watch a wrecking ball and crane take down an old building.

This summer, I'll go downtown with my kids and grandkids. We'll see a play at Spirit Square and have dinner at La Vecchia's Seafood Grille. We'll divide an afternoon between Discovery Place and the library. Maybe we'll see a show at the North Carolina Blumenthal Center or a new exhibit at the Mint Museum of Craft + Design. This fall, we'll come for a football game, and we'll walk the busy streets, mingling with thousands of Charlotte residents who have made the Center City their home.

Center City Charlotte, in short, has become a livable community. Its success poses a challenge to communities across America facing unmanageable growth and sprawl. The challenge is to build communities on a human scale, in which proximity to people and shared activities creates feelings of shared ownership, trust, respect, and interdependence.

I am pleased that Bank of America has had the opportunity to take part in the creation of livable communities across our great country. I look forward to the work we'll all do together to make all our communities even better places to live.

Hugh L. McColl, Jr.
Chairman and Chief Executive Officer
Bank of America

Introduction

Anyone who tries to define the challenges confronting America's cities today and determine how well communities overcome them will be frustrated by two pervasive elements: rapid change and a growing diversity.

Demographic and social changes will test the capacity of most American cities to adapt to a new century. Communities built, organized, and operated to meet the needs of a relatively homogenous population now serve very different people. Our communities have grown more international and more economically diverse. As a result, in many significant ways, communities do not *fit* their populations. Institutions pursue outdated goals. Inappropriate services are provided, and potentially useful services are delivered ineffectively. The physical community—housing, roads, schools, recreation facilities, and water and sewer systems—may be inefficient, costly, and inadequate to serve expanding community needs. Images of a desirable quality of life remain distant from the realities of daily life.

Generalizations, however, mask tremendous differences among communities. Problems related to children, the elderly, racial minorities, health, and physical development prove important everywhere and lend themselves to national overview descriptions. Nevertheless, the problems are not identical in any two places, and the solutions, as well as a community's ability to effectively implement them, may require adapting national solutions to local conditions.

Yet, these problems—and their solutions—are national only in an abstract sense. Few people live *nationally*. They live in neighborhoods, where communities either succeed or fail to ensure most people can work, enjoy adequate health care, or retire with sufficient earnings. An effective national jobs-training program does not guarantee the availability of well-paying local jobs, for example; the absence of a national program does not condemn local communities to joblessness.

American communities represent two stories: the first involves growth, revitalization, and prosperity; the other, poverty, despair, and decline. A single community can incorporate both stories; and both are likely to be true.

Even in some communities that display general well-being, the long-standing social and economic conditions of minorities and the poor has deteriorated. The rapid expansion of wealth led by high-technology industries has often excluded the very young and the very old.

Children and the elderly now top America's list of urgent domestic concerns. Following closely are the goals of uniting the nation's multiracial and multicultural society and providing adequate and affordable housing in decent neighborhoods for all Americans.

The significance of these concerns has been well-documented. In America today, too many children are born unwanted and live in poverty. They will pay a lifelong price for poor medical care and inadequate nutrition during their early years. They live in families under strain and will likely enter school already behind their classmates, forcing them to play a game of educational catch-up that most cannot win.

At the same time, at the other end of life's journey, too many elderly lack funds to pay for satisfactory health care. They must face long terms of physically and mentally debilitating solitary confinement as their friends and close relatives die, and they can expect to be dislocated from their familiar surroundings for the final years of their life.

Characteristics of color and nationality cut across age groups. On average, minority young and old are likely to face the most severe problems and have the least promising prospects. In addition, widespread segregation of residential neighborhoods into poor and rich, minority and majority, sentences many of the most vulnerable families to lives in the most problematic neighborhoods. Despite record national growth and prosperity during the last decade, solid evidence indicates poverty has become more persistent and more highly concentrated in many of America's communities.

Partners perceives these problems not only as moral dilemmas communities are obliged to resolve, but also as economic challenges: Their resolution can help communities become stronger, attract more income-generating enterprises, and enrich the quality of life for all residents. Today's policies have not deviated from our 1994 *State of the American Community* recommendations on *local solutions to national problems*. We reaffirm our conviction that livability is people, requires place-based strategies, focuses on the family, and entails both leadership and a vision that encompasses diverse communities, diverse priorities, and diverse goals. We must think regionally and act locally to achieve quality cities. Partners also urges communities to consider new caveats and new emphases in the development strategies of the first decade of the twenty-first century.

Jobs and Community Innovation

Partners believes the creativity of our community expressed through arts and culture, design, entertainment, food, and high technology may well be the hothouse and incubator of our communities' competitive future. We applaud the European Community for exploring the *Creative City* concept and examining how downtowns can be transformed to creative industry districts by creating new building and street designs, and blending industries such as music and the arts, food, entrepreneurship, youth-development, and E-commerce. A *Creative City* can foster a new image that not only evokes excitement, but also draws capital, intelligence, and quality-of-life resources.

Partners has long recognized the importance of the quality of community life in attracting lucrative enterprises and industries. As early as 1979, the Rand Corporation concluded that in an information-based economy, "jobs increasingly follow people." Employers seek locations that attract residents.

In 1980, Partners launched its Economics of Amenity program to provide evidence of the close link between community livability and economic vitality. We urged cities to incorporate cultural facilities, parks and open space, natural and scenic resources, architecturally distinctive buildings, and preserved or restored historic areas in their planning for economic development. Thirty-seven pilot cities adopted amenity projects, including a cultural district in St. Louis, streetscape improvements in

Richmond, Virginia, and a linear park in Oakland. Partners provided these locally financed programs advice and technical assistance, information retrieval, and networking assistance—and showcased their achievements through media relations and program publications. By preserving local physical and cultural amenities, we concluded, cities can attract both people and jobs.

In the twenty years since Partners launched the Economics of Amenity program, the nation has moved from the postindustrial era into the electronic era. Partners still believes that, as we enter the new century, attracting commerce to cities will depend more than ever on the quality of our urban community life—in the new century *commerce* chiefly will mean *E-commerce*.

As corporations locate in new communities, the *capitals of our regions*—our downtowns— will increasingly be defined as interesting and diverse twenty-four-hour gathering places for exchanging ideas, culture, language, and values. These downtown *beehives* or magnets will attract people to a sense of citizenship, defined by the downtown of the central city, rather than by the commuter cities where people sleep. The quality of life of our central cities is absolutely key to fostering both citizenship and creativity.

The image of the city is the key to the entire metropolitan area. We must rediscover amenities as investments. Denver Mayor Wellington Webb, president of the U.S. Conference of Mayors, says parks and recreation, cultural amenities, and team sports build the kind of civic spirit that "allows our central cities to gain loyalty and regional investment."

Smart Growth and Communities

America has reached an era Partners could not have imagined when we wrote the *State of the American Community* in 1994. Problems of sprawl, growth management, and congestion have moved from the environmental and transportation agendas to become the common concern of private, nonprofit, and public-sector leadership. Places are increasingly being defined in a negative sense by congestion, caused by people moving to and from their homes, workplaces, schools, and entertainments. A truly amazing variety of civic organizations—the Silicon Valley Manufacturing Group, the National Trust for Historic Preservation, the Surface Transportation Policy Project, the Sierra Club, and the American Association of Retired Persons—now focus on growth management. Defining and controlling sprawl has advanced to the presidential agendas of both parties.

New Leaders and New Teams

In 1994 Partners urged communities to create teams to work together, set a vision, and move ahead. We now affirm our view that the region is the unit of the collective will and the neighborhood is the unit of action. Will refers to commitment by diverse leaders among the region's elected officials, faith communities, private businesses, philanthropies, media outlets, citizen activists, universities and colleges, and cultural institutions to foster equity-based collaboration. Our mutual interests will be good for whole communities.

Partners' view that civic achievement is the result of civic action—it is neither the government's job nor the private sector's job, but is everyone's job—stems from helping thirty-seven cities build amenities such as parks, cultural districts, and public art projects during the early eighties. The most notable accomplishments in these cities stemmed from teamwork involving government agencies; community groups; business groups; advocates for the environment; and civic, cultural, and philanthropic organizations. An entrepreneurial leadership style emphasizing action, results, innovation, and responsiveness also defined the most successful cities. Calling such teamwork and entrepreneurship the *new civics,* Partners added it to the tenets of its expanding definition of livability.

Partners' *new civics* will increase in importance with the massive transfer of wealth expected in the next decade. Philanthropies will play a wider role in American leadership. The faith community will expand exponentially in its ability to not only serve its flock on faith issues, but also to help guide the region through the broader civic agenda. The private sector, in pursuit of a quality labor force, will be innovative and imaginative in forming new coalitions. New opportunities for collaboration—stimulated and rewarded by the federal government, nurtured by state governments, and executed by city and county elected officials—will help business and religious institutions meet their overriding goal: a livable community.

New Financial Sources and New Communities

Citizens are increasingly willing to levy new local taxes to pay for projects they believe in such as open-space conservation, cultural venues, sports fields, recreational programs, and transportation projects. Increasingly, we will reach out to our citizens for investments, not levies, by asking them to identify the quality-of-life factors they consider most important and to define how to achieve those factors. We will also encourage citizens themselves to mount campaigns for funds to sponsor civic investments.

The Community Reinvestment Act has been of great value. It has been reauthorized against great opposition. Partners urges lawmakers to consider banks as part of an infrastructure that creates unique opportunities for inner-city development. When these financial institutions were forced to focus upon reporting their lending activities in central cities and with people of color, they actually discovered a potentially profitable community they had ignored for years, to their detriment. Continued improvements in the Community Reinvestment Act may help bankers view the Act as a tool for building profit rather than as an obligation to the government.

New Americans and New Communities

We highlighted, but not with sufficient depth in 1994, a multicultural America as our greatest future asset. The city of Dalton, Georgia, provides a potent example of the benefits of multiculturalism. When the leaders of the city's many carpet factories realized that a growing proportion of the labor force had emigrated from the Monterrey, Mexico region, they helped make those workers and their families feel comfortable in their new community. Some of the Mexican-American workers had lived and worked in Dalton for twenty years—and had already changed the city's cultural identity. Rather than fighting the changes, the Anglo community and its leaders embraced diversity by declaring Dalton a bilingual, multicultural region where both American and Mexican cultural values would contribute to its economic growth and quality of life. If we had more Daltons in America with more leaders like Erwin Mitchell and Robert Shaw, we would expand our ability to market multicultural workers as competitive assets in the world market. We would also expand our ability to create a livable community for all citizens.

Partners heralded the importance of our diverse communities in 1994 with its America's Most Livable Community awards to sixteen communities that managed effective strategies to improve the quality of life. The awards highlighted community commitment to programs for children, increases in real family income, reductions in poverty, and multicultural economic development. Partners' multicultural awareness has evolved since the eighties when board members began to question the definition of livability. At that time, downtown development seemed to carry more weight than human development. Design solutions trumped social issues. Large pockets of poverty and despair persisted untouched by the reinvestment and renewed vitality in the cities that Partners had lauded for livability. "Livability for whom?" asked these board members.

Partners answered with the Shaping Growth program that aimed to balance redevelopment with social equity and we used planning charettes to involve all citizens in efforts to revitalize urban economies and enhance livability.

The Shaping Growth experience convinced Partners that livability is more than a matter of physical design, more than a matter of amenities. It is a matter of essentials—safety, health, jobs, justice, and environmental concerns—that build a sense of community and of individual worth within the community. Without these essentials, amenities become frills and quality of life is an empty concept.

A second issue we noted in 1994 was the aging of our population. As baby boomers reach their mid-fifties, a large number of healthy people are moving towards social security. Increasingly, however, they are hardy enough to participate in and lead their communities' economic life. We face a unique opportunity—the elder community is changing from a lobby on retirement issues to a broad constituency on livability issues. Yet, politicians often fail to understand the importance of livability to people in their seventies, eighties or nineties.

We need to launch a national agenda of rethinking, retrofitting, and redesigning our existing cities, suburbs, and small towns so we can age in our own homes. Preserving home places for the elderly will also cut the national healthcare budget by preventing a massive migration to healthcare facilities, as boomers grow frail. Partners believes communities designed to serve the needs of youngsters, elders, and citizens with special physical and mental conditions are livable communities for everyone.

Conclusion

Livability cannot be measured in indices, benchmarks, or in the number of golf courses per 100,000 people. Partners believes livability stems from the arduous teamwork required to improve a system; that livable communities can augment economic development and benefit all segments of the resident population; and that regions—led by vibrant central cities—create livability through participatory planning. Livability encompasses attention to both places and the people who live and work in them. Livability is mobilizing change; livability is action for the good.

Robert H. McNulty
President
Partners for Livable Communities

The Twenty-First Century American City:
Impediments and Promises

New Community Design for a New Century

1

Here in the city the goods of civilization are multiplied and manifolded; here is where human experience is transformed into viable signs, symbols, patterns of conduct, systems of order; here is where the issues of civilization are focused; here, too, ritual passes on occasion into the active drama of a fully differentiated and self-conscious society.

—LEWIS MUMFORD

As the European

Union adds polish

to its concentrated

trade network,

U.S. communities

continue to squabble

for lesser turf.

Older Cities Offer Lenses for Tomorrow's Communities

The denizens of great nineteenth-century American cities would discover many surprises should they reappear today in a typical community. People drive in automobiles along wide streets and usually at high speeds. The size and scale of our retail stores, high schools, and supermarkets would amaze the residents of cramped tenements. They would marvel that most people own single-family homes, something only the wealthy could afford in 1900, and they would be surprised by the lack of pungent animal odors. At first glance, they would conclude that urban dwellers enjoy a better life than did their ancestors.

Yet, a closer examination would show them a more familiar world. They would understand the social and political fragmentation heightened by metropolitan America's continuing growth. They would view the separate territories of the *haves* and the *have-nots*. They would recognize tensions among immigrants from all over the world. They would realize that for millions, metropolitan existence remains a daily contest for economic security, good housing, and a decent way of life.

Cities remain, as Lewis Mumford observed more than sixty years ago, the central focus of human civilization, the places where people,

NEW COMMUNITY BUILDERS

- Offer citizens and industries tangible decision-making opportunities in the design, creation, and maintenance of communities and institutions.

- Mend economic, ethnic, and racial divisions heightened by suburban growth, the politics of exclusion, and the rapid accumulation of wealth by a small population.

- Use transportation, information technology, and telecommunications to unite fragmented communities and expand opportunities for economic success.

- Manage housing to adapt to complex changing family structures, unite disparate communities, and stabilize and restore inner cities.

- Create communities of knowledge that attract businesses and expand job access through continuous learning, from early childhood education programs to senior citizen classes.

- Offer communities opportunities to rebuild, re-create, and centralize human engagement by building cultural centers and strategic open-spaces.

commerce, culture, and ritual intertwine to enact the drama of human existence.

No matter how cities and towns have changed since Mumford studied them, civic leaders' obligations have not altered. Leaders must create peaceful and prosperous communities. Technological advances, rapidly shifting demographics, and changing social structures require leaders to retool to meet the demands of the twenty-first-century citizenry.

The last decade of the twentieth century has transformed the global political and economic environment, creating new challenges for communities. Once islands of stability and predictable expansion, cities now rapidly absorb changes in the worldwide economic and social environment.

Chattanooga, TN. Pedestrian walkways, overcome features such as cliffs and highways of Chattanooga's Riverwalk, a 7 mile landscaped path along the Tennessee River that connects the city's diverse neighborhoods to the river.

Taxpayers—and global

markets—expect good

value for money spent.

New citizens and

enterprises will pay

for community

improvements but, in

return, exact high

performance standards.

NEW TECHNOLOGIES CREATE GLOBAL COMMUNITIES

The Wired World. Like the telegraph and the railroad in the nineteenth century, modern information technologies and telecommunications reduce the constrictions of time and location, fundamentally altering the relationship of people and business to their communities and the world. Anyone can communicate instantaneously with anyone else anywhere in the world. Companies and consumers can seek out and acquire information and products through the World Wide Web. Technology has liberated individuals and businesses from the confines of geography, giving expanded freedom to choose where they live and work. Technology makes place more important as a residence and less so as a business location. A community's performance in the ruthless global competition for resources and its attractiveness to business leaders replace geographic and technological elements in determining which cities thrive and which die. Most communities compete for businesses by offering low-cost capital and labor (a task made difficult by overseas competition); proximity to beaches, mountains, or lakes; or distinctive and historic neighborhoods and business districts.

The Glocal World. As technology wires the world, it blends global and local—glocal—priorities. Unique geographical features remain attractive to new businesses. At the same time, localities are becoming less distinctive, more homogenized, and more dependent on global influences such as trade and population shifts. America's multicultural society, for example, is often seen largely as the result of continued immigration from Latin America and Asia. Yet, immigration represents only a tiny element in the changing composition of U.S. cities. The emergence of Third-World trading partners such as Korea and China and the universality of technical advances create innovative international fusions and enterprises. But globalization also has destroyed industrial-city economies and eliminated manufacturing jobs as imports have dominated the U.S. marketplace. Even before China joined the World Trade Organization, for example, exports from that country tipped the United States-China balance of trade toward China. In the glocal world, people live in specific geographic settings with unique histories, topographies, and cultural amenities. But people, goods, and ideas stream in from all over the world, undermining old structures, re-creating relationships, and altering political and economic landscapes.

The Fragmented World. Despite global homogenizing, the old problems of fragmentation and disjointedness remain. In many ways, these problems are worse than ever. Municipal reformers once consolidated boroughs such as Brooklyn and Queens into a metropolis like New York City by annexing them. Today, populations concentrate in vast urban conglomerates such as the New York City region, which extends from New Brunswick, New Jersey to the northern tip of Long Island and beyond Westchester County. Suburbs circuit once centralized cities, and each municipality vies for residents, businesses, amenities, and tax revenues. The fragmentation is one of the most destructive influences on American community life today. Political jurisdictions endlessly jockey for limited government funding, rich suburban dwellers shun impoverished urban communities, races mingle only in the workplace, and the elderly seek isolated fortresses far from the din of productive activity. Such fragmentation undermines the competitiveness of U.S enterprise. As the European Union adds polish to its concentrated trade network, for example, U.S. communities continue to squabble for lesser turf.

The Accountable World. Civic leaders who want to market their city's cultural amenities and streamlined infrastructure must win voter approval and find new financing for community improvements. Yet, raising funds and rousing political support for public investments can be difficult. Over the past two decades, American taxpayers have proven increasingly reluctant to pay for urban construction and rehabilitation. Since the passage of California's Proposition 13 in 1978, public investment in development has declined. Civic leaders now must seek out specialized funding mechanisms such as enterprize-zone financing, assessment districts, special taxes, the reselling of mortgages, and the repackaging and reuse of government resources. The competitive global environment tolerates little fat in a community's financial system. No city—indeed, no nation—can afford to finance improvements and amenities using an uncompetitive tax structure. Rather, taxpayers—and global markets—expect good value for money spent. New citizens and enterprises will pay for community improvements but, in return, exact high performance standards.

New Leaders for a New Century

Twenty-first century communities require from leaders a candid and sometimes painful self-evaluation—and a willingness to lead the citizenry in discarding comfortable structures and illusions. Political leaders in some dwindling mill towns, such as Weirton, West Virginia, lobby the federal government to restrict the international competition that stripped plant profits. But politicians in Pittsburgh, Pennsylvania and Pueblo, Colorado, have accepted the reality of changed economic conditions, cast off the industrial mantle, and fashioned new tourist and technology centers.

Leaders can garner political capital by transforming risky community-development innovations into government initiatives, but only the bold make the attempt. In 1996, Governor Parris Glendening of Maryland pursued a *Smart Growth* initiative—to curb urban sprawl, save farmland, and protect existing communities—he believed would

Memphis, TN. The Memphis International Airport, home of Federal Express, anchors the city as the regional center for commerce, finance and culture in western Tennessee and the bordering states of Mississippi and Arkansas.

Chattanooga, Tennessee leads in synthesizing the desires of disparate community groups, businesses, and government agencies to develop revolutionary housing and business-development programs. A community dialogue launched twenty years ago by the Lyndhurst Foundation has resulted in ambitious and effective land-use and business and housing development plans. The city transformed a depressed and heavily polluted industrial center to a *green* business park, for example, and mandated on-site waste recycling.

Shelby County, Tennessee Mayor Jim Rout united government planners, politicians, and business leaders in the Governors' Alliance for Regional Excellence to make region-wide plans for the Memphis suburbs and exurbs in Tennessee, Mississippi, and Arkansas.

Southern California's Natural Communities Conservation Planning program joins federal environmental experts with state and local government planning officials. Together, they plan for future endangered species preserves as they direct urban growth. In past years, state and federal biologists defended their own regulatory power and local governments zealously guarded their ability to promote urban growth. To better the prospects of both the human and animal populations, these agencies ended their turf wars.

New York City had to treat its water supply—long cherished as pristine and untainted. So, the city collaborated with farming communities, upstate New York cities, and the downstate metropolis. Conjoined communities created a rural development fund, protected the city's water source, and saved state taxpayer money.

cost him his job. Despite vociferous opposition from some landowners and builders, *Smart Growth* instead proved politically practical. In 1998, Glendening won reelection by a considerable margin.

Leadership emerges not only from the political sector. More than 400 businesses formed the Sierra Business Council in northern California to promote business development and preserve the picturesque landscape that attracts new workers to the region. The Council works to prevent the repeated subdividing of rural lands. In Silicon Valley, computer-manufacturing companies promote affordable housing, public transportation, and other controversial public priorities overlooked by politicians anxious about careers.

Nonprofit-sector organizations—churches, foundations, and civic groups—unrestricted by reelection exigencies and unsatisfied with corpo-

rate attainments seek government and private financing to form new communities. Local newspapers and television news teams also can shed the trappings of objectivity and use information resources to guide lasting political and neighborhood development. Catalysts for change, these new leaders can fuse previously unconnected constituencies—urban and suburban dwellers, for example—or tap new sources of neighborhood intelligence and resources to mold new communities.

In Cleveland, corporations concerned about deteriorating neighborhoods that flank commercial districts created Cleveland Tomorrow, a funding and development agency that leveraged community investments of $122 million. After the 1968 riots that fractured Newark's neighborhoods, a parish priest helped create a neighborhood housing coalition called New Community Corporation to rebuild neglected urban residential districts throughout suburban New Jersey.

The sustenance and vibrancy of these new leaders and the programs they initiate hinge on their ability to engage stakeholders in decision-making, minimize their own ascendancy over the community design, adapt strategies to economic conditions, and reallocate power positions to retain community focus.

The new leaders also must help fragmented communities select a distinct development path among dozens of competing routes. As America's communities have matured, factionalism has intensified. Cities and counties compete for control of institutional and geographical authority. Federal agencies such as the Environmental Protection Agency vie with state environmental departments for purview over brownfields, protected lands, industrial regulation, and preservation strategies. Business associations and community nonprofits compete to be the prime movers in civic life.

The country's decentralized political system inevitably leads to splintering priorities. But increasingly, leaders recognize they must bridge separate constituencies—states, and even countries—to build and maintain successful communities.

A century ago, America's young urban communities displayed changing political power structures and fluid economic bases and geographical boundaries. Today, these communities often suffer from the problems of maturity: aging physical infrastructure and neighborhoods, and calcified political and bureaucratic institutions that slow

new development. By focusing political will, leadership, creativity, and collaboration, America's communities can overcome the obstacles of age. They can create adaptable political leadership, develop new resources, and create amenities to keep the new city viable in the new century.

Thinking Globally and Acting Regionally

The American metropolitan explosion commenced with the beginning of the twentieth century. New York and Chicago emerged as gigantic metropolises—dense, crowded, dirty—deeply divided between rich and poor. New financial services regulation prompted by the Great Depression and new labor standards resulting from decades of agitation helped usher in an era of economic stability and measured growth unprecedented in the young country. Labor union success, coupled with federal programs like the GI Bill, which supplied veterans funds for college, helped create and expand the middle class. Low-interest federal home-loan programs and massive national highway-construction projects helped class members transfer from

the city to suburbs. The swell of urban minority populations attracted by the new stability of industrial employment and the government-mandated mixing of minority and majority group members only intensified white out-migration. As suburbs became symbols of affluence and independence, the new African-American middle class joined whites in their flight from city centers.

But the resulting rapid, unplanned growth has generated ugly, mismatched suburban communities crosshatched by inadequate road and highway systems, isolated industrial and office parks, and anonymous strip malls. The primacies of the automobile and widespread planning principles based on segregating commercial and residential zones have helped create isolated suburban islands. Many suburban communities have lost historical centers and discarded downtown congregation points in favor of shopping, civic activity, entertainment, and business. In the place of homegrown businesses, developers consolidate homogenous chain retail outlets in monstrous shopping malls enclosed by vast asphalt parking lots. Metropolitan regions—once cramped and con-

St. Paul, MN. The Lowertown Redevelopment Corporation provides a successful mix of housing for diverse incomes, age and ethnic groups of St. Paul. The focus of Lowertown is to provide amenities as well as housing for neighborhoods.

Philadelphia, PA. An arts festival is held on North Broad Street of the city's Avenue of the Arts, a major economic development effort using arts and cultural facilities as the catalyst for revitalizing over 4 miles of Broad Street.

gested—have evolved into sprawling, complicated, and inefficient conglomerates.

Our biggest metropolises stretch more than a hundred miles from end to end. Easy-to-miss highway signposts delineate jurisdictions often indistinguishable in architectural style, ethnicity, or commercial orientation. Only geographical indicators—palm trees, mountains, and salt marshes—distinguish the commercial corridors of suburban Miami, Florida; Denver, Colorado; and Newark, New Jersey. Residents of these urban conglomerates, hard-pressed to even define their own communities, understandably avoid the clash of turf and cultures required to form interconnections or fail to join in planning and improving what to many are distant, anonymous—even intimidating—inner cities.

But the quality of life in the twenty-first century and the success of our metropolitan communities will rely on new urban-suburban bonds, the streamlining of city and suburb—the development

of unified *regions*. As is detailed in succeeding chapters, the metropolitan *region* has emerged as the basic building block of the global economy. Only by operating as single *regions*, will communities overcome the parochial barriers to success and compete effectively in the global marketplace for residents, businesses, amenities, and ideas.

Social equity and the securing of all communities' economic interests also hinge on linking the often-impoverished center cities with their more affluent suburban neighbors. Many homogenous individual communities remain isolated from both the vibrancy and the responsibility that a diverse society requires. Communities will realize their potential as economic engines and centers for human congress by building comprehensive *regions*.

Where will the engineers of these diverse *regions* congregate? The answer explains the importance of a region's center. Paradoxically, amid the globalization and homogenizing of human enterprise, distinguishable city centers have gained significance.

As electronic connections dominate communities, residents long for new face-to-face interactions.

In Spain, civic leaders and politicians instigated an inner-city revival by financing the construction of a unique architectural landmark—the Solomon R. Guggenheim Museum in Bilbao. A bold composition of monumental geometrical shapes circuiting an atrium, the museum already has ignited the city's tourist trade, and leaders hope it will also attract new businesses, and encourage new residential development. Other cities also have used the arts to revive exhausted downtown commercial districts. Providence and state leaders retain former Rhode Island School of Design students as residents by converting old warehouses to artists' lofts and granting tax advantages to artisans and their patrons. Orlando, Philadelphia, and Pittsburgh have constructed cultural corridors that concentrate entertainment and artistic ambition downtown. Leaders in Memphis, Denver, and St. Paul rebuild powerful business-residential alliances by constructing downtown housing.

Robust city centers can consolidate and take advantage of *regional* assets—such as the availability of universities and colleges—for the benefit of each community. Some *regions* will revive their historical geographical centers because they retain social diversity and irreplaceable cultural heritage. Other *regions* will fashion newly constructed town centers or consolidate rambling suburbs. Many communities will forge complex—but understandable—hierarchies of centers.

The interplay of extensive *regions* and consolidated city centers will inform and energize the communities of the twenty-first century. The City of Memphis—with its three-state development alliance—has created a new *regional* community. In Kansas City, the Greater Kansas City Community Foundation engages distinct Kansas and Missouri communities in *regional* development by financing neighborhood improvement projects. International accords like the North American Free Trade Alliance (NAFTA) and the concentration of populations along traditional national borders create new international *regional* centers. The San Diego Dialogue, a University of California think-tank, compiles statistics and regulations and devises policies to define and advance a single *region* extending north from Mexico's Baja Peninsula to the southern boundary of suburban Los Angeles. In Europe, three historical commercial and residen-

tial centers, Turin, Italy; Geneva, Switzerland; and Lyon, France, hope to realize the potential benefits of traditional cultural and linguistic connections by creating the Alpine Diamond, an informal think tank that develops *regional* transportation, culture, and economic initiatives.

Creating the Twenty-first Century *Polis*

No one can predict the outcome of twenty-first century region and city-center alliances. We cannot accurately predict the consequences of the global telecommunications revolution. We cannot say, for example, whether our communities will reflect a rich and diversified world culture, or will result in the alienation so many urban and suburban dwellers deplore. Neither can we predict whether the rise of the global market economy will bring prosperity to billions or continue to concentrate wealth among the few.

However, we can define the rough outlines of what Lewis Mumford would call the *containers* of human activities—city centers and *regions*. Civic leaders face new challenges in the decades ahead even if the basic tasks of community life have changed little in the past millennium. The *polis*— the geographical setting and the very essence of human congress—will forever require consolidated centers of commerce and governance. But, as the following chapters reveal, their definitions will reflect the energy and vitality of communities, their civic leaders, and their institutions.

The polis—the geographical setting and the very essence of human congress—will forever require consolidated centers of commerce and governance.

Cleveland Gets the Rust Out
by Forging New Deals

By the late 1970s, the city of Cleveland had become synonymous with every-thing negative about urban America. Characterized by burning neighbor-hoods and a burning river, its jobs and population migrating into the hinter-lands, the once-mighty industrial city with a toe in the southern end of Lake Erie was regarded nationwide as the flagship of American urban decay. A city of one million at its peak, its population crashed to 500,000. Major indus-tries fled to the suburbs, the South, and the Third World. On December 17, 1978, Cleveland became the first city since the Great Depression to default when it failed to repay $14 million in municipal loans from six banks. The city remained in default for almost two years.

Cleveland's decline—while spectacular in its own way—was widely regarded as entirely unremark-able. One more rust-belt city had followed the inevitable course of decay and dissipation that accompanied the collapse of the country's manu-facturing base.

But if those charting Cleveland's slide regarded it as inevitable, they missed the true story. Undeni-ably buffeted by tangible and powerful socioeco-nomic forces from the fifties to the seventies, the city also had a significant hand in its own meltdown. For years, it had suffered from a funda-mental lack of civic and political leadership. Indifference, incompetence, internal and external conflict, and a powerful lack of vision character-ized its civic organizations and government. Neglected city streets proved a symbol of the city's ineffectual leaders.

"We had fire hydrants in my neighborhood that were lying on their sides, not even hooked up," says Linda Hudacek, the city's current community devel-opment director, recalling city life in the seventies.

Arson and urban renewal destroyed much of Cleveland's architecture and housing stock. A desegregation order in 1974 emptied the city's neighborhood schools and created a chasm in the already fraying social fabric.

The city's loan default helped the city bottom-out, says Hunter Morrison, city planning director. Large employers such as the Cleveland Clinic found they could not attract quality employees. A local bank went so far as to take the word Cleveland out of its name. And no financial institution would lend the city the money it would need to emerge from default.

"That's when people realized we had to do something," Morrison says. "Yes, the suburbs had drained off a lot of Cleveland's energy, but not the feelings that those still living in Cleveland had for the city. Those Clevelanders who had stayed put their shoulders to the wheel to erase this collective shame."

Committed residents decided to buck the conventional wisdom that urban decay was inevitable. The election of Mayor George Voinovich in 1979 helped launch improvements. A fiscal pragmatist with close ties to both state government and business, Voinovich reorganized city government, restructured municipal finances and, under state supervision, worked out a $36 million, fourteen-year debt-restructuring package backed by eight banks. As the city regained financial stability, residents and government got to work.

The Big-Hole Theory of Urban Revival

If Cleveland is known for anything today, it is for its waterfront revitalization, which includes the much celebrated Rock and Roll Hall of Fame, the city's sparkling Great Lakes Science Center, and a new football stadium constructed on the site of the old Cleveland Indians ballpark for the recently repatriated Browns. Set on a vast expanse of green space at the foot of downtown, it is the sort of waterfront configuration that may lure other cities into concluding that municipal revitalization is as simple as the Big Project.

In the case of Cleveland, big, bold projects have certainly stimulated the city's redevelopment, but few actually know about the one *big project* underpinning the waterfront revival, or how much work and study went into the plan. The *big project* building that started the waterfront revitalization rolling was a massive $8 million dredging and construction effort completed in 1986, aimed at bringing Lake Erie—the city's most prominent and powerful geographical feature—closer to the city.

It seemed audacious, at best, to approach the state legislature for $8 million to build an inner harbor at the foot of a city just coming out of fiscal default, still struggling to provide basic services to citizens, still ravaged by crime and blight. But such cockiness symbolized new thinking in Cleveland: If the city were to come back, it would have to first rebuild its civic self-confidence and its civic image. Inspired by the

success of Baltimore's inner harbor, Cleveland decided it was time for a change of attitude.

"We were sick of people saying, 'Baltimore can do that, but we're not Baltimore,'" says Morrison. "Or 'Boston can do that, but we're not Boston.' We decided to prove that if Boston or Baltimore can do it, so can Cleveland."

The city organized a blue-ribbon panel to study the inner harbor plan. Detailed hydrological modeling showed that the inner harbor would experience some of Lake Erie's nastiest weather. When the city finally pitched the plan to the state legislature, however, it was seamless. Lawmakers agreed to fund it. But it was still a gamble.

The campaign for an inner harbor represents the hard-nosed approach to urban redevelopment that continues to stir controversy today. Like Baltimore—Cleveland's waterfront-based redevelopment twin to the east—Cleveland has been accused of focusing on downtown to the detriment of its neighborhoods. Spending $8 million to move mounds of lakefront muck represents a speculative investment that critics of center-city redevelopment strategies question. But neighborhood activist and Cleveland Community Development Director Tom Yablonsky dismisses such criticism as hopelessly off the point.

"Without the redevelopment downtown, none of what you're seeing here would be taking place," says Yablonsky, who is also the executive director of the center-city Historic Gateway Corporation, a nonprofit redevelopment organization.

Once the western anchor of Euclid Avenue— the local equivalent of New York's Fifth Avenue— the Historic Gateway is undergoing a remarkable transformation a few blocks from the waterfront. Once a wasteland of abandoned hotel, office, and retail buildings, the Gateway has become a prime commercial, hotel, residential, restaurant, and entertainment district. A resurgent theater district and the reopening of Jacobs Field, the city's new old-style downtown baseball stadium, help anchor the redevelopment of the Gateway and of Cleveland's entire downtown.

There is no better guide for that redevelopment than Yablonsky. As he explains, at Gateway he analyzes a project's market potential in relation to the availability of federal historic rehabilitation tax credits; federal, state, and local loans and grants; tax abatements; and private funding. Yablonsky measures this package against likely construction

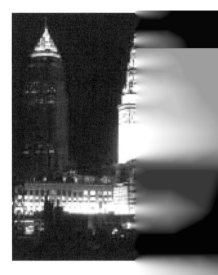

Cleveland's Tower City Center is one of the city's most prominent architectural landmarks (photo above). The city's waterfront revitalization includes the celebrated Rock and Roll Hall of Fame and Museum that attracts visitors from all over the country to view exhibits like "Roots, Rhymes and Rage: The Hip Hop Story" (photos left).

costs, which, in Cleveland, are reduced by the passage of an alternative state building code in the eighties to encourage rehabilitation projects. Yablonsky's downtown tour offers a blur of new projects:

1. Development of the much-celebrated Tower City downtown festival marketplace, which turned one of the city's most prominent architectural landmarks—an ornate 1927 railroad station and skyscraper (the third tallest building in the country when constructed)—into a thriving retail, restaurant, office park, and transit terminal in the late 1980s.
2. Conversion of the National City Bank Building, a gorgeous brownstone near the Tower City marketplace, into a 140-room Holiday Inn. (The deal was a bargain for Holiday Inn because the state's revised building code made the rehabilitation $20,000-per-room cheaper than new construction.)
3. Renovation of two of the city's classic arcade buildings—The Arcade and The Colonial Arcade—each characterized by a soaring, glass-covered atrium running from street to street, linking multistory commercial, living, and office space.

Each project represents another step in the city's downtown comeback, Yablonsky says. Nevertheless, a decade and a half ago, those kinds of projects were a hard sell. In the early 1980s, no commercial banks would risk investing in downtown, and neighborhood redevelopment activists frequently turned to labor union pension funds for financing. But gradually, as the waterfront work materialized, and as developers revived buildings in the city's warehouse district to the northwest, the Historic Gateway neighborhood turned around as well.

"Volume begets volume," says Yablonsky. "These projects used to come one at a time, now they're coming two-by-two."

Gateway has fashioned new financing packages by adding a project-specific twist to the twenty-percent federal tax credit for certified historic rehabilitation. As part of the arcade restoration (it will become a combination of office, restaurant, and retail in the arcade and a new Hyatt hotel in its main towers), for example, Historic Gateway

accepted a conservation easement with a tax benefit of $1.8 million to the five-story, vaulted arcade connecting Euclid and Superior avenues. The investment made the project financially viable, while ensuring that a grand public space in Cleveland would remain accessible to all.

More important, the Historic Gateway neighborhood also is witnessing a resurgence of what urban turnaround artists covet most: housing. Developers are converting unused downtown office buildings to spacious market-rate apartments, a direct spillover of ambitious and now pervasive apartment rehabilitation activity that started in the early 1980s in the city's adjacent warehouse district.

Yablonsky honed his ability to facilitate commercial real estate deals in that warehouse district starting in the early eighties. As with most preservation efforts, the push to establish the historic district was galvanized by the disastrous demolition of some of the city's most spectacular buildings, including the architecturally magnificent Blackstone Building demolished in the sixties and the historically significant Board of Trade Building torn down in the early eighties. The warehouse district now includes 1,200 housing units, along with dozens of restaurants, offices, galleries, and markets, including a sumptuous Italian market that replaces a 25-cent pornographic movie house. Typical of the new activity in the district is the adaptive reuse of the massive Otis Terminal complex, a series of huge warehouse buildings that, on a recent tour, were swarming with construction workers and filled with sounds of hammers and power tools. Overlooking the Cuyahoga River and its spectacular series of steel-truss bridges, the building is being developed into lofts featuring high ceilings and fashionable faded brick walls, all buttressed with giant wood beams. The expansive warehouse buildings include adequate space to provide housing on the building's lower floors with no significant structural alterations or foundation reinforcements.

Neighborhood Activists Stop Agitating and Start Dealmaking

Yablonsky's facility for commercial rehabilitation projects characterizes the evolution of neighborhood activism in Cleveland. Once concerned with social issues and neighborhood empowerment in the 1960s and 1970s, the movement in Cleveland has evolved into a no-nonsense focus on community redevelopment. Activists do deals.

"When Dennis Kucinich was elected mayor in 1977, neighborhood activists were more confrontational; it was the whole era of neighborhood empowerment," says Reid Robbins, executive director of the Shaker Square Development Corporation, one of the city's twenty-one community development corporations. Today, more neighborhood groups understand the importance of long-term political power, and they establish their own power, not by fighting local government, but by working with city officials and private developers, Robbins says.

Neighborhood Progress Incorporated (NPI), created in the early 1980s by a group of the city's leading corporate foundations, led the new approach. Tired of seeing money sprinkled around Cleveland to little apparent effect, NPI refocused resources on tangible redevelopment projects, strategically chosen for the greatest impact.

Tensions persist among neighborhood activists and real estate developers, says Laura Noble, a planner with the Ohio City Near West Development Corporation, which coordinates housing and commercial development projects on the city's west side. Noble says her organization constantly confronts issues of social equity. Home to a very rundown single-room occupancy hotel and a high-end microbrewery, the Ohio City Near West neighborhood has to balance gentrification with basic housing.

"It's a lively dynamic," Noble says with considerable understatement. "The debate [is] between those who want to keep a community open to everybody versus those who want to do market-rate housing and upscale commercial development."

Nevertheless, gentrification has pushed out few low-income inner-city residents in the citywide push for redevelopment. Even in Ohio City Near West, home to the spectacular West End Market, a huge vaulted airplane hangar with a gorgeous interior of terra cotta and tile that draws hundreds of thousands of people every weekend, low-income residents face little danger of getting priced out of the housing market. There is an ample supply of housing to be developed or redeveloped.

Mill Creek Inner-city Subdivision Attracts the Middle Class

In fact, today the city campaigns to attract middle-class residents. Mayor Michael R. White has supported an aggressive, ambitious policy of offering inexpensive land—complete with utilities—to developers willing to risk building in the city to create moderately priced housing (and some high-end housing, as well). City government, more than any other civic entity in Cleveland, has led the resurgence of downtown housing, putting together ambitious packages of abandoned or tax-delinquent land along with targeted financial assistance for redevelopment. New foundations and frames mark the housing projects that would be considered folly ten years ago.

In consultation with the city's hands-on planning department, the Slavic Village Development Corporation acquired land for only $21,000 to launch a middle-class subdivision called Mill Creek. The ensuing demolition of nineteen buildings and the cleanup of a decades-old landfill and three leaking underground gasoline storage tanks would end up costing the city $1.2 million. The development's total price tag: $37 million, including $6 million in city funds.

The experiment in city housing redevelopment has so far succeeded. With low Community Reinvestment Act mortgage rates, and fifteen-year property tax abatements, buyers can purchase homes priced from $120,000 to $300,000. The neighborhood's proximity to a large municipal park and bike trails linking it to the Ohio and Erie Canal National Heritage Corridor heighten its appeal. The historically incendiary issue of race represents a nonissue in Mill Creek. Half the households are white; half are African American. Half the subdivision's residents came from other Cleveland neighborhoods and half from outside the city limits.

Mill Creek also has generated interesting residuals, adds Nathan Zaremba, the developer.

"You're seeing housing values in surrounding areas go up, and suddenly people who had no equity in their houses before now do," he says. "But rather than take that equity and run to the suburbs, people in those homes seem to be hanging in because they're seeing good things happening around them. In fact, they'd be crazy to sell now with everything that's going on."

Zaremba did not begin his career as a downtown development advocate. His involvement in the project signals new times in Cleveland. His father built thousands of suburban houses to which a generation of Clevelanders fled, and the younger Zaremba followed his father's example until approached by the city about transferring his business downtown.

Shaping Cleveland's Destiny by Seizing Control

Viewed from the ground level, redevelopment in Cleveland, while certainly widespread, apparently resulted from random activity, mostly fostered by a new breed of sophisticated and aggressive community redevelopment corporations. Seemingly unrelated efforts include:

1. A gorgeously restored bank building in Ohio City with its historically accurate reconstructed marquee of pale blue and yellow neon;
2. A turn-of-the-century triangle building in the theater district soon to be stripped of its aluminum skin and restored to its brick-faced glory;
3. New loft housing in the warehouse district;
4. New homes in Beacon Square on the city's near east side; and
5. A theater comeback in Shaker Village.

The city actually has tightly orchestrated the revival with a series of Cleveland Vision 2000 comprehensive plans. Looking at the first plan, now ten years old, it is easy to see its influence from the waterfront to the theater district. Likewise, the "Cleveland Civic Vision 2000 Citywide Plan," published in 1991, guides neighborhood redevelopment projects.

A recent scene in an architect's conference room helps to illustrate how redevelopment gets done in Cleveland today and displays the relation between neighborhood rejuvenation and comprehensive planning. The architect hosts a meeting with a local developer, a rails-to-trails advocate, a neighborhood community development corporation representative, a neighborhood activist, and a member of the city planning department. They are polishing their proposal to the city for a redevelopment project. The group will pitch a planned

development project in south-central Cleveland to a tripartite of municipal officials called the *development cluster*.

The *development cluster* in many ways represents the new power in Cleveland and has Community Development Director Linda Hudacek, Economic Development Director Chris Warren, and Planning Director Hunter Morrison as its members. They marshal money, regulatory relief, and technical assistance for neighborhood restoration initiatives. Such coordination among city departments with common interests has led to a whole new era of strategic redevelopment.

"In the old days you'd have projects sprinkled all over the city with no context," says Morrison, "and so they would have no collective impact."

Now, when a neighborhood development group presents its plan to the development cluster, the group must prove the project will be viable, fit into the city's comprehensive plan, and improve neighboring districts. Hudacek displays a frankness common among the cluster's hard-nosed reviewers.

"We're no longer interested in funding Don Quixote," she says bluntly.

City officials in Cleveland today are not shy about their desire to run the show. That willingness to take control has fueled the city's comeback, argues the city's director of economic development, Chris Warren. An untold story, in his opinion, has been the city's ability to seize control of vast derelict properties held by tax delinquent and absentee landowners. Using expedited condemnation procedures—the city now has a mechanism for instantly condemning property—Cleveland has pulled together large and strategically situated parcels for redevelopment.

As a consequence, since 1992, Cleveland has built more housing than it has torn down, Warren says. The ability to control land also has enabled the city to reclaim contaminated industrial sites and lure small businesses—a critical and growing segment of the city's economic base.

The city is taking control in other ways, Warren adds. For example, it has gained influence over transportation funding. Instead of using municipal money to pursue the sprawl-inducing practices of the past—including widening or extending interstate highways—the city invests in downtown transit and street improvements. State and Cuyahoga County officials endorse the city's transportation agenda and have become active partners in Cleveland's redevelopment effort. The region's new governmental partnerships reflect one of the more positive consequences of the city's loan default, says Morrison, the planning director.

"The core city's problems all of a sudden became everybody's problem," he says. "It affected a lot of folks' bottom lines, and so the state and county both saw that it was in their direct interest to work with us."

The county contributed significantly to the theater district comeback, for example. The city's aggressive land condemnation procedures were, likewise, worked out in conjunction with county officials.

Paying Mortgage and Tuition

At the same time, the city is taking control in one other important area: education. In 1997, after years of watching Cleveland's public schools spiral into decay and dysfunction, the state dissolved the school board and handed the mayor's office control of the city's public schools. Observers regard the school takeover as absolutely crucial to the long-term sustainability of the city's revival of these buildings and neighborhoods.

"In the past, those considering moving to Cleveland had to make a key financial decision," Economic Development Director Chris Warren says. "Can I afford a mortgage and tuition for private school?"

Mill Creek has been successful in attracting families in part because of its proximity to private schools, Bobbi Reichtell, executive director of the Slavic Village Development Corporation, admits with sadness.

It is too early to describe the impact of the schools on Cleveland's long-term redevelopment prospects. Few urban public-school turnaround stories exist. But redevelopment officials argue that the city comeback will never be complete unless the city retains control of the schools and improves student outcomes.

Cleveland Developers Walk a Pitted Road

To travel from Mill Creek in the south end of Cleveland to Jacobs Field in the north, the straightest path is Broadway Avenue, one of the city's old trolley corridors. Once lined with handsome turn-of-the-century commercial buildings bustling with business and life, Broadway today is a study in how much work remains to be done in Cleveland. Dilapidated commercial buildings and vast expanses of vacant property along the boulevard offer evidence of still-struggling neighborhoods.

For those who focus on the downtown-versus-neighborhoods investment debate, the blighted areas along Broadway are proof enough that the water that flowed into the city's new inner harbor in 1986 did not float the entire city. Yet Broadway also shows signs of life. Locally based, the Third Federal Bank is building a huge new corporate campus midway along the corridor. Just off Broadway, multiple neighborhood redevelopment projects are in the works.

City Planning Director Hunter Morrison acknowledges that Cleveland's revival must include more than downtown mega-projects, and he admits the city has a huge amount of work ahead. Yet, he remains adamant that little development would occur beyond the center city core without aggressive downtown projects to demonstrate the city's commitment. Morrison never will forget April 4, 1994, when throngs of city and suburban residents entered Jacobs Field for the first time.

"That day," says Morrison, "was the end of Cleveland's Great Depression."

The successful opening of Jacobs Field proved Cleveland had rebounded. The city had become a place where plans don't languish on the drawing board. City and suburban dwellers had joined in a remarkable show of civic pride and activism, fostering Cleveland's revival by pulling together and making deals.

Charlotte Advances from Trading Post to City of the Future

LEADERSHIP
PROFILE

The original trading post at the intersection of Trade and Tryon Streets in downtown Charlotte, North Carolina, closed almost two centuries ago. Still, that crossroads remains a potent symbol of this city's mythic origins and reflects its aspirations.

Today four twenty-four-foot bronze statues mark the corners. The statues represent four aspects of historic Charlotte: gold mining and banking; hydropower and textiles; transportation; and the future, represented by an archetypal mother and child. Independence Square, a public plaza often used as a celebrity stage, opens onto the intersection. The North Carolina Dance Theater and the local symphony orchestra sometime perform at the lunch hour. The symbolic power of the intersection is further heightened by the presence of the city's tallest building, the fifty-one-story Bank of America Center. Designed by Cesar Pelli, the opulent, red-marble tower houses the world headquarters of the city's largest employer.

Although imposing, the Bank of America Center is not the only notable feature on Tryon Street. The North Carolina Blumenthal Performing Arts Center, a two-story steel-and-glass pavilion, is affixed to the corporate tower like a mushroom at the base of a tall oak. The sidewalk has recently been widened, one of many concessions to pedestrians. The former Belks Department Store, with its Carrara marble facade, has been converted into the Museum of Craft and Design. The street resembles a three-dimensional brochure for the city's newfound affluence, corporate prestige, and urbanity.

Welcome to Charlotte, a city on display. Despite its eighteenth-century roots, most of the display has its origins in the past decade. In addition to the Bank of America Center and the bronze statues by sculptor Raymond Kaskey at the intersection, the city has undertaken staggering developments:

- The $250 million Gateway Village, a complex of offices and condominiums with its own park.
- The overhauling and transformation of a depressed U.S. Housing and Urban Development (HUD) project into housing for families with a range of incomes.
- The privately financed $187 million Carolina Panthers stadium and nearby practice field on formerly contaminated industrial sites.
- The renovation of the historic, formerly decaying Victorian neighborhood in the Fourth Ward, now occupied by middle-class families.
- A new bus terminal financed by Bank of America and its predecessor, NationsBank. The impressive, A-frame structure is hemmed by street-level restaurants and shops.
- Fifteen new downtown nightclubs that reflect the newfound popularity of the downtown housing market.
- Five million-square feet of new downtown office space.

According to one account, no fewer than sixteen construction cranes were visible against the Charlotte skyline in August 1999; that number would have been impressive for such metropolitan behemoths as Los Angeles or Chicago during boom times.

The city's conversion from a midsize regional economic hub into a national economic center has

been a well-planned act of self-transformation. Charlotte is a classic example of cooperation among city officials and corporate stakeholders in the remaking of an American city. Here, Bank of America, First Union, and Duke Energy assume the roles the Bass family played in developing Fort Worth and the Eli Lilly Corporation played in improving Indianapolis.

Corporate urban showcases may seem overly clean and manicured for people who value urban grit and spontaneity. On the other hand, Charlotte has shown an ability to tackle problems directly and quickly and a willingness to reshape itself to a degree almost unimaginable in many other American cities.

Charlotte follows relatively conservative design conventions; only a few projects display elements unseen in other locations. Charlotte's development process is almost radical: The city wants, all at the same time, a mass transit system, major sports teams, new museums, and new mixed-use neighborhoods to replace its deteriorated housing. Civic leaders and private developers pursue this vision at breakneck speed.

Charlotte Builds a City Among Farms

Historically, Charlotte has grown fitfully. The first Europeans arrived in the 1750s, and the city incorporated in the 1790s. An anonymous surveyor laid out the still-surviving downtown street grid to create about 100 large-scale residential lots.

Charlotte's strong public/private partnerships are responsible for the Ericsson Football Stadium, home of the Carolina Panthers (photo left) and a new mixed income housing complex, located in the heart of City Center (photo above). Both projects have contributed to the revitalization of downtown and to building community pride.

With a single natural asset—farmland—the city attracted two centuries of economic and industrial growth. Farmers accidentally discovered gold in 1802, precipitating the young nation's first gold rush. Despite the wave of prospectors, Charlotte remained a village of a few thousand people until the 1850s, when the railroad linked it to the major industrial centers of the northeast. The city became a rail depot for cotton bound for the mills in the North and in Europe. Spared almost entirely by the Civil War, landlocked city dwellers aided the war effort, surprisingly, as a center of naval industry. (The Confederacy located its shipbuilding activities well inland to minimize the risk of Union attack.)

After the war, the doctrine of economic self-reliance in the South helped turn Charlotte into an industrial center dominated by textile mills. Since the Second World War, banking has supplanted industry as the city's economic engine.

"It is almost as if the descendents of the textile entrepreneurs gradually purified their trading activities to the point that the cotton disappeared, leaving a trade purely in money," wrote Thomas W. Hanchett, historian and director of the Museum of New South in Charlotte. Today, he continued, Charlotte "has become the financial center of the Carolinas. Deposits held by banks operating in Mecklenburg County exceed that for any comparable area between Philadelphia and Dallas, and bank offices dominate the Charlotte skyline."

When Charlotte-based NationsBank merged with BankAmerica Corporation and the new financial service conglomerate decided to remain in the city, already the home of First Union Bank, Charlotte became the second largest banking center in the country. Only New York employs more people in banking.

Charlotte's postwar history follows a conventional American pattern:

- Suburbs emerged and expanded as residents depended on automobiles and neglected the inner city.
- Construction of the interstate highway system in the 1960s and 1970s circumscribed downtown. Interstate 77 and Highway 277 encircle the city, creating a ringstrasse around

the downtown, isolating it from outlying residential districts.
- The typical exodus of retail and corporate office tenants from the urban center in the 1960s was abetted by the construction of a large HUD housing project, Earle Village, in the city's First Ward.
- Much of the city's downtown area fell prey to the bulldozers of Urban Renewal.

Despite a prosperous business base, downtown Charlotte in the 1970s was an eight-hour city deserted after dark, recalls Mayor Patrick McCrory.

"Downtown was basically a business park, which emptied out after 5 p.m.," he says.

Downtown Charlotte boasted some resources. The revenue of the growing suburban property tax base could be redirected toward downtown projects. State annexation law allows Charlotte to absorb new residential subdivisions without the approval of local homeowners. The law forces suburban communities to pay attention to downtown, McCrory says.

"The suburban tax base does not escape the responsibility of rebuilding the inner city," he says.

Corporations Build Downtown Charlotte

Corporate activism by Bank of America and its predecessors also helped preserve the city center. In the late 1970s, the North Carolina National Bank (an early incarnation of NationsBank) led the revival of the downtown near bank headquarters. In an era when interest rates were hovering near twenty percent, the bank offered very low-interest loans, in the three- to four-percent range, for neighborhood property purchases. Despite considerable resistance and local skepticism, a few urban pioneers took the bait. The city provided new street lamps and sidewalks.

Today, the Fourth Ward is a middle- and upper-middle-class neighborhood notable for its many restored Victorian houses and generates the highest property tax revenues of any Charlotte community, according to Bank of America.

The transformation of Earle Village into First Ward Place reconfigured a failing HUD project and attracted new financing for important African-American institutions in a district formerly known as Little Brooklyn. Well-intentioned efforts to create housing and eradicate poverty failed in the sixties and seventies. In the name of Urban Renewal, the city and developers bulldozed many historic black neighborhoods.

In the early nineties, the city removed the undesirable image of the dilapidated Earle Village housing project and replaced it with a mixed-income neighborhood. In 1995, HUD provided the city with a special, one-time grant of $42 million to reconstruct the entire neighborhood. Nations-Bank served as the project manager.

The city tore down most of the old units and turned them to rental apartments and condominiums. Residents also gained recreation and child development centers. In an unusual move, the city also made some funds available to the First Baptist Church of Christ, an important neighborhood institution.

"We had to convince them not to leave the downtown area," McCrory recalls.

Today a shopping center and two other important institutions, the Afro-American Cultural Center and Little Rock African Methodist Episcopal Zion Church, serve the neighborhood.

Since the completion of First Ward Place, the city has moved forward with three new residential projects, including town homes and condominiums.

"It's a very desirable place to live, which you wouldn't have believed if you had seen it five years ago," says Mayor McCrory. "It is not uncommon to see yuppie bankers walking down the streets of the First Ward."

Bank of America also helped finance the Gateway Village in a venture with a real estate developer, Cousins Properties. A few blocks west of the downtown core on Trade Street, the mixed-use development contains nearly a million square feet of office space, 120 condominiums and a one-acre park. Businesses have leased all of the offices.

The construction of Ericsson Stadium in 1996 was a defining moment for the city in terms of building civic self-confidence, according to Ed Wolverton, vice president of operations of Charlotte Center City Partners, a business improvement district supported by downtown businesses.

"People began to think, 'Hey, we are really able to make things happen,'" Wolverton says.

The city's construction of the football stadium also is a case in redeveloping a brownfield, a plot of land contaminated and abandoned by industry. Cancer-causing PCBs—the legacy of transformers

dumped by Duke Power and batteries dumped by other users—contaminated this federal Superfund site. Cleanup cost $4.1 million. The city provided $1 million in cash up front, while Duke Power provided $500,000 and the State of North Carolina another $50,000. The city absorbed the remaining costs, in exchange for the property owner's agreement to sell the land to the city at a discount that included cleanup expenses. The city leased the stadium site to Panther owner and stadium developer Jerry Richardson for $1 a year.

The majority of the $187 million to build the sports stadium came from Richardson, his investors, and his lenders. The city contributed $56.4 million toward construction, plus another $8 million in bond financing. Richardson raised about $160 million (or about $100 million after taxes) from the sale of special seating arrangements. Now, the city is considering a downtown basketball arena.

Charlotte's Future: Uniting Suburb and Central City

City planners will not stop at developing sports arenas to generate downtown revenues. The city has extended its reach into the suburbs by embracing the regional growth strategies of urban planner Michael Gallis. Gallis & Associates maps of surrounding population centers define Charlotte as the hub of a metropolitan region nearly fifty miles in diameter.

Gallis also has designed a planning model to protect the historic characteristics of outlying city centers and rationalize the corridors—rapidly expanding suburban subdivisions—by preserving green space, focusing economic development, and building transit hubs as centers for future commercial and residential construction.

Charlotte's regional development began with improvements in an outlying city, Rock Hill, South Carolina, a historic textile-mill town. As textile fortunes changed and production moved overseas, the city's economy faded. But in the late eighties, Gallis showed city leaders how to develop a new economic base. First, the principals of the city's institutions —the chamber of commerce, Winthrop College, York Tech, and city and county governments—pooled their resources and planning ideas. They redefined and marketed the city as a Gateway to the Charlotte metropolitan region and as a center for higher education. They also developed plans for preserving its historic character while attracting millions of dollars in development.

The city invested $1.2 million in its downtown, commissioning four neo-classical sculptures and erecting the columns rescued from the demolition of Charlotte's former Masonic Temple to represent the Gateway and to launch a ten-year public art campaign. The city also developed a landscaping model and built new business parks, funding the infrastructure with taxes collected on new businesses. Developers recycled a former textile mill, and the city also plans to renovate a downtown mall and preserve the city's historic character by uncovering the antique storefronts the mall encloses.

South Carolina invested $50 million in highway construction and renovation, improving Rock Hill's links to a circle of outlying cities and emphasizing its new role as a Gateway and educational center for the region, according to *The Charlotte Observer*.

The work in Rock Hill led Gallis to his understanding of the region's development structure—and his firm mapped the concentric circles of population extending from Charlotte outward. Rock Hill's success inspired Charlotte's civic and business leaders to redefine the city as a regional hub. In 1989, *The Charlotte Observer* examined the South Carolina city's strengths and weaknesses as a model for Charlotte and in multiple editorials explored the concept of regional development, probing Charlotte's new image as a regional cultural, business, and educational center.

In 1994, Gallis helped Charlotte's planners and civic and business leaders define critical decisions required during the coming decade to take advantage of Charlotte's assets, and he urged the development of:

- Regional parks, wastewater treatment plants, and landfills.
- High-tech businesses to profit from the concentration of financial centers in Charlotte.
- A research center linking the educational resources of Winthrop College in Rock Hill and the University of North Carolina, Chapel Hill.

- Coalitions of city councils and planning commissions to regulate land use and zoning.
- A comprehensive and integrated transportation network.

The planner's focus on regional transportation gained influence as traffic congestion heightened. By 1997, the Charlotte-Mecklenburg County area of North Carolina had the fourth highest level of traffic congestion among large U.S. metropolitan areas, according to the Texas Transportation Institute.

City planners estimated the region's population would rise by 57 percent over the next twenty years, and Gallis's maps proved invaluable in planning future land-use. Gallis helped the municipal government, civic organizations, neighborhood activists and government officials redefine themselves as part of a region—and showed how growth in the entire region would influence the quality of life and the commercial success of Charlotte and its residents.

"Political boundaries are less relevant than ever before. Large economic regions, not the cities or towns in them, are the competitive units in the new global marketplace," Gallis says.

After a spate of public hearings and town meetings, transportation engineers, academics, and real estate specialists created the Charlotte-Mecklenburg 2025 Regional Integrated Transit/Land-Use Plan. The plan provides for a governing structure to evaluate proposed land use, concentrates commercial development and housing at transit hubs, conserves green space, and sets benchmarks for development. The twenty-five year plan defines three central transportation modes—light rail, bus rapid transit, and diesel multiple units—designed to more efficiently move residents from one transit hub to another and link outlying suburbs with the central city.

Rail transit has a special meaning for Charlotte, where trains played a major role building an industrial center and regional transportation hub. The city built a downtown trolley and now proposes a $19.7 million expansion.

Charlotte Mayor McCrory also used Gallis & Associates research to back his push for a far more ambitious light-rail system to connect the central city with five neighborhoods on the city's periphery. The $1 billion transit plan will be financed by a half-penny sales tax endorsed by county voters. Charlotte's newly named transportation director, Ron Tober, has put Gallis's planning theories to work by creating new zoning ordinances to concentrate development along the rail and bus lines. Nevertheless, city officials do not view the planning models or the new transportation lines as regional panaceas. Tober has acknowledged it may be difficult to persuade residents of southern Charlotte, with its historically suburban character, to endorse increased density near the transportation routes.

Developing a New Downtown History

Despite extraordinary public will and corporate initiative, downtown Charlotte still suffers certain deficits. The legacy of Urban Renewal has left the city without a recognizable downtown historic identity—a strange lack in a city with such a long history (although Civil War sites are duly noted).

Mayor McCrory, a human-resources professional who describes himself as an urban-planning junkie, points out his favorite projects from his City Hall office window. He frankly describes unsuccessful or outdated downtown ideas.

"It doesn't work," he says of Marshall Park, an isolated park in the city's 1970s-era civic center.

McCrory says the park should be reduced, redesigned, and surrounded by housing. He also criticizes the sky bridges that connect major downtown buildings. A visit to Minneapolis by a group of city officials inspired the idea in the 1970s, but those officials apparently failed to appreciate that Charlotte's warm climate made such bridges unnecessary. He believes the civic center would be best located downtown. Downtown residents need a supermarket and other retail outlets. Parking lots consume too much downtown property, he says.

The draft version of Charlotte's 2010 Plan, a twenty-year growth blueprint, identifies new goals, most based on successful projects and urban designs in other cities. Plans include a new Amtrak station and baseball stadium as well as a light-rail line to the Charlotte/Douglas International Airport. The city also wants to create an academic quadrant accommodating the expansion of a local

college and connecting it to a planned downtown high school.

McCrory would like to build a network of pedestrian and bicycle bridges over freeways that surround and isolate the downtown. That futuristic image is hard to reconcile with the city's genesis as a primitive trading post founded before the Declaration of Independence. Then again, Charlotte has chosen to define itself more by its aspirations than by its past.

"Downtown is unrecognizable from what it had been before," McCrory observes. "And it will become even more so in the future."

Patrick McCrory, mayor of Charlotte

Rochester Discovers
Inner-City Resilience

A map of New York State from west to east, Buffalo to Troy, charts a course of precipitous urban decline. The list of former models of manufacturing muscle and economic might makes for depressing reading: Syracuse, Rome, Utica, Amsterdam, and Schenectady.

Rochester, just south of Lake Erie, breaks the pattern. Battered by industrial downsizing and relocations, the victim of the population's suburban exodus, Rochester nearly died a decade ago. Its population declined from 400,000 in the sixties to roughly 220,000 today. City planning officials expect the decline to level off at just over 200,000 by the year 2010.

Yet, unlike many upstate industrial counterparts whose slow demise continues, Rochester has survived the fall of a great manufacturing empire and discovered new strengths in its neighborhoods. Energized by a leadership team that arrived in the early 1990s—a team dedicated to the notion that city comebacks are never the result of quick fixes or one-formula prescriptions—the Flower City, with historical roots in the seed and nursery business, has stabilized its downtown and its neighborhoods in the last few years.

"We still have a declining tax base, businesses poised to move out, and an aging population tired of seeing their taxes go up," admits Rochester Mayor William A. Johnson, elected the first African-American mayor in 1992. "But we've had the opportunity to make fundamental and significant change, and those things are now taking root and getting established."

Balancing Competing Localities and Purposes

Rochester's long-range revival hinges on a deliberate balancing of downtown business interests and residential neighborhood demands. A handful of powerful corporations, including Eastman-Kodak and Xerox Corporation, dominated the Rochester economy much as industrial fortunes determined

the fates of many other rust-belt cities. As family-owned businesses, such corporate powerhouses once understood that cities without vibrant neighborhoods were like pits without the peach. But in the mid to late 1980s, with the rise of global competition and the ascent of an upper-level management lacking community roots, the partnership between downtown and neighborhoods became tenuous.

Rochester's city leaders realized the partnership had to be rewoven.

"Rochester has always been a city of neighborhoods," says Tom Argust, the city's director of community development. "Involving them is key to the city's long-term success."

The city's focused and sustained effort to make

neighborhoods the central drivers of the urban comeback distinguishes Rochester from other cities making revival attempts. Nevertheless, transferring power and development to multiple neighborhoods requires the city to spread itself a little thinly when investing scarce capital and economic resources. In the nineties, as the city built a downtown sports arena for its minor league baseball and soccer teams and refurbished its downtown convention center and indoor arena, it also reinvested in housing and commercial development outside the downtown core. This investment focused resources in some of the city's most troubled neighborhoods.

But bricks and mortar alone did not cement new and better working relations between the city

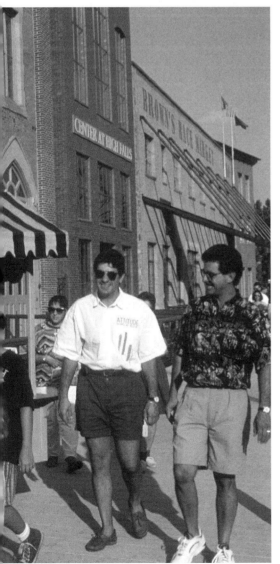

government and its neighborhoods. A sweeping and remarkably ambitious program launched in 1992 called Neighbors Building Neighborhoods (NBN) provided the engine for revitalization. The city made neighborhoods equal partners—and central resources—in the city's long-term economic revival plans.

The Nuts and Bolts of NBN

The city organized thirty-six neighborhoods into ten sectors, and representatives from each were allowed input into a long-term plan for citywide economic development and renewal. Although consolidating neighborhood interests in a city with a history of neighborhood activism caused turmoil, city officials and neighborhood activists say the government never dictated how NBN would be organized or administered. All NBN plans result from the full participation of city and neighborhood representatives. Argust describes the operating philosophy as simple.

"You can't have city revitalization without the involvement of neighborhoods," Argust says. "You'll never get meaningful neighborhood involvement unless you give them real power to decide on the direction the city should go and the strategies for getting there."

The city defused explosive us-versus-them controversies by allowing neighborhoods to create and design the NBN, says Hank Herrera, executive director of the Northeast Neighborhood Alliance, a development organization that represents three neighborhood associations in the blighted northeast part of the city.

"All along the city has indicated a clear willingness to listen to us and work with us," he says. "Before NBN we'd have to fight for a voice within the city bureaucracy, but with NBN it's a whole new way of doing business."

Neighborhood activists expressed some initial skepticism, Herrera observes. They had been promised a seat at the table before; they had been promised help with specific economic and housing development projects. Only when the city delivered on a promise to aggressively—and successfully—push for a major neighborhood supermarket did Herrera and his constituents realize the government would follow through on its pledges.

Rochester, NY. The Neighbors Building Neighborhoods Program launched in 1992 provided the engine for revitalization. The city made neighborhoods equal partners in its long-term economic revival plans.

The World Changed

Established in the early 1800s as a mill-based industrial center powered by the Genesee River, Rochester reflects well-known patterns of urban growth and collapse. With river, Erie Canal, and railroad links to the expanding Northeast and the burgeoning Midwest, the city attracted waves of immigrants, new manufacturing techniques, and breakthrough technologies. Kodak and Xerox would transform Rochester into the image-making capital of the world. The city became a Mecca for investors, inventors, and business leaders. As businesses thrived, the city's neighborhoods rose from surrounding fields. They now include clapboard colonials and Queen Ann, Victorian, and Tudor houses, sized and situated to fit either blue-collar workers at the Genesee Brewery, middle-managers, or top Eastman-Kodak executives.

The growth prompted the development of parks, theaters, hospitals and museums. Civic leaders founded the venerable Eastman School of Music, Rochester University, Rochester Public Library, and Rochester Institute of Technology.

But city fortunes fell as steeply as they once had risen. In the early sixties, the city cleared large sections of stable and slum neighborhoods to build a segment of an ill-conceived urban interstate highway called the inner loop. It still surrounds the city like a moat or a wall. Rochester's leaders are discussing creative ways to reconfigure the loop and reconnect key pieces of the city. The east-west Interstate 490 took out even more commercial buildings and homes and severed vibrant commercial and residential districts. The 1964 riots sent upper- and middle-class residents scurrying to suburbs.

Despite the flight, the city retained some stability as late as 1984, says Edward J. Doherty, commissioner of the municipal Department of Environmental Services and a long-time Rochester resident. In 1984, the city celebrated its sesquicentennial, in part by negotiating a new sales tax-sharing plan with the county that put it on a considerably healthier financial footing.

"That year was a real high for the city," says Doherty. "And then the world changed."

Some businesses departed for the suburbs, or moved south to save on labor, overhead, and material costs. But the image-making capital of the world held its own through the mid-1980s, thanks to its most prominent corporate citizens, Eastman-Kodak, Xerox, and Bausch and Lomb. But the bulwark cracked in the mid-eighties as Kodak and the others struggled—and often stumbled—in an increasingly competitive global market place. The eighties brought layoffs and retrenchment. The new world order had changed Rochester in direct and sobering ways, Doherty says.

"From 1984 to 1994 we went from having the thirty-fourth highest median income of citizens in an urban area to one hundred and thirty-seventh," Doherty says. "It was indicative of big change."

Engineering a Comeback Block by Block

Although its corporate foundation had crumbled, Rochester had not lost its fundamental civic ethic. The home of Susan B. Anthony and Frederick Douglass and a terminus of the Civil War-era Underground Railroad, the city had long refused to settle for the status quo. When Rochester and other upstate cities hit bottom in the early nineties, residents and government fought back.

With the launch of NBN, the city tapped its homegrown civic power. The ten city sectors designed strategies for long-neglected blocks to come together and clean up streetscapes. Residents and the city joined to combat quality-of-life crimes like petty drug dealing and prostitution, violations of the city's noise ordinance (barking dogs and booming car stereos), and violations of the codes requiring property maintenance and removal of abandoned vehicles. Although the city worked to prove it would do its part in the cleanup, officials showed unequivocally that government could not do it all.

"What we discovered was that it wasn't so much serious crime that was impacting neighborhoods as it was quality-of-life issues like barking dogs, abandoned vehicles, derelict and abandoned properties, and cluttered and untended vacant lots," says Terry Borshoff, who heads the newly established network of six neighborhood-based service centers. "But the city can only do so much. At some point citizens have to get involved. Neighborhoods were ready to participate.

"The city has a history of active neighborhood associations," says Lois Geiss, president of the Rochester City Council, who entered Rochester politics as the director of her neighborhood association, a group that coalesced in the mid-1970s to prevent the neighborhood's finest old houses from being partitioned into apartments. "If anything, it has been the downtown that has been getting weaker as the neighborhoods were getting stronger."

Geiss employs a simple formula to promote civic engagement.

"It has been our experience that when neighborhoods are encouraged to be involved, they contribute," she says.

Geiss displays little concern that by building neighborhood activism, she may be nurturing future political opponents. The council's chief legislative assistant, Bill Sullivan observes, Rochester's activists prefer opposition to inattention.

"Neighborhoods where people are happy are much less likely to produce political competitors than neighborhoods that feel ignored and neglected," Sullivan says.

A New Future for Rochester

The NBN proposed 1,000 projects and goals, including renovating housing, building neighborhood schools, fixing sidewalks, and redesigning streets. The NBN also wanted to lure small businesses to commercial strips outside the city center. Work with the NBN also prompted the city to establish the six Neighborhood Empowerment Teams (NETs) to coordinate citizen action and promote the newly established Police and Citizens Together Against Crime (PACTAC) teams. The city plans eventually to open a NET office in each of the city's ten sectors.

"We use the NET offices not just to coordinate city and citizen action, but as think tanks for how to solve certain problems," says NET director Borshoff. "For example, working through a NET team we came up with a more aggressive and effective way to deal with private property owners who weren't taking care of their property."

Compliance with the city's tall grass ordinance jumped from fifty percent in 1997 to ninety-two percent in 1999 when the city developed steep fines for noncompliance and citizens realized the government had listened to complaints about sloppily maintained yards.

At the same time, city and neighborhood officials worked with NBN to create a system for surveying community assets—identifying and tapping volunteers with specific technical expertise and

pointing out cultural and business strengths and opportunities. The NBN also developed a system for measuring improvements in community vibrancy and livability.

NBN created a new neighborhood power structure in partnership with the city. When the city in 1997 turned its attention to its long-neglected comprehensive plan, which hadn't been updated in twenty-five years, city officials expected neighborhoods to lead its redesign. Dozens of meetings incorporating hundreds of ideas for neighborhood and downtown revitalization and stabilization blossomed into the Rochester 2010 plan. The plan includes: A Renaissance of Responsibility; A Renaissance of Opportunity; and A Renaissance of Community. Each describes strategies for enhancing civic engagement and outlines regional partnerships to broaden and sustain economic and civic vitality.

The new comprehensive plan adoption brings changes to the city's zoning ordinances. For example, the plan requires businesses to build out to sidewalks with parking relegated to the rear, allows a wider mix of uses in commercial corridors, and gives the city more control over the design of commercial construction and renovation.

Progress and Challenges

A tour of Rochester reveals the impact of just a few years of intensive and coordinated neighborhood and government action. A warehouse district is filled with construction equipment as laborers convert huge old buildings into lofts. A mix of market-rate and moderately priced housing is being built within walking distance of city hall. Farther out, where the Genesee River spills over a spectacular 100-foot waterfall, an emerging entertainment and restaurant district rejuvenates beautiful old brick and stone warehouses and mill buildings. In the city's more defined outlying neighborhoods, a campaign to restore commercial life is in the works. Public works crews are narrowing intersections to slow traffic and create sections of on-street parking to serve businesses. New schools, new supermarkets, new houses on vacant lots, and abandoned houses newly renovated for sale reverse the city's decline.

Home sales rose eleven percent from 1998 to 1999. Rochester has proved so adept at building, rehabilitating, and selling housing that HUD allows only this city to directly dispose of foreclosed federally owned properties. The privilege enables the city to aggressively package and sell derelict properties in concert with the local real estate community. Last year, the city sold nearly 100 vacant HUD properties to new owners and provided as much as $10,000 per house to help with renovation.

The city's work has resulted in both minor and major successes. Mike Piehler, who runs the city's only major car dealership—all the others have fled to the suburbs—says he remained in Rochester because the government joined with city residents to rebuild. Blue Cross and Blue Shield considered moving its Rochester regional office to the suburbs, but instead built a new office headquarters downtown, retaining 1,100 jobs.

Bringing Schools into the Neighborhood Mix

But difficult campaigns persist. Vibrant cities require good school systems, and Rochester's fails to attract families. Neighborhood leaders say the school system avoided working with the NBN though some school staff supported collaboration. In 1999, a frustrated Mayor Johnson dispensed with the apolitical approach to school board politics and primed his own slate of school board candidates. These candidates are more inclined toward broader cooperation between neighborhoods and the city.

"I figured that if I was going to take the blame for bad schools, I might as well get involved in who is elected to the board," the mayor says.

The Regional Connection

But one other troubling trend—a decade of flat growth—influences Rochester's development and threatens all of Monroe County.

"We in this region have the most pernicious kind of sprawl," says Johnson. "It is sprawl without growth."

To counter flat growth, the mayor and other city officials have reached outside city limits. They want to stimulate broader discussions of a very stark reality: Rochester and its neighboring jurisdictions will live or die by their ability to work together. Working separately has accomplished a zero-sum game of economic and social musical chairs, as the same jobs and people trade one place for another. To date, discussions have been very

preliminary and general, says Johnson. Nevertheless, opportunities abound for working across borders in the Rochester area and opportunity often knocks in unpredictable ways.

In 1992, when Sandra L. Frankel was elected supervisor of the Town of Brighton, just south of Rochester, she inherited the traditional gift bestowed on newly elected officials by their predecessors in New York: a crushing debt. Looking to save money, she wanted to contract with other municipalities for certain services—such as building inspections. After a rebuff from the flanking townships, she looked north, to Rochester, and found a very willing partner in Mayor Johnson. The city and the town agreed that Brighton could take full advantage of Rochester's broad building code and architectural and engineering expertise.

But Brighton had other problems in addition to big debts. In particular, the main commercial

A public market located in one of Rochester's 36 neighborhoods (photo left). Rochester's Mayor, William A. Johnson, elected in 1992, is a strong supporter of the city's neighborhood program (above).

corridor—Monroe Avenue—was crumbling.

"Brighton citizens were concerned that the town seemed to be fraying a little bit near the city border," Frankel says. Frankel did not close off the town. Building on her earlier relationships, Frankel joined with Rochester planners to update Brighton's comprehensive plan. Together these city officials have sketched the potential redevelopment and revitalization of Monroe Avenue, proposing a single marketing scheme for the entire corridor.

"We're seeing decreased storefront vacancies, more businesses doing facade improvements, and at the same time the whole corridor is developing a more residential feel," Frankel says.

Vision Great, Perseverance Mandatory

The Rochester comeback is slow and deliberate. The city has laid the foundation not with solitary, big-splash projects like museums or sports stadiums, or with the promise that corporate angels will someday bestow the city with bountiful jobs and buckets of tax dollars. City officials instead maintain a vision of a vibrant city, where revival begins with the existing people and resources. Rochester also has marshaled remarkable civic energy and expertise.

With dozens of new development projects under way, and with new and revitalized partnerships spanning the city and the region, Rochester bears close watching as it struggles to escape the fate of so many aging towns in the industrial Northeast. Its comeback will point the way for other regions suffering fallout from the rise of global competition and the dwindling importance of old-style corporate anchors in local economies. There is no shortage of similar communities in the United States.

2 | Building the Future by Boosting Today's Families

"I have seen the dual reality of the time that we live in," HUD Secretary Andrew Cuomo told the National Press Club as he released a report detailing how urban impoverishment thrives amid the country's unprecedented economic expansion. "Cities are the geography, the temple of community," he said. Yet, he related, ". . .the poverty, the despair—is just as bad in some places as it has ever been. And the sense of hopelessness is just as bad as it ever has been. For all the progress we've made, Lord knows we have longer to go."

" We can do this together. We can live together, all colors, all races, all classes. That's what cities say."

– ANDREW CUOMO, SECRETARY, U.S. DEPARTMENT OF HOUSING AND URBAN DEVELOPMENT

Cuomo's May 1999 report, "Now is the Time: Places Left Behind in the New Economy," exposes the resilience of urban poverty. Despite regional and national growth and prosperity, central cities experience a poverty rate of 18.8 percent, while only 9 percent of suburban residents are poor.

Urban communities that make progress in ameliorating poverty, and many do, still retain a disproportionate share of the country's racial and cultural strife and inequity. They do so while receiving the lion's share of immigrants from Eastern Europe, Asia, Africa, and Latin America—immigrants who enrich the cultural and business communities and increase the cultural complexity of cities seemingly to the breaking point. They do so while sheltering their children from the menace of bigotry and the subtler peril of poverty.

Cuomo argues that the success of our communities in this new millennium hinges on our ability to develop a new generation of educated, self-reliant workers and leaders. For the continued progress of our cities, he says, their leaders and communities must create safe, economically viable environments for all families.

Many communities already have begun turning distressed environments into livable neighborhoods. Police departments are joining forces with churches to make cities safe. Governments are training welfare recipients for the workplace by

employing them in community service. Businesses are securing their workforces by providing parents with quality day care. Foundations are directing their donations to job training and family security. Arts organizations are opening whole new vistas for troubled children by encouraging them to build and create. Schools not only are opening their doors to community organizations, but also are acting as catalysts for improving the health of communities.

These projects and programs share common change mechanisms. They pool federal, state, and private resources; build partnerships and leadership among disparate neighborhood-based organizations; and help restore the power over their own destinies that some families may believe they have lost.

Cuomo recognizes a community's ability to help recharge and rebuild families when he says: "We can do this together. We can live together, all colors, all races, all classes. That's what cities say."

The Faces of the New City

Cuomo's challenge to rebuild American communities in the twenty-first century resounds amid the powerfully divisive forces unleashed during the final decades of the twentieth. Federal highways have crosshatched communities—leaving desolate atolls in center cities and furthering the creation of outlying suburbs. Home-ownership subsidies help the middle class build in outlying grassy havens; new high-tech corporations locate at highway hubs linking distant suburbs. The race, economic class, and ethnicity of communities follow the highway arteries—with disparate groups clustering near off-ramps the way nineteenth-century communities clustered near ports and along rivers. The challenge of the twenty-first century is to harmonize the factions—creating communities with blended races, classes, ages, and economic groups.

Seek prosperity, and follow a direct path to the nation's suburbs—where the rise of technology and telecommunications firms has created a voracious demand for well-educated employees. Seek

Seek poverty, and the path leads through America's central city streets.

Table 1.

Welfare Receipt in 1989 for U.S. Natives, Foreign born

Group	Number	Recipients (Over 15)	Percent	Income
Native	176,529,000	7,476,000	4.2	$3,535
Foreign*	18,228,000	862,000	4.7	$4,485

Source: Tabulations from 1990 census
* These include all foreign-born persons from countries where refugees represent a large proportion of the immigrant flow during the 1980s. These countries include Afghanistan, Albania, Cambodia, Cuba, Ethiopia, Iraq, Laos, Poland, Romania, the Soviet Union, and Vietnam. From: "Immigration and Immigrants: Setting the Record Straight," The Urban Institute.

Table 2.

U.S. Crime Victimization (percent)

		White			Black		
	Total	Urban	Suburban	Rural	Urban	Suburban	Rural
Total crime	23.4	27.7	22.7	17.4	29.7	25.2	18.6
Personal crime	6.5	7.6	6.4	4.5	9.1	7.3	5.6
Property crime	19.9	23.8	19.2	14.8	24.7	20.8	15.5
Households (number)*	101.5	23.7	42.0	20.4	6.8	3.6	1.8

Note: Detail does not add to total because of overlap in households experiencing various crimes.

"We looked at gun violence in Boston in two ways. There was a demand for guns—an underlying dynamic that made [youths] seek out guns. There were also supply problems—identifying dealers and reducing the flow of guns."

—ANTHONY BRAGA, JOHN F. KENNEDY CENTER, HARVARD UNIVERSITY

poverty, and the path leads through America's central city streets. One can recognize the neighborhoods by their outward emblems: anonymous public housing complexes, graffiti-defaced public spaces, boarded windows of abandoned buildings, and overgrown vacant lots. Few businesses brave these dilapidated corridors where young people sometimes linger even in the wee morning hours. School buildings share the worn, unkempt appearance of the housing stock.

These outward images illustrate the social upheavals of the last two decades as the manufacturing base that drew millions of rural dwellers to the cities crumbled, middle-class whites and minorities migrated to the suburbs, and increasingly parsimonious federal leaders capped entitlement and other programs for the urban poor. The numbers living in concentrated poverty nearly doubled between 1970 and 1980, from 4.1 million to 8 million, according to the Brookings Institution Center on Urban and Metropolitan Policy. Even the most prosperous cities—New York and Chicago—that boast low overall unemployment rates—hide pockets of hopelessness, Cuomo notes

in "Now is the Time." In one of every six cities, the unemployment rate tops 9 percent, compared with the 4.5 percent average unemployment nationwide.

Many cities are losing population. Former manufacturing centers in Ohio, Illinois, Pennsylvania, and Indiana suffered the most dramatic losses. East St. Louis, once a working-class enclave, lost nearly a third of its population during the last decade and a half. The exodus of factories that depleted these Midwestern cities has not ended; in 1999, the country lost 500,000 manufacturing jobs. Cuomo attributes the higher poverty rates to structural barriers, including a lack of marketable skills among residents and rapid disinvestment in urban commercial centers.

Twelve years ago, then University of Chicago sociologist William Julius Wilson warned about a growing urban "underclass," of unemployed workers, isolated in desolate enclaves. A decade later, in his 1996 book, *When Work Disappears: The World of the New Urban Poor*, Wilson frets that for the first time in the twentieth century, in a typical week, most adults in inner-city neighborhoods will not work.

Although changes in the economy have created islands of austerity for thousands of poor families, for many immigrants, U.S. cities signify wealth and opportunity. Immigrants arrived in this country in record numbers during the eighties and early nineties, and by 1993, 22 million American residents were foreign-born, according to a 1994 Urban Institute analysis, "Immigration and Immigrants: Setting the Record Straight." Some immigrants are fleeing persecution in their own countries, but many journey to America to gain an education and find well-paying employment.

In inner cities and older suburbs, these foreign-born residents join large African-American populations, and can displace low-skilled American-born workers. When the local economy is weak, the influx can cause a depression in wages for low-level jobs, according to the Urban Institute. The majority of immigrants dwell in seven metropolitan areas—Los Angeles, New York City, Miami, Anaheim, Chicago, Washington, D.C., and San Francisco.

In these cities, immigrants brave their own challenges, securing profitable employment despite language and cultural barriers and preparing their children for schooling in a foreign tongue.

Though only a tiny percentage of immigrants depend on welfare or other government entitlements (Table 1), the number who are poor and who live in neighborhoods with high poverty concentrations has grown faster than has the number of natives in those communities. A Johns Hopkins University study of immigrant children in Miami and San Diego concluded that Latin American and Haitian children were more likely than natives to attain low-levels of achievement in U.S. schools and more likely to drop out.

"The dearth of opportunity and investment in these environments increase family isolation and undermine families' confidence and competence," note researchers from the Annie E. Casey Foundation in Baltimore. The foundation, which supports programs for children, now finances counseling and mentor programs to assist troubled families. It also has mounted a national research campaign on welfare reform. "These conditions also strain and sever connections to the contacts, relationships, and resources families so urgently need to do their jobs well."

Annie E. Casey researchers describe a nation that remains divided after nearly four decades of progress on race and poverty. The have-nots, who are disproportionately African American and Hispanic, occupy the central corridors where high-paying jobs are hard to come by. The *haves*—among whom whites predominate—dwell in the newer suburbs and exurbs reaching further into a countryside that now rarely sustains traditional rural communities.

The *haves* may still fear to tread the urban neighborhoods of the *have-nots*, where the violent crime rate runs higher than in the surrounding cities. The *have-nots* may still dream of inhabiting the safe green islands of the prosperous suburbs—but they cannot get a bus. Innovative communities overcome these obstacles and bring both groups together to build a common landscape.

Securing Neighborhoods

The first step to building a community is to free families from fear of violence and crime. The growing awareness among police officers of the relation between a neighborhood's economic health and its crime rate has generated new approaches to crime fighting. The focus has turned from solely arresting offenders—who may serve short sentences and return to the streets—to also improving relationships in neighborhoods. Officers try to work as peacekeepers as well as law enforcement authorities.

Police officers serving as peacemakers and problem-solvers help families and youths learn new strategies for living. Building networks among neighborhood organizations and churches help police work directly to heal the social fragmentation and chaos that define neighborhoods with high crime rates (Table 2).

New police programs highlight community problem-solving, a crime prevention approach

Operation Cease Fire, a community policing program initiated by the Boston Police Department, successfully works with community-based organizations and church members to reduce crime and curb youth violence.

originated by Herman Goldstein, a professor emeritus at the Wisconsin School of Law. Goldstein suggested that teaching police officers to be problem-solvers would enliven their work and engage them in the community; in turn, they would reinvigorate police crime prevention by providing executives and administrators fresh insight from neighborhoods.

Inspired by Goldstein's work, during the late eighties and early nineties, cities pioneered a new problem-solving technique called Scanning, Analysis, Response, and Assessment (SARA). SARA begins with a comprehensive examination of crime victimization and offender patterns and engages communities in defining neighborhood crime problems and their solutions. Tactics range from assigning each officer to a single neighborhood so they become familiar with the community, to working in collaboration with community groups, to providing after-school programs for children.

"Analysis and problem solving are the keys," says John Welter, assistant chief of the San Diego Police Department, which first explored community-policing techniques in the seventies. "Otherwise what you have are great relationships."

Justice Department officials considered the techniques so effective that President Bill Clinton decided to provide federal funds for the hiring of 100,000 new police officers; he ordered them primed in community-oriented problem solving. As a preliminary step in May 1999, Clinton announced the award of $66 million to sixty-five communities to finance the 882 community-policing officers through the Community Oriented Policing Services (COPS) of the Department of Justice.

One promising community program is Operation Cease Fire, an antigang project created in 1996 in Boston. The Boston Police Department, alarmed about the rise in gun violence among youths, began to explore new prevention approaches in 1990. The department joined with federal law enforcement agencies and invited community-based organizations and church members to help guide neighborhood problem solving.

The Kennedy School of Government at Harvard University assisted the department in examining crime patterns across the city and developing techniques for understanding and treating them. Their investigations revealed a concentration of violent crime, perpetrated mainly by fifteen- to twenty-one-year-old African-American males, in the city's poorest minority neighborhoods. By examining hospital records of gunshot wounds and deaths, and talking with neighborhood residents, clergy, and probation officers, the police were able to identify and track the gangs and target their leaders.

"We looked at gun violence in Boston in two ways," says Anthony Braga, a senior researcher at the Kennedy School. "There was a demand for guns—an underlying dynamic that made [youths] seek out guns. There were also supply problems—identifying dealers and reducing the flow of guns."

Community-based organizations and clergy gathered information from youths in their neighborhoods and helped the police broadcast a simple message: gang warfare would not be tolerated. When gang violence flared, the department substantiated its warnings through aggressive enforcement. Officers also targeted the most resilient gangs by ticketing their members for public

Table 3.

"Slow," "Same," and "Fast" Cities and Counties Broken Down by Concentration of State Welfare Caseload

% STATE CASELOAD In City/County (1996)	City or County Caseload Decline Compared to State Caseload Decline (1994-1997)		
	SLOWER Than State	SAME As State	FASTER Than State
60%-75%	Cook County New York		
45%-60%	Chicago Milwaukee County		Maricopa County (Phoenix)
30%-45%	Detroit Los Angeles County Philadelphia County Wayne County		
15%-30%	Boston Suffolk County Hartford Cuyahoga County (Cleveland) King County (Seattle) Dade County (Miami) St. Louis	Marion County (Indianapolis)	Denver County
0-15%	Bridgeport St. Louis County Allegheny County (Pittsburgh)		Mecklenburg County (Charlotte) San Francisco County

Source: The Brookings Institution

drinking and motor vehicle violations, as well as arresting probation violators and others with outstanding warrants.

"We tied harsh enforcement methods to violence," Braga continued. "We let them know that as long as they continued being violent they would get special treatment."

The police also referred 500 youth to a network of child service providers who placed them in drop-out prevention, counseling, and other programs. The John Hancock Mutual Life Insurance Company sponsors a summer internship program giving youths an opportunity to work with mentors and learn new conflict resolution skills to replace violence.

"For kids who wanted to step away, we have programs—job training, General Education Diplomas," Braga says.

Boston police credit the program for reducing the annual number of homicides by men below the age of twenty-four from 152 in 1990 to 43 in 1997. Boston's program has won accolades from the Justice Department for reducing crime and uniting neighborhood organizations.

Building an Economic Safety Net

Another federal program—welfare reform—also promises to help connect poor families with the community of businesses, government, and non-profit organizations that can end isolation. In the place of individual cash assistance to children, states now receive block grants called Temporary Assistance to Needy Families (TANF) under a law Clinton signed in 1996. Gone is the entitlement to as much cash assistance families may need in perpetuity—in its place are strict time limits on aid.

For poor families the new regime engenders unprecedented opportunities—states are training more welfare mothers for work than ever before—and unprecedented risks. The country's burgeoning economy has created jobs to employ roughly sixty-one percent of the former welfare mothers. New job skills and new relations with corporations and governments are emerging.

But the prognosis, so far, is less promising in inner cities (Table 3). Although the welfare rolls in the city have shrunk along with the rest of the country, the city's share of the total welfare burden has grown, according to the Brookings Institution.

Roughly twenty-nine percent of the total U.S. population lives in central cities, but forty-four percent of the nation's welfare recipients now reside in these areas, Brookings reports.

Even those families who are considered a success under the new anti-welfare regime have a tough time surviving. In Boston, for example, a single parent with a preschool child has to earn $15.28 an hour, or $32,000 a year, working forty hours a week, fifty-two weeks a year, just to make ends meet on a no-frills, no-subsidy budget, according to the Self-Sufficiency Standard for Massachusetts, produced by the University of Washington. Former recipients earn an average of $5.18 to $7.90 an hour.

Yet, for all the risks forcing families off the welfare rolls, this new discipline also holds promise; mothers who are compelled to join the workforce may gain new skills. They may create both social and economic networks that give them greater confidence and self-sufficiency. Children who witness their mothers working may develop expectations about their own abilities to hold jobs.

"For those families that have left welfare and joined the work force [sic], success will depend on whether they move into jobs with higher wages and benefits," writes Pamela Loprest of the Urban Institute in *Newsday* (September 1, 1999). "The goal is for them not merely to be better off than when they were on welfare, but also able to move further toward self-sufficiency."

Where Welfare Reform Works

A blueprint for successful welfare-to-work programs is emerging, according to studies by the Manpower Demonstration Research Corporation (MDRC), a nonpartisan research group, and other organizations. Effective state programs impose financial penalties on recipients whose collection of benefits exceed time limits and provide generous cash and other incentives for joining the work-force, according to MDRC and other researchers. Community mentors and responsible business leaders help families keep on track; transportation assistance shortens the distance between home and work. Such partnerships between worker and job, individual and community unite the poor with their otherwise isolated working neighbors.

The Minnesota Family Investment Program (MFIP), created in January 1998 from an earlier pilot program, requires families to begin preparing

Philadelphia@work will generate part-time community jobs for 3,000 hard-to-employ people during the next two years. A local nonprofit organization supplies specially trained job coaches or mentors who oversee the former recipients' job search and help them find unsubsidized jobs. Participants work twenty-five hours a week at minimum wage and spend another ten hours in training.

Chicago's Suburban JobLink transports former recipients to temporary jobs in the suburbs where they develop the work skills they need to compete for full-time positions.

Cleveland city planners changed the bus routes to connect former welfare recipients to the places where work thrives.

for work within six months of enrolling for assistance. The state has simplified food stamp and other benefit rules and pays child care directly to providers.

MFIP allows recipients to receive a declining share of their cash assistance until they earn twenty percent more than the federal poverty level—$19,760 for a family of four. Mothers who do not work or care for infant children are expected to participate in employment and training. If they do not, they lose a portion of their benefits.

After eighteen months, pilot MFIP participants enjoyed a forty percent higher employment rate and a twenty-seven percent earnings increase when compared with other Aid to Families with Dependent Children clients, according to MDRC. Because welfare administration costs were also higher, the state reduced the maximum earnings-with-benefits from 140 to 120 percent of the poverty level.

But such promising results elude many who collect welfare because they lack the job skills or mental stamina to remain employed. Sending mothers to the workforce cannot tear down geographic barriers—and related lapses in transportation—that isolate the poor in the cities. Communities are trying to mend these gaps.

Some states and cities use TANF funds to provide community-service jobs for hard-to-employ welfare recipients who lack job experience and readiness. Washington's Department of Community, Trade, and Economic Development contracts with local groups to provide case management and find education and training for participants

who earn part-time wages from the state while working in public and nonprofit organizations.

Many states also are piloting programs to help participants thwarted by learning disabilities, physical limitations, mental illness, or drug or alcohol addictions. Oregon integrated drug and alcohol treatment into its welfare program before Clinton enacted TANF, according to a study by Mathematica Policy Research Inc. of Cambridge.

In Oregon, TANF participants with addictions receive cash incentives for staying in treatment and financial penalties for withdrawing. During a year-long examination of Portland, fifteen percent of all TANF recipients were referred for a drug or alcohol assessment, the Mathematica study found. Of the forty-two percent who showed up for the assessment, eighty-two percent enrolled in treatment. Fifty-two percent of those who enrolled completed treatment. Oregon's welfare staffers believe the carrot-and-stick drug-treatment incentives boost the success of welfare reform in that state.

Corporations also have joined in the campaign to reduce welfare dependency. Marriott Corporation not only trains former recipients, but also includes them in their corporate-assistance programs that provide access to counselors. The Home Depot, in partnership with the Enterprise Foundation in Baltimore, is developing a comprehensive training and support strategy for former welfare recipients.

Religious communities that have traditionally assisted the poor through charitable works may now have a more formal role. Provisions of the 1996 Welfare Reform Act also allow states to contract with faith-based community organizations to provide services to welfare recipients, according to the Welfare Information Network. Churches and public agencies across the country are developing joint programs to provide mentor service or training to poor families. For example, a group in Alexandria, Virginia called Alexandrians Involved Ecumenically (ALIVE!) pairs volunteer mentors from congregations, community groups, and businesses with low-income individuals moving from welfare to work. Funded by the Robert Wood Johnson Foundation, ALIVE! employs a director and case manager to support and train the volunteer mentors.

According to the Urban Institute's Loprest and other researchers, the real test of welfare reform will come after the expiration of Medicaid and subsidized child care, adding to families' reliance on scarce community resources. In anticipation, foundations, government officials, and charities are trying to find ways to make families more self-sufficient. The Annie E. Casey Foundation sponsors both child-welfare and welfare-reform programs, linked with national evaluations, to identify programs that allow families to prosper and maintain their living standards.

The Ford Foundation seeks to build equity in neighborhoods. The Foundation's Delaware Valley Reinvestment Fund—which provides loans for houses and businesses in impoverished Philadelphia neighborhoods—is an example of Ford's worldwide campaign to help poor families build permanent resources of cash and economic security. Working with Philadelphia church groups, the Fund's community-loan program provided financing to build 159 affordable town homes in one of the city's impoverished neighborhoods.

Strategies to Save Children

With more mothers in the workforce, careproviders in community centers, parks, libraries, and recreation programs become central to families. Working parents need the support of such networks now more than ever because the workday absorbs time and saps energy; single parents have even greater needs to share their questions and concerns with other adults.

The earlier families forge connections with networks of adults who support parents, informally instruct children, and help set behavior limits, the better their children will fare—that's the conclusion of sociologists and child-development experts. New evidence indicates that children acquire verbal and other skills long before they enter school. Early education programs that expose preschool children to rich learning environments and allow them direct contact with adults who are not family members can help develop communication skills that will serve them for a lifetime and arrest the progress of habits that can be self-destructive.

Quality early childhood education yields benefits for more than the people directly served. For companies experiencing difficulties recruiting adequate workers, the availability of day care frees parents for work. Parents can better focus on their work if

they are confident that their children are safe and are developing appropriate skills. A host of studies even suggests that a quality early childhood education may help the nation in its perpetual battle to prevent crime.

Hirokazu Yoshikawa, a researcher at New York University, examined forty studies of preschool children in 1997 and concluded that the combination of early childhood education and family support services for parents reduced teenage delinquency and adult criminality.

The results can be startling. At Perry Preschool in Ypsilanti, Michigan, in the 1960s, researchers found dramatically lower delinquency rates among children who attended preschool compared to those with no early childhood education. By the time the 123 children studied had reached adulthood, only seven percent of the preschool-trained children had been arrested five or more times, compared with thirty-one percent of their peers. Studies at the Syracuse University Family Development Research Center, the Yale Child Welfare Project, and the Houston Parent-Child Development Center show similar results.

The overwhelming advance of mothers into the workforce—which will only increase as welfare reform takes shape—heightens the demand and need for such quality early education programs. But with price tags of $4,000 to $10,000 a year per child, they can be too costly for the poorest families who need them. Many of the poorest depend on family members or pay for poorly designed preschool programs. A 1995 study of child-care settings by University of Colorado researchers found that fewer than one child in ten receives excellent care, while more than half of child care is "fair," at best, according to the Children's Defense Fund.

The federal government provides $11 billion a year for child care through tax credits, subsidized day care, Head Start, and other family assistance programs, according to Isabel Sawhill, a senior fellow at the Brookings Institution. Yet, while forty-five percent of the families who benefit from these programs earn more than $50,000 a year, only one in ten poor families receive assistance, Sawhill found. Sawhill and other advocates propose that the government spend an additional $19 billion, or a total of $30 billion a year, to provide quality early education to all children.

Communities across the country already are

The Arts Incubator Program of Arlington County, Virginia, supports programs like the Hip-Hop poetry workshop with students from the Thomas Jefferson Middle School.

Top photo. *Babyland, an initiative of the New Community Corporation in Newark, NJ, is a community-based program that cares for preschool children and links families to a network of neighborhood services.*
Bottom photo. *The Brighter Futures for Families Christmas Party in Alexandria, VA. Alexandrians Involved Ecumenically (ALIVE!) pairs volunteer mentors with at-risk families seeking self-sufficiency.*

filling the gaps in federally financed services by forming partnerships with schools, business leaders, and churches. Nonprofit foundations, corporate donations, the United Way, as well as the federal and local governments, finance the programs.

Babyland, a child-care center founded to help working families reverse the economic distress caused by the devastating Newark riots in 1967, illustrates how a community-based program for preschool children can link their families with networks of services available in their neighborhoods. The program provides medical and mental health care, parent education, and assistance to abused or neglected children as well as those with AIDS or HIV. The staff also recruits, trains, and supports family child-care givers so that even the poorest parents have access to quality care.

Babyland draws expertise and support from federal and state agencies, Essex County Community College, the University of Medicine and Dentistry of New Jersey, and a variety of nonprofit and religious organizations. Fleet Bank, Prudential, AT&T, Blue Cross/Blue Shield, the Athletes Association, and others provide some financing and Lucent Technologies donated computers.

Corporations also are developing their own early childhood education programs. Butterball Turkey Company, a subsidiary of Con-Agra Corporation, implemented a child development/day care program as a way of recruiting workers to its new factory in Huntsville, Arkansas. The Butterball program and the Madison County Child Development Center also work in partnership with a host of nonprofit and government agencies.

Communities Use the Arts to Build Families

Similar community partnerships also are integrating child and family services with the traditional services of the public schools. The 21st Century Community Learning Centers, financed primarily by grants from the U.S. Department of Education, combine public schools, out-of-school enrichment programs, community service, and often adult education programs. They are meant not just to serve the children and youth, but also to engage parents and community members in designing the programs they believe will best serve families and communities. At the Lillian Emery 21st Century Learning Village in New Albany, Indiana, children can practice gymnastics and sports, and learn crafts

or dance after school, while their mothers get their high-school diplomas or get help applying for jobs.

The school draws many of its students from a nearby 600-unit public housing complex. When parents complained that gangs terrorized the neighborhood, school officials organized meetings with police, neighbors, and community groups to help break up the gangs.

As the New Albany example illustrates, parents' and children's needs for quality community relationships do not end when the day's last school bell rings. Yet, many parents have no choice but to leave their older children at home alone after school. Busy parents commute from the workplace, shop for food, clean their homes, and pay their bills during their precious few after-work hours. That leaves children to fend for themselves—making tough decisions in an increasingly complex world.

Adolescents wield discretion over forty to fifty percent of their after-school hours, reports the Carnegie Corporation of New York. Those are the hours from three to eight p.m.—when they are the most susceptible to criminal victimization, according to Carnegie's 1992 report on adolescence called "A Matter of Time." A later Carnegie study shows that children left alone during these hours spend only fifteen to twenty minutes talking to adults each week. These children make their own decisions about how to spend their time and with whom, but lacking supervision, they also lack the training and preparation they need to make the right decisions and plans.

The answer may seem simple—keep kids in school longer. But youths can only concentrate on school activities for so long, and many after-school programs only make children feel they are being punished or detained, says the March 1998 study "The Arts in Non-School Hours." The decade-long study, financed by the Carnegie Foundation for the Advancement of Teaching, examined 120 national and community-based organizations serving 30,000 children.

The study showed that after-school arts programs—unlike homework sessions or some recreation—offer promise. They provide adolescents a safe way to practice solving problems for themselves. Practice in self-expression also can boost children's mental development. In sum, arts programs increase adolescents' self-confidence, as well as boost the likelihood that they will attend college (see Leadership Profile).

Community arts programs are as varied as the groups who run them. In Washington, D.C., the Levine School of Music works with the public housing authority to provide music lessons for tenants. Children attend free forty-minute music lessons once each week and have an opportunity to perform in three neighborhood recitals. The Kinara Quartet, an African-American music ensemble, also performs at the public housing properties and spends time talking to and advising the music students. The Levine School also operates music programs for preschool students and teaches child-care workers and others how to use music to help motivate children to learn.

The University of New Mexico Institute of Public Law operates a television and video program for youths from ages twelve to nineteen. The youths help write, edit, and produce segments on social issues like alcohol abuse, verbal violence, and teen/parent relationships in a format that also includes audience participation and Saturday-Night-Live-style skits.

In Philadelphia, youth on probation conceived and designed a comic book. In a project sponsored by the Pennsylvania Prison Society, the students learned how to develop a story line and illustrate it. Professional artists, storytellers, and cartoonists not only provided artistic training, but also talked to the students about living by values other than material ones. The students also produced a rap tape and a selection of short stories. Each project required the students to analyze the technique, talk with professionals, and make the finished project.

After-school arts projects and community-based early childhood education programs share goals and desired outcomes with community police forces and job programs for former welfare recipients. Where economic status and racial heritage divide people, innovative community members—in churches, government agencies, or nonprofit organizations—can unite them. Where disinvestment results in neglected neighborhoods, shared self-expression and creativity can renew them. Community school staff can invigorate their learning environments by making the parents both bosses and beneficiaries. State welfare agencies can help even the most inexperienced welfare mothers get jobs—by first hiring them to staff community-service programs.

Communities across the country are even demonstrating that, when united, they can deflect

the inexplicable rise of bigotry in a country more culturally complicated than ever before.

In *10 Ways to Fight Hate*, The Southern Poverty Law Center of Montgomery, Alabama, depicts communities across the country who have used their strength in numbers to cull hate groups from their cities. When a landowner attracted white supremacy groups to his ranch near Yukon, Pennsylvania, for example, the townspeople fought back by holding vigils and demonstrations near the property. The owner eventually sold his property and left town.

It's not kumbayah," says the book's author, Jim Carrier. "Fighting hate in a community is a protracted, ugly, scary job. [Approaches] can vary from holding a candlelight vigil to going door-to-door to spread information. The most important is for communities to band together and speak out, with their [F]irst [A]mendment rights, against hate. [The antihate group] should include the mayor, school principals, and congressional representatives."

Andrew Cuomo ended his report on poverty and urban decline with an impassioned call to build communities. Neighborhood groups across the country already have answered by joining forces and solving problems. Family by family, officer by officer, neighborhoods can provide the new century's next generation an economically and spiritually secure place to mature.

Top photo. *Capital Commitments in Washington, D.C. provides a telecommunications training program for unemployed residents. Lucent Technologies, Bell Atlantic, Nortel Networks and Marconi Communications donate equipment, funding, and instructors.*
Bottom photo. *Port Discovery, The Children's Museum in Baltimore, provides interactive exhibits that are fun and educational. It also houses a public library that attracts children from surrounding downtown neighborhoods.*

A Philadelphia Story:
Culture Builds Community

LEADERSHIP
PROFILE

The Point Breeze Performing Arts Center shows how the arts not only can inspire and uplift audiences, but also can unite neighbors to better their communities. When the innovative Point Breeze Center Positively to the Point dance troupe was invited to perform at the National Conference on Community Development in Australia in 1996, parents raised $6,000 from candy and bake sales. Focus on the immediate goal of sending the young dancers abroad converted parents into advocates for their kids, the dance troupe, and the center.

The Australia trip illustrates the role that culture can play in building community and in spurring grass-root support for community-development initiatives. Culture Builds Community (CBC) is the name of a program for forty community arts organizations in Philadelphia. Managed by Partners for Livable Communities and financed by the William Penn Foundation, CBC recognizes the power of local cultural institutions to anchor a community, supplement learning for populations neglected by the traditional school system, and drive economic activity. Three of four children younger than eighteen live within a mile of a community arts facility, and CBC shows how the arts can be agents for invigorating and restoring a community's character and sense of identity. As Point Breeze demonstrated, arts can serve as a rallying point for reviving diminished civic enthusiasm.

In 1997, the William Penn Foundation established multiyear grants worth $3.5 million to community-based arts and cultural centers in the greater Philadelphia area with the following components:

Core support. Assisting select organizations to improve their financial management, fund-raising, and operations while strengthening bonds with the surrounding community;

Earned income demonstration projects. Offering technical assistance and seed money to help grantees build an entrepreneurial spirit that can provide a much-needed revenue stream for often cash-strapped enterprises while spurring local economic development;

Artistic enhancement. Funding residencies, teacher training, and materials that strengthen core programs; and

Youth Access. Supporting programs that reduce the barriers to participation in arts and cultural programs for youth ages five to eighteen.

Youth Collaboration. Helping arts and non-arts organizations develop joint programs for young adolescents ages ten to fifteen.

But CBC intends to do more than strengthen arts and cultural organizations in the Philadelphia area; it plans to document the ways community arts programs can add value to the lives and economies of city residents. Hence, evaluation must be part of any program if arts and cultural organizations are to succeed in proving their worth to funders and to the larger community. To expand research indicating that arts programs sell more tickets than sporting events and student musicians and artists score higher on achievement tests, CBC enlisted two researchers from the University of Pennsylvania's School of Social Work to design and carry out an evaluation of the Penn Foundation project. The resulting three-year study called the Social Impact of the Arts Project (SIAP) explains the arts' impact on social structure and neighborhood development.

SIAP researchers Mark Stern and Susan Seifert compiled a massive database measuring the impact of 15,000 noncommercial and voluntary social organizations, including art centers, churches, and social service agencies. They sought to explore:

Culture and civic engagement. To identify networks of trust and collaboration within neighborhoods;

Communities and the metropolitan area. To examine the links between Philadelphia's downtown Center City—home of large arts and cultural institutions—and local neighborhoods; and

Culture, diversity, and the quality of life. To assess the relation between demographic diversity and arts and cultural organizations.

The evaluation team's initial findings add quantifiable weight to the proposition that strong arts and cultural programs strengthen communities. When the team finished correlating the nonprofit organization's data with census information, voter registration records, and measures like school achievement, they concluded that arts and culture are strongly linked to quality-of-life indexes. SIAP found that neighborhoods with many arts groups also had an increased number of other voluntary organizations. Individuals engaged in the arts are more likely to be active in other forms of civic participation. Arts particularly flourished in diverse neighborhoods, while rates of poverty declined and population increased in neighborhoods where residents participated in different arts and cultural organizations.

Over the duration of the CBC project, the people involved have bcome aware of both the power of community arts and their under-representation at a national level. CBC is not just about developing individual organizations and their ties to local communities. It is also about engendering a community arts network that has a voice in national conversations on issues such as youth and community development. CBC participants are developing a structure that will continue beyond the life span of the project, to build that voice and spread their message outside Philadelphia.

A dance troupe from the Point Breeze Performing Arts Center gives a performance at a Philadelphia neighborhood festival. The Arts Center, part of the Point Breeze Community Development Corporation, provides a safe haven and creative environment for neighborhood children.

After-School Arts Programs Expand
Children's Confidence

LEADERSHIP
PROFILE

A team of researchers from Stanford University and the Carnegie Foundation for the Advancement of Teaching led by Shirley Brice-Heath recently completed a decade of research (1987-1997) on youth development during non-school hours. The key question guiding the analysis was "What happens in community-based organizations that draws young people to sustained participation and achievement?" The researchers studied 120 community-based organizations in thirty-five locations involving 30,000 children.

ArtShow: Youth and Community Development is a resource guide on the success of after-school cultural programs in assisting at-risk youth.

The researchers examined three types of after-school programs: athletic-academic, community service, and arts. All programs cost nothing and encouraged voluntary participation by youth.

The researchers found similar organization priorities among the successful programs; they:

- Depend on young people to be resources not problems.
- Expect everyone to play different roles.
- Ensure young people learn to expect the unexpected.
- Provide a structure of planning, practicing, performing, and evaluating.
- Require youth to imagine future possibilities through if-then and what-if questions.
- Demand self-assessment.
- Demand accountability to excellence.
- Allow the work of the program to go hand in hand with play.
- Provide a sense of safety and predictability.

In its initial seven years, the study paid no special attention to arts organizations. But the data suggested that arts provide youth with a particularly comprehensive range of opportunities for development. A selection of young members completed the National Educational Longitudinal Survey (NELS), enabling a comparison between youth participating in arts-based organizations and a national database of students attending schools across the United States. Youth in arts programs are:

- Twenty-five percent more likely to report feeling satisfied with themselves.
- Thirty-one percent more likely to say they plan to continue education after high school.
- Eight times more likely to receive a community service award.
- Four-and-a-half times more likely to win an award for writing an essay or poem.
- Three times more likely to win an award for school attendance.
- Four times more likely to participate in a science or math fair.
- Twenty-three percent more likely to say they can do things as well as most other people can.
- Twenty-three percent more likely to believe they can make plans and successfully work from them.

In comparison with other activities, arts intensify the characteristics of effective learning environments; they:

- Expose young people to a greater range, degree, and frequency of risk.
- Provide an opportunity for the development of individual identity within a group.
- Ask youth to suspend disbelief, deal with intense emotions, and explore vulnerabilities.
- Demand that youth take a high level of responsibility.
- Require discipline and flexibility.
- Focus on the present activity while looking forward to future possibilities.
- Allow young people to bring their perceptions of daily life into the creative work.

The Stanford research concludes that the arts offer rich opportunities for learning. The arts feed motivation. Their fundamentally expressive base requires youth to interpret and produce individually and in groups. The necessity of critique ensures analytical attention. Facing audiences gives young people incentives to explore with restraint. The opportunity to move through work cycles—from practice through display—requires young artists to explore many roles in different media with varying levels of responsibility.

Urban Health Initiative

7900 E. Greenlake Dr. N. Suite 302
Seattle, WA 98103-4850
www.urbanhealth.org

Contact: Charles Royer,
National Program Director
206.616.3637

Five U.S. cities, in partnership with a foundation, work to improve children's health and opportunity. The Robert Wood Johnson Foundation initiated the Urban Health Initiative (UHI) in 1995 when the foundation invited community leaders in twenty cities to apply for two-year planning-and-development grants.

The application process, a single letter of interest from each city, is designed to foster collaborative thinking and to unite previously unconnected or mutually disinterested groups toward a single goal. Eight cities—Baltimore, Chicago, Detroit, Miami, Oakland, Philadelphia, Richmond, and Sacramento—each received approximately $200,000 a year for two years of planning and development.

As many as five cities also would receive funding for eight years of implementation. Throughout this planning-and-development phase, the sites could access technical support and coordination from the University of Washington in Seattle. New York University's Robert F. Wagner Graduate School of Public Service evaluated the projects.

Each city participating in the Urban Health Initiative developed separate implementation plans based on local conditions, with no mandates from the university or the foundation. The local focus enables each city to select its own project leaders, build community collaboration, establish specific priorities, select and prioritize interventions, and work with local communications consultants to design strategies. Baltimore, Detroit, Oakland, Philadelphia, and Richmond each received grants averaging an annual

$1.2 million for four years. Each will be eligible to apply for four more years of Foundation funding.

The Baltimore project provides pre- and postnatal care for children, hosts after-school activities, involves the entire community in promoting literacy, and works to take guns away from kids.

Monitoring the success of the initiative is key: Project participants document and share their accomplishments and best practices; they also alert others to strategies proven less fruitful. The goal is to improve health and safety for all city children. Each city must develop leadership, collaborative processes, and data response systems. They must build flexible rules and create bridges between affluent and poor neighborhoods. Strong communications plans also are required. If cities develop according to these core principles, the UHI asserts, children's lives can be improved and the improvements can be sustained.

Denali Initiative

Manchester Craftsmen's Guild
1815 Metropolitan Street
Pittsburgh, PA 15233
www.denaliinitiative.org

Contact: Joetta Adams
412.322.1773 x187

The Denali Initiative was established to provide *know-how* to aspiring social entrepreneurs. Nonprofit organizations today are expected to address complex social needs. But even when strong vision, powerful ideas, and sufficient funding are in place, the entrepreneurial skills to implement and sustain programs may be lacking. Clearly it is not enough to have good intentions for social impact. Nonprofit leaders must understand how to make their social programs effective.

Based in Pittsburgh, the Denali Initiative awards fellowships to teach a new generation of social entrepreneurs how to envision improvements in their comm-

unities and to mobilize the necessary resources. The program identifies outstanding nonprofit leaders based on their commitment to social enterprise and the viability of their proposed projects. Denali Initiative Fellows and their organizations are expected to launch a major social enterprise midway through the three-year program. The Denali Initiative provides technical assistance and mentoring throughout the program.

To select the most outstanding nominees, a panel of leaders and non-profit and private-sector entrepreneurs invites candidates to complete detailed applications. Applicants must propose a major social enterprise project, demonstrate the support of their board of directors, and supply community-support letters and other evidence of achievement. The panel then reviews applications, identifies applicants to be interviewed, and selects participants who will serve as fellows.

The Denali Initiative evolved from a collaboration among the Manchester Craftsmen's Guild and various foundations, including the E.M. Kauffman Foundation and the W.K. Kellogg Foundation. The guild provides opportunities for young people to experience high quality visual art and music, and to study art making under the guidance of local masters. William E. Strickland, Jr., the guild's president and chief executive officer, leads the Denali Initiative. The initiative offered its first round of fellowships in the spring of 1999 and will name new fellows every eighteen months.

The New Hope Project, Inc.

2821 N. 4th St., Suite 516B
Milwaukee, WI 53212
newhope@execpc.com

Contact: Julie Kerksick,
Executive Director
414.267.6020

Project New Hope extends assistance and training to low-income workers and their families in Milwaukee. Milwaukee created this innovative welfare-reform program in two city neighborhoods in 1994 to increase families' incomes, financial security, and access to full-time employment. Beginning in 1994, all low-income workers in the two target areas, and those not employed but willing to work full time, received New Hope benefits. New Hope used broad eligibility rules intended to serve the most diverse population possible—spreading benefits equitably. To enable its participants to comprehensively attack poverty, New Hope offered access to four distinct program components: an earnings supplement, affordable health insurance, child care subsidies, and full-time job opportunities for those unable to find paying work.

New Hope is designed to parallel the existing public assistance system. Financed by a consortium of local, state, and national organizations involved with work-based antipoverty policy, New Hope also receives money from the State of Wisconsin and the federal government. New Hope also trains its volunteers. A nongovernmental agency, New Hope provides a model for and an insight into the role of nonprofits in family income-support programs.

New Hope contracted with an independent research corporation to evaluate its program and provide credible information to policymakers on the implementation, effectiveness, and expense of welfare reform. The research revealed that New Hope increased the work effort and earnings of those not already working full time, improved people's lives, and reduced poverty among low-income workers and their families in Milwaukee.

Operation Cease Fire

Boston Police Department
1 Schroeder Plaza
Boston, MA 02120

Contact: James Jordan,
Director
617.343.4507

Operation Cease Fire encourages safety and peace of mind among city residents. From 1990 to 1994, Boston counted 155 homicides among teenagers. In the last two years, thanks to an innovative new policing program, Operation Cease Fire, the homicide rate has dropped to zero. The police department, cooperating with city clergy, formed a coalition of probation officers, community workers, educators, and school police who identified potential "hot spots" of gang trouble. Once a community is identified as a hot spot, police convene a meeting of gang members and "lay down the law." The gang members must sign a nonviolence pact and renounce possession and use of guns or ammunition. Failure to meet requirements results in severe penalties— federal and local sentencing as recommended by Boston's district attorney and the U.S. attorney.

The central philosophy of Operation Cease Fire is that punishment is not the ultimate solution to the problem of gangs and youth violence. The program emphasizes education, provides alternatives to violence, and creates opportunities for youths to develop skills that will lead to well-paying jobs. Boston religious institutions decided to participate after gang violence erupted at a funeral in Roxbury. The incident demonstrated the gang members' brazen disregard for peace, civility, and the sanctity of the church. In Operation Cease Fire, serious troublemakers are prosecuted, while the rest are steered into churches that offer after-school programs and summer jobs.

The program has been designated as a model for the nation and was awarded the prestigious Ford Foundation Award and a $100,000 grant. The grant money will enable the Boston Police Department to share its knowledge with other law enforcement agencies and promote replication of Operation Cease Fire in other cities. Operation Cease Fire's success at curbing youth violence is due to the program's roots in the religious community as well as in community collaboration to help at-risk youth and provide committed leadership. The result of these efforts is nothing short of miraculous and an inspiration to cities across the nation struggling to make their neighborhoods safe.

Self-Enhancement, Inc.

3920 N. Kerby Ave.
Portland, Oregon 97227

Contact: Kelly Mohr,
Assistant to the Director of Development
503.249.1721

Portland's Self-Enhancement, Incorporated (SEI) harnesses youthful energy and boldness to create a state-of-the-art youth center. SEI staff persuaded donors and local governments to spend millions to create a place for kids to hang out. The SEI Center for Self-Enhancement in North Portland provides programs for at-risk youth in education, recreation, and the performing arts. To build the Center, SEI first obtained land in a location easily and safely accessible via public transportation. SEI hired architects, designers, and contractors and obtained materials.

To attract donors and local officials, SEI's development director took prospective funders on a bus tour through low-income neighborhoods, ending with SEI's in-school programs for youths. These potential donors met the kids benefiting from, and really enjoying, SEI programs. This experience proved to be the clincher for many donors who could see the value of their investment in the accomplishments of these children. Many of the youths in SEI programs improved their grades and graduated with honors as a result of their participation.

The SEI's site choice also proved successful. When the staff chose an abandoned and decrepit lot, Portland Parks Bureau secured $1.2 million in state lottery funds and restored it. A major corporate donor, US Bankcorp, signed on to help when the head of their corporate giving program convinced the bank's president, Ed Jensen, to give $1 million to initiate development. Jensen's credibility among Portland's big money donors inspired large one-time donations as well as sustained giving. The most notable gift has been the $5 million, ten-year endowment builder from Portland businessman Eli C. Morgan. Portland philanthropists Ed and Sue Cooley contributed $1.2 million for construction of the center, and a further $1 million for an endowment. SEI is committed to helping Portland youth head off serious social problems.

YouthFriends
1000 Broadway, Suit 302
Kansas City, MO 64105
www.youthfriends.org

Contact: Lisa Ashner Adkins,
Executive Director
816.842.7082

Created in response to research showing children in Kansas City needed caring, adult role models, YouthFriends' mentors work with more than 40,000 young people. YouthFriends is a school-based volunteer effort in Greater Kansas City that connects young people, ages five through eighteen, with caring, adult volunteers in schools. Volunteers serve as mentors, tutors, readers, coaches, storytellers, homework helpers, special project directors, and career counselors to groups, classes, and individuals.

Created in 1995 as a pilot project in six districts by the Greater Kansas City Community Foundation, YouthFriends grew to include school districts throughout the greater Kansas City region. Kansas City's city manager endorses the program by allowing city employees ninety minutes of paid time each week when they volunteer in schools. Currently more than 6,000 adults have been screened, trained, and placed as YouthFriends volunteers in more than twenty-one school districts. In 1999, YouthFriends launched an expansion effort into the state of Kansas through a partnership with the Southeast Kansas Education Service Center-Greenbush. YouthFriends has been able to expand so rapidly and achieve such success because of the willingness of school districts and employers to allow their workers an hour each week for volunteer activities.

Ray Chambers provided the original funding through a gift from the National Mentoring Partnership. YouthFriends now is sustained through grants and educational funds.

The Georgia Project
101 N. Thornton Ave.
P.O. Box 886
Dalton, GA 30722-0886

Contact: Erwin Mitchell,
Director
706.281.1530

Demographic shifts can precipitate a crisis or fuel a dream. The Georgia Project has transformed a crisis into a tremendous cultural opportunity. The presence of a new Hispanic immigrant labor force in Dalton, Georgia necessitated performing the intricate task of educating Spanish-speaking children. The crush of new students began in 1994, when Hispanic workers who had steadily filled the job opportunities in the Dalton carpet industry imported their families. The difficulties of working with so many students for whom English was a second language overwhelmed the schools. Erwin Mitchell witnessed the communications breakdown and decided to help. He sought usable models by observing other school systems with similar language challenges. United business leaders, educators both in Mexico and Dalton, and new teachers helped Mitchell create The Georgia Project.

Mitchell modestly credits self-interest as the motivation for the education project. He understood that, in the long-term, education reform would ensure a well-educated workforce. But long-term, progressive views require active, committed communities to ensure equity. Financial commitment came first from the local government; federal officials anted up later, and, finally, area businesses donated funds, creating a private-public partnership.

Bilingual education projects are a perennial source of controversy, but rather than succumb to negative pressure, educators in Dalton created an equitable solution for the newest citizens of the area. The program sends city and county teachers to Mexico for intensive summer programs in language and culture, as well as helping Dalton to develop a bilingual program for students. Bilingual teachers from Monterrey, Mexico are also placed in Dalton schools to serve as essential translators, role models, and cultural liaisons between public schools and Hispanic parents. Everyone hopes The Georgia Project will become a new, progressive model for schools across the nation faced with similar changes, making a cultural opportunity out of a crisis.

Best Practices

Lifetime Sports Academy

City of Fort Wayne
One Main Street
Fort Wayne, IN 46802
www.cityoffortwayne.org

Contact: Joan Goldner,
Executive Director,
Ft. Wayne Sports Corporation
219.420.1305

The Lifetime Sports Academy teaches area children sports they can play for life. Although swinging a golf club may not be everyone's idea of a necessary skill, the development of sports skills and, as a result, self-esteem, have broadened and enriched the lives of thousands of Fort Wayne kids.

The Lifetime Sports Academy kicked off during the summer of 1998 under the leadership of former Fort Wayne Mayor Paul Helmke. The program helped youths learn tennis, golf, and swimming—all sports that can be enjoyed for a lifetime—at no cost. The Academy operates for six weeks during the summer, offering free classes at a central city park. Along with free sports lessons, eight- to eighteen-year-old children also receive free lunches from the local public school system.

In 1998, the nonprofit Ft. Wayne Sports Corporation successfully raised nearly $200,000 in-kind and monetary donations for the Lifetime Sports Academy program. These funds helped pay the salaries of instructors as well as helping to finance construction of new tennis courts and a driving range. Area businesses also donated equipment provided free to participating children.

Thousands of Fort Wayne kids now know how to drive a golf ball, swim the breaststroke, and serve a tennis ball. In future summers, the Academy hopes to increase enrollment and funding to ensure that more children will have the opportunity to learn a sport they can enjoy for the rest of their lives.

Northlake Community School

City of Orlando Florida
400 S Orange Ave.
Orlando, FL 32801

Contact: Paul S. Lewis, AICP,
Senior Planner
407.246.3358

The Northlake Community School demonstrates an innovative public-private partnership that builds schools to keep pace with a growing community. Touted as an original among American schools, Northlake is more than just an elementary school; it is a neighborhood center/gathering place, city park, and family wellness/recreational facility. To achieve this appealing mixture of uses, the City of Orlando, Orange County Public Schools, Central Florida YMCA, Orlando Regional Healthcare System, and Lake Nona together provided a "thoughtful development" scheme for the 19,300-acre green-field area east of the airport. The school is the centerpiece of new residential areas designed using Traditional Neighborhood Design concepts by the Lake Nona Land Company. Lake Nona oversees and finances the design and construction of the facility. The City, school, and YMCA will pay user fees for the first four years to purchase the building. These user fees are calculated according to the development pace of the surrounding neighborhood. Because Lake Nona will pay impact fees for homes constructed in a designated area, beginning on the date of project completion through 2004, the school user fee collected is calculated to remain below $1,300,000. Additionally, the YMCA pays $1 million annually for its user fees. On the transfer date, each party pays Lake Nona in-full and assumes ownership of the land and facilities.

In adjusting the cost over a four-year period, the city, school, and YMCA gain substantial savings, essentially by purchasing land and structures in 2004 at contemporary prices. The total cost, $12,300,000 for land and facilities, apportions $8.6 million for the school and $3.7 million for the YMCA and city. Combining costs in a multiuse structure saved nearly $1.5 million. Furthermore, new families are provided with quality education and recreational services within their own neighborhood, encouraging community building.

The center's proximity to new housing at Lake Nona and to a major highway ensure access for both local and regional users. The 130,000-square-foot school, accommodating 762 students, is in a twenty-two-acre park. In addition to classrooms, the school will have art, music and skills development labs, resource rooms, a media center, and specific learning disability labs. The full-service YMCA includes a food court, ball fields, and a pool. The club will also include tennis and basketball courts and aerobics, weight, and game rooms. These facilities will be complemented by health maintenance and education services. By building a facility that is more than simply a school, the first significant civic component of this new growth area, the contributing partners have managed to create a true community-building amenity.

City of Seattle Family Centers

City of Seattle, Human
Services Department
Alaska Building – 6th Floor
618 Second Avenue
Seattle, WA 98104

Contact: Patricia Wells,
Manager
Family Support Programs
206.386.1001

Stemming from a 1990 citywide Education Summit, the Seattle Family Centers offer a place where families can strengthen both familial and community ties. Family centers are informal, community-based places to welcome families. To avoid helping create family dependency, organizers designed the family centers to be inviting places for families to participate in programs and learn, while at the same time encouraging autonomy. The centers' goal is to foster long-term stability among families, and by extension, in the community.

The first family centers were funded by a families and education levy supported by voters. Located in the north, west, and south neighborhoods of Seattle, the demonstration projects included a high degree of evaluation, supplying needed data concerning project effectiveness. With positive results, the following year the City's Parks and Recreation program provided funding so that space in four new community recreation centers could be dedicated to family-support activities. Additionally, the program added two new centers. One, a result of grassroots organizing, demonstrates the ground swell of admiration and positive community reaction to the project. The other was a satellite of the original program. By 1998, almost 1,900 families were engaged in support activities at Seattle's family centers.

The philosophy behind the centers is that families have needs, face rough times, and can benefit from support.

At the same time, families bring their unique strengths to programs. Furthermore, "family" is an ethnically, religiously, and culturally diverse category that can not always be divided into neat stages according to gender or age. Family centers in Seattle rely on residents' active participation in developing their own programs and activities. The centers aim to strengthen families, attend to children's education, and make parents a part of their child's learning readiness. These goals are pursued with a careful balance in mind: increasing families' self-sufficiency while providing support.

Tailored to the neighborhoods that surround them, the centers offer programs and activities designed to attract participants, including parent education, parent and child activity times, English as Second Language classes, and topical workshops. The centers pay particular attention to responding to each participant. For example, a group of Spanish-speaking young mothers wanted to form a support group, so the family center offered them a free meeting space, child care, and source material in Spanish. Their range of programs also includes four different East African education groups, as well as Teen-Parent High School completion programs. The changes in the welfare law brought multiple requests for programs to promote family self-sufficiency. The New Citizen Initiative aids immigrants and refugees in preparation for citizenship exams. The Teen-Parent Self-Sufficiency Project helps teenage parents complete high school equivalency programs and teaches them to balance employment and good parenting.

The Seattle Family Centers emphasize evaluation and promote equity. The centers use parent surveys, translated into ten common languages, to gather information to improve and expand their programs. The multilingual surveys ensure that participants of family center programs feel comfortable discussing their experiences.

3 | Home Ownership in the Center City

Twenty years ago, few middle–class residents lived in downtown Memphis, Tennessee. Like nearly every other major American city during the fifties and sixties, Memphis had directed its growth toward the suburbs by annexing new residential communities. Despite a large daytime population of office workers, downtown Memphis remained virtually empty at night. Although the downtown area had a rich inventory of historic buildings, many sat empty.

In the past two decades, public officials in many American cities recognized that downtown housing is a critical component—perhaps the most critical component—of vital cities.

Today, housing dominates downtown Memphis. Subdivisions of single-family houses for upper-middle-class residents can be found at the northern and southern edges of downtown. In the city center, historic office buildings and warehouses have found new life as apartments and residential and office quarters. Newly confident developers build apartments and condominiums downtown, particularly along the Mississippi River, where a new park along the riverbank has attracted downtown residents. Housing has become so popular downtown, in fact, that prices have risen sharply and city officials are working to bring affordable homes onto the market.

The growth of downtown housing in Memphis stemmed from a fortunate confluence of several factors. Chiefly, a strong municipal government policy encouraged downtown living and the city provided incentives to home buyers and developers to buy and rehabilitate buildings. Market conditions, particularly the strength of the downtown employment base, were also favorable enough to attract private-sector home builders. Low-cost land and buildings were available.

Today, the density and residential ambiance of downtown Memphis have created an atmosphere attractive to pedestrians, which is unusual for a city of about 600,000 people. "It's difficult to find

a city of our size, where you can live without a vehicle, and walk to the office and the grocery store," says John Lawrence, the director of business development for the Center City Commission, a local nonprofit organization that is involved in downtown revitalization. "It's a big-city lifestyle in a relatively small town."

Downtown Memphis is not an isolated example. In the past two decades, public officials in many American cities recognized that downtown housing is a critical component—perhaps the most critical component—of vital cities. Housing is the glue that binds communities, the guarantor of urban vitality.

The History of Urban Housing

Historians may find it ironic that present-day public officials must argue that housing be woven into the urban fabric. Housing had almost always been synonymous with center-city areas, at least until the twenties, when zoning codes created arbitrary divisions between residential neighborhoods and the workplace. Even today, many European cities (and some American ones, as well) allow and even encourage mixed-use development. With the

Gayoso House (left) and Riverset (above), new housing complexes in downtown Memphis, TN, attract residents to a pedestrian-friendly city for work and entertainment. The Center City Commission, created by the governments of Memphis and Shelby County, promotes the development of housing as part of its revitalization plan for downtown Memphis.

This growing suburban dissatisfaction has coincided with dramatic shifts in the demographics of the American family: the rise in single-parent households, the tendency of people to marry and have children later in life, and the trend toward smaller families.

exception of large, specialized buildings, most urban structures throughout history effectively functioned as mixed-use buildings, with street levels devoted to business and trade, and upper stories or rear rooms set aside as dwellings. In his book *Home*, Witold Rybczynski describes the house of medieval times as an open room used as a workshop by day, a kitchen in the evening, and a bedroom at night. Clearly, flexibility has historical roots.

Zoning, in part, represented a response to urban life during the industrial age, when planners segregated the foul air and water byproducts of industry from living space. Some historians also speculate that zoning protected the character of upper-middle-class neighborhoods. Such segregation of uses, however, seems less necessary in the postindustrial age, with the obvious exception of rendering plants, food packers, paint factories, and other similar industries. The static quality of

postwar-American cities, with housing relegated to the suburbs, business to separate subdivisions, and shopping to enormous, fortress-like buildings, has led to discontent. Now, city residents increasingly long for handsome streets, less intense traffic, the streetcars of yesteryear and, above all, the sense of sociability—to be near to and interact with other people. These experiences were best replicated in the suburban shopping mall, with its dense crowds of people strolling down internalized streets lined with shops.

Although many Americans seem happy with their suburban lifestyle, they spend an increasing amount of time in the car. Breadwinners must commute increasingly long distances between new residential subdivisions and the downtown workplace. Additionally, most daily tasks—from music lessons to grocery shopping and picking up a suit at the dry cleaner—necessitate the use of a car. The suburbs seem to discourage walking or bicycling.

Long distances to schools, shopping centers and business centers are possibly part of the problem. More to the point, perhaps, is an observation made by the late William Whyte and others, that people enjoy walking along a continuous "street wall." A walk along a city street lined with attractive buildings can be stimulating; the stroller may say hello to an acquaintance, window-shop, or loiter in front of a newsstand. A walk in a suburban neighborhood, however attractive, can sometimes be depressing. The streets supply few social contacts and create a sense of isolation intensified by locked houses sequestered behind vast green lawns that keep outsiders at a forbidding distance.

This growing dissatisfaction has coincided with dramatic shifts in the demographics of the American family: the rise in single-parent households, the tendency of people to marry and have children later in life, and the trend toward smaller families. Pedestrian-friendly urban housing, which offers the possibility of a supportive social network, appeals to smaller households.

Urban housing has a clear appeal for young, single professionals fresh out of college, who often work downtown. For this population, urban housing offers proximity to entertainment, places to socialize, and the stimulation of downtown life. The presence of people who live downtown is indispensable for the creation of so-called 24-hour cities. And the presence of a well-educated workforce provides an incentive for major employers to locate in downtown areas.

Housing can take many forms. The choice of housing types is dictated by the prevailing housing market, the scale and style of the surrounding neighborhood, land economics, existing density, and the cultural preferences of a given neighborhood or community. Some people prefer high-density housing; others prefer low-density. New high-rise apartment construction has been success-

The First Ward Place in Charlotte, NC, combines single family living in the center city with rental units and condominiums for mixed-income residents.

ful in New York, Chicago, and most recently in San Francisco's Yerba Buena area. In smaller cities, developers may prefer to rehabilitate older commercial buildings or build new low-rise units.

Individual residential projects cannot be considered ends in themselves, but rather building blocks of a comprehensive housing strategy. Successful strategies define a goal: introducing housing into downtown, helping raise the level of home ownership in an area, or providing a wider range of housing choices.

Housing Secures Communities

Communities have long understood that housing conditions contribute to the safety, stability, and perceived value of both high-density developments and suburban-style tracts. Residents also have understood that neighborhoods dominated by low-rent, poorly maintained units with a rapid turnover rate will become blighted. The goal of an urban housing policy must be to strengthen existing neighborhoods while creating successful new neighborhoods.

Encouraging downtown home ownership helps stabilize urban neighborhoods. Local governments have long recognized that ownership creates safe and stable neighborhoods by giving residents a

financial stake in the city—and hence a deeper motivation to maintain property and guard against crime. Cities can choose from a number of strategies to increase ownership. One strategy is a loan program to make mortgages more affordable to first-time buyers, or to provide below-market loans to home owners for renovation and upkeep.

In St. Louis, Missouri, the Mercantile Bank operates an innovative home-ownership program called Project Opens Doors. Buyers in select communities can purchase homes with no money down (although buyers must provide $500 in earnest money). Residents of neighborhoods with a median household income of $41,600 annually or less can qualify for the loan program.

In Santa Fe, Neighborhood Housing Services of Santa Fe helps residents buy homes in tony neighborhoods that otherwise would be too expensive. Drawing on a $5 million mortgage pool, the program enables conventional lenders to provide below-market loans for mortgages and home repair. To date, more than 1,000 New Mexico home owners have used the loan program.

In Washington, D.C., Howard University developed a similar program to help a neighborhood that inadvertently had been harmed by the university's acquisition of forty-three houses.

Howard had purchased those properties in the

LeDroit neighborhood over several decades in anticipation of a campus expansion that never occurred. Local residents protested the plans and criticized the degradation of the neighborhood caused by the university's decision to keep the houses empty and shuttered. After consulting with the Fannie Mae Foundation, the university set up the Howard LeDroit Housing Program. The university is providing below-market home loans in the neighborhood to a preferred list of buyers. Howard staff and faculty top the list, followed by teachers and firefighters employed by the District of Columbia, and city residents.

Uniting Downtown Dwellers

In addition to encouraging home ownership, cities can also regulate housing types and create incentives for developers to build a relationship between housing and other neighborhood elements, including neighboring houses or apartments, commercial buildings, parks, open space, and transit stops.

One strategy is to combine different kinds of housing in the same zones; another is to encourage different income groups to live in the same area. These are challenging goals because American society has long segregated its residences by class and income. Nonetheless, communities understandably dislike the ghettoizing effect of low-income or public housing projects, which are often dense, poorly maintained, and further set apart from the larger community by being different in design.

A small number of communities have reduced crime levels by reconfiguring housing projects as mixed-income areas. The mixing also stabilizes property values and replaces the image of depressed projects with that of well-maintained buildings and landscaping. A notable example is First Ward Place in Charlotte, North Carolina, where officials partly demolished a former HUD project and built both rental units and condominiums. As a result, a housing project once feared has attracted a more stable population.

Residential mixed-use development is an increasingly popular strategy to bring together activities of city life—the workplace, the marketplace, and housing—that generations of zoning had divided. In some areas, traditional apartments over stores have attracted downtown populations without new construction. In other areas, housing

is one among several ingredients, including office space, restaurants, stores, clinics, and child-care centers, attracting residents downtown.

Creating new housing in existing downtowns or industrial areas helps create safer streets, as well as supplying built-in markets for local merchants. Live/work housing—apartments that hug office spaces—promotes start-up businesses and housing in the same location. Live/work housing has become so popular in some cities, including Los Angeles, San Francisco, and Memphis, that developers, who formerly limited themselves to rehabilitating existing buildings, are now building all-new live/work units.

Providing housing near transit stations is a way of encouraging increased use of light-rail and buses, while making otherwise desolate station areas into attractive neighborhood centers. In Oakland, California, developers in a joint venture with Bay Area Rapid Transit (BART) are building the Fruitvale Transit Village. The project incorporates 200 apartments, 35,000 square feet of neighborhood-serving retail, a senior center, a new branch of the Oakland Public Library, a child-care and Head Start center, and an adult health-care center, which provides day care for the elderly.

Mechanisms for Housing Downtown

Private-public partnerships like those in Oakland are promising and have played key roles in prominent urban revivals.

In Memphis, the commercial construction of two high-end, single-family neighborhoods, Harbortown and South Bluffs, jump-started the revival of downtown housing. In the mid-1980s, developer Belz Enterprises bought a multiblock area of downtown Memphis and turned it into Peabody Place—including several old office buildings that Belz refurbished as housing.

A close-knit group of public and private civic organizations has fostered much of the new housing in downtown Memphis. The Center City Commission, a private nonprofit organization, manages a business improvement district (BID) covering four square miles. Businesses inside the BID pay a special assessment.

Some of the funds from the BID assessment go to the Center City Development Organization, which provides loans of up to $100,000 for both structural and facade improvements on commercial property and multifamily buildings. Many borrowers were small business owners who bought apartments and leased business property in the same building. Another group, the Center City Revenue Finance Organization, is a state-chartered group authorized to freeze property tax payments on individual properties. The tax freezes, which last as long as twenty years, help property owners pay for building improvements. The tax incentives have had a terrific impact on multifamily development, according to Lawrence of the Memphis Center City Commission.

In Denver, the creation of housing in the former warehouse area known as Lower Downtown (LoDo) coincided with massive public and private investment in the area, including the creation of the Coors Field baseball stadium, a new performing arts center, and new landscaping along the Platte River. Dana Crawford, a local developer, may deserve the credit for kick-starting the housing trend in the late-1980s. Taking advantage of the city's new zoning designation, which provides incentives for historic preservation and allows residential conversions, Crawford converted several warehouses into market-rate condominiums.

The city provided much of the financing for those initial projects. The city also issued bonds for new sidewalks, landscaping, and street lighting. Soon, the housing market expanded, and the private sector took over. (North and west of the Platte River, a land developer recently obtained approval for a project that will include 2,000 housing units.) The city has focused its efforts on low-income housing in lower-downtown Denver, and is renovating several older buildings, including a former single-room-occupancy hotel, into units for low-income, elderly, and handicapped renters.

In St. Paul, Minnesota, a warehouse district became a 180-acre urban village in the city's Lowertown. The Lowertown Redevelopment Corporation, a private, nonprofit organization initially funded by a $10 million grant from the McKnight Foundation, sparked the downtown housing revival.

The St. Paul effort differs from efforts in other cities, according to Lowertown Redevelopment President Weiming Lu, because his organization has worked hard to provide public amenities as well as housing. In addition to helping finance the 1,500 housing units built during past years, the corporation has also helped create parks, neighborhood retail projects, tot lots, street lighting,

and a skyway system of covered bridges connecting Lowertown to the rest of downtown St. Paul. To date, the former industrial area has attracted $450 million in investment.

As communities provide a variety of housing types, encourage ownership, and ensure that residential developments complement other land uses, it is important not to overlook the importance of project design. Even architecture can address such problems as social isolation and its manifestations in crime, vandalism, and neglect.

In Norfolk, Virginia, careful design decisions in the rebuilding of the Diggs Town public housing project have created not only a more attractive neighborhood, but also encouraged a sense of ownership and a feeling of community. Starting out with unattractive, barracks-style public housing, architect Raymond Gindroz added front porches and new wooden window details. These details not only made the housing more attractive, but encouraged social interaction among neighbors, who could talk to each other from their porches. The architect also fenced in the front yards, separating the houses from the streets and creating a sense of privacy. The architects designed backyard patios, storage sheds, and side fences that helped establish a sense of ownership among the residents. A new street grid breaks up the project's enormous blocks.

Today, community has replaced anonymity, and residents have taken responsibility for maintaining the apartments because they have a stake—places to call their own—in the greater neighborhood.

Crime and neglect are not the only urban problems that can be remedied through housing development. Urban housing also can play a role in the difficult problem of finding new uses for formerly contaminated sites, popularly known as brownfields.

If such land is to be used for home building, the cleanup of toxic substances must meet a much higher standard than is acceptable for industrial or commercial use, and that added cost may well influence the feasibility of such projects. In addition, home buyers might understandably attach a stigma to formerly tainted land even after it has been made safe.

Nevertheless, developers in Dallas have located a multifamily complex called Jefferson at North End on a brownfield. The project is a model of a high-end residential neighborhood located on a former no-man's-land of industrial contamination. Residential development also is expected on brownfield sites in the lower-downtown area of Charlotte, North Carolina.

The experience of home builders and local government officials offers lessons for other cities that want to make housing a key component of urban renewal:

Cities should mix types, prices, and ownership arrangements: loft conversions, apartments, condominiums, detached single-family homes, for sale and for rent. Some cities, including Los Angeles and San Diego, suffer from a lack of high-end housing in downtown areas. Other cities—Charlotte, Denver, and Memphis, need more affordable and low-income units where downtown housing has gained acceptance by middle-class residents in order to provide downtown housing for the elderly, for single-parent households, and for low-paid service workers.

It must be easy to get around on foot. Pedestrian access to basic services is a benchmark of successful urban housing; transit, medical clinics, social-service providers, and neighborhood stores should all be a short walk from housing.

Urban dwellers need beautiful open spaces as much as suburbanites do, although that space need not take the form of big, private yards as in the suburbs. Downtown areas, in fact, need different kinds of open space for different needs: green space, plazas, tot lots, pocket parks, and large-scale urban parks for active recreation.

Security is a paramount issue. Communities that police themselves—because their residents feel they have a stake in the neighborhood and are willing to take responsibility for conditions—enjoy the best and most reliable type of security.

City dwellers also need privacy. In urban terms, privacy need not depend entirely upon locked gates and high walls, but on architecture and urban designs that provide a clear demarcation between the street, the semipublic areas (e.g., yards), and private areas (e.g., porches and front steps).

Conclusion: The New Meaning and New Form of Urban Housing

As these examples suggest, urban housing constitutes more than the number of units produced or the number of people who live in a certain area. Housing has a larger and subtler importance to urban areas.

In a 1995 article, Robert D. Putnam of Harvard University coined the concept of social capital. He defined social capital as "features of social organization such as networks, norms and trust that increase a society's productive potential." Unlike conventional capital, Putnam writes, "social capital is a public good, that is, it is not the private property of those who benefit from it. Thus, like other public goods, from clean air to safe streets, social capital tends to be under-provided by private agents."

Cities are ultimately held together not by laws, or security patrols, or buildings, or urban design, but by a delicate fabric of human relationships. Making neighborhoods, then, is not just a matter of the right real estate economics or architectural design, but of providing a set of strategies to foster cooperation and mutual trust among residents. Obviously, neither city officials nor home builders can provide the social capital essential to urban housing. At their best, however, well-conceived projects may provide the conditions, and the confidence, that make healthy neighborhoods possible. In this way, the design of housing becomes the visible expression of the relations that create cooperative communities.

Diggs Town in Norfolk, VA, was once a dangerous, decaying public housing project. Thanks to the collaboration among city leaders, tenants, and architects it has become a neighborhood with a sense of community.

Fannie Mae:
Building Home Ownership

LEADERSHIP
PROFILE

Created by Congress during the Depression in 1938, the Federal National Mortgage Corporation (Fannie Mae) works with lenders to make mortgage funds available for Americans to realize home ownership. Launched under the Federal Housing Administration (FHA), Fannie Mae acquired FHA-insured loans to supply funds to lenders. From the beginning, Fannie Mae functioned as a secondary market; it lent no money directly to home buyers, rather, it purchased mortgages from lenders to provide capital for future loans.

The government sold Fannie Mae to private shareholders in 1968 and its role has since burgeoned. Today it is the nation's third largest private corporation. Not only the largest provider of funds for home mortgages, with more than 12 million mortgages on the books, Fannie Mae also has emerged as a model of corporate responsibility and a leader in breaking down barriers to African Americans, Hispanics, and women.

Fannie Mae's charter mandate, established by Congress, is to increase the availability and affordability of home ownership for low-, moderate-, and middle-income Americans. The corporation depends entirely on private risk capital, with no government funding or backing. Traded on the New York Stock Exchange, the company is consistently profitable, demonstrating that its mission of putting Americans into their own homes can be more than financially self-sustaining. The corporate profits allow Fannie Mae to invest in the effectiveness of its mission. The Fannie Mae Foundation makes grants and operates outreach programs to help transform communities through innovative partnerships and initiatives that revitalize neighborhoods and create affordable home ownership and housing opportunities across America.

During the 1970s and 1980s, Fannie Mae broadened its activity in the housing market by purchasing conventional mortgages in addition to loans guaranteed by FHA and the Veterans Administration, adding adjustable-rate and second mortgages to its portfolio, and starting up a mortgage-backed securities business. When James A. Johnson became Fannie Mae's chairman and chief executive officer in 1991, he launched a $10 billion "Opening Doors to Affordable Housing" initiative. Two years later, Fannie Mae accomplished its goal of producing $10 billion in purchases for low- and moderate-income home buyers sixteen months ahead of schedule. The corporation expanded the Opening Doors program in 1994 with the Trillion Dollar Commitment, a pledge of $1 trillion in targeted housing finance to serve ten million low- to moderate-income families. Since it went private in 1968, Fannie Mae has helped more than 30 million Americans purchase homes.

Recognizing that families of modest income often lack money for a down payment, Fannie Mae created Flexible 97, a mortgage product designed to expand home ownership through a low three-percent down-payment requirement. Fannie Mae requires that borrowers enroll in a prepurchase home-buyer education session to qualify for loans. For many of the nation's underserved neighborhoods, Fannie Mae has invested nearly $40 million in Community Development Financial Institutions (CDFI) to help fight discrimination and build an economic infrastructure in deteriorated neighborhoods. In 1997, CDFI added a vehicle for loaning money to nonprofit organizations. The CDFI provided a $1 million line of credit to Collaborative Lending Initiative, Inc. to supply development financing for affordable housing in Philadelphia and its suburbs.

In partnerships with other lending institutions, Fannie Mae has leveraged loans to minority-or women-owned businesses traditionally ignored by financial institutions. The corporation has joined partnerships with educational institutions and industry to train minorities for housing finance jobs, while its own workforce of 3,800 is noted for diversity. CEO Franklin D. Raines is the first

African-American chief executive of any Fortune 500 company. Moreover, women make up fifty-four percent and minorities forty percent of Fannie Mae's workforce. *Fortune* magazine ranked Fannie Mae second on its 1999 list of the best companies for Asians, Blacks, and Hispanics.

Under the umbrella of the Trillion Dollar Commitment, Fannie Mae's many local offices have become laboratories to test the effectiveness of innovative mortgage products and investment tools. The labs provide the groundwork for partnerships with local lenders, government officials, housing organizations, and community and nonprofit groups to expand affordable home ownership and rental opportunities. In communities across the nation, Fannie Mae functions as a catalyst for local community development. By making home ownership a reality for more people of limited economic means, the company provides families an equity stake in their neighborhood's overall quality of life.

In 1998, Fannie Mae financed $260 billion in mortgages for households most in need and helped push overall U.S. home ownership to an all-time high of 66.8 percent with a record 69 million home owners. The corporation also recognizes that for some people, home ownership will not be an option. Hence, Fannie Mae focuses on rental housing as well. One of the Trillion Dollar Commitment initiatives is the $50 billion commitment to multifamily housing for people who rent while preparing to buy a home. The corporation leads in developing ways to take over some of the risks shouldered by HUD, which will translate into more affordable multifamily rental units.

But to truly appreciate the work of Fannie Mae, a look at a real-life story demonstrates the impact of this behemoth financial services corporation. In Orlando, Florida, Farid and Nancy Sharifi were looking for a larger house near quality schools because they needed room for the children's grandparents' yearlong visits from the Middle East. An agent from Prudential Reality Florida helped Farid identify the new home on a Fannie Mae list of foreclosed properties. The Sharifis qualified for the 5-percent down-payment option available under the Fannie Mae Community Home Buyer's Program, which resulted in a low monthly mortgage payment. The Sharifis ploughed the savings into renovations. Fannie Mae helps thousands of families like Sarifis invest in their future by buying new homes.

In addition to helping millions of Americans purchase affordable homes, Fannie Mae has helped transform communities through innovative partnerships that revitalize neighborhoods and leverage loans to minority- and women-owned businesses.

Chattanooga Attracts
Living Downtown

LEADERSHIP
PROFILE

Across the country, midsized cities like Chattanooga, Tennessee, saw their fortunes decline during the 1970s and 1980s as the country adjusted to a new, automated, services-centered economy and left behind once-thriving center cities built on heavy industry and transportation. A former major railroad hub with foundries and a large warehouse district, Chattanooga differed from its national counterparts in the willingness of its business and civic leaders to join partnerships. They called their enterprise Chattanooga Venture and drew a new map for the city's future called Vision 2000.

Flight to the suburbs, disinvestments in the inner city, and deteriorating housing stock meant that Chattanooga Venture would have to expand or rehabilitate center city housing to realize its goal of urban revitalization. Chattanooga Neighborhood Enterprise (CNE) emerged as a Vision 2000 initiative in 1986 to tackle the city's housing situation. Planners gave CNE the mandate to develop, finance, renovate, and manage affordable housing for Chattanooga and Hamilton County's low-to-moderate income citizens.

With technical assistance from The Enterprise Foundation, the newly formed nonprofit set three immediate tasks:

• to increase the effectiveness of existing rehabilitation programs;
• to initiate a financing program for home buyers; and
• to undertake real estate projects to revitalize inner-city neighborhoods.

Because much of Chattanooga's inner-city housing stock was (and remains) inexpensive, the strategies CNE developed over the past fourteen years allowed low-income families to become home owners.

CNE's success relies on a partnership among major sectors with a stake in improving the city's quality of life. The collaboration includes the city, local banks and businesses, foundations, and the federal and state government. Its funding comes from city general revenue, federal programs, the

Lyndhurst Foundation, and other private organizations. It also receives revenue through loan origination and developer fees. The city committed resources for home-owner rehabilitation loans, while the county participated by issuing mortgage revenue bonds offering financing for first-time home buyers. CNE's strong financial track record has attracted other investors and favorable loan rates from lenders.

CNE's philosophy eschews rigidity in favor of flexible programs that tailor financial assistance to the needs and economic ability of the client. Its programs benefit from being customer driven and responsive to the community. For example, CNE created an innovative lease-purchase program to

Rental homes located in the 5th Street and Mitchell Avenue area of Chattanooga, TN, a project of the Chattanooga Neighborhood Enterprise (CNE). CNE develops, finances, renovates and manages affordable housing for low-to-moderate income citizens.

help low-to-moderate-income families buy homes. Under the program, CNE buys a home on behalf of qualified families, who then assume the mortgages when they can qualify for a Federal Housing Administration mortgage. Low-interest home-improvement loans help (often elderly) residents fix up their homes, while CNE's involvement in owning and managing rental properties satisfies a critical need in the inner city where affordable units are at a premium.

All of CNE's programs are highly leveraged with local and private-sector funding. For example, CNE formed a partnership with a local Catholic hospital to develop a program for hospital employees. By 1995, 262 first-time home buyers had received financial assistance and 144 home owners benefited from rehabilitation assistance. The organization exceeded its own goal of rehabilitating seventy rental units, with 170 made available for occupancy. A year later, CNE had assisted in 1,486 home purchases involving nearly $70 million in financing. One reason for the program's strength is the fact that the city commits general revenue funds to housing. Future plans are to increase rehabilitation financing and participate in a three-year comprehensive revitalization effort in a near-downtown neighborhood. The plan calls for $33 million in financing for housing, small businesses, and community improvements.

The largest community development corporation in the United States grew from the ashes of the civil disturbances that rocked Newark in July 1967. Days of rioting left the Central Ward in ruins: no homes, no jobs, no hope. What better opportunity to preach about loving thy neighbor? What better place to teach the power of faith to heal wounds of hatred and foster understanding?

Reverend William J. Linder, Founder and CEO of the New Community Corporation (NCC) in Newark, NJ.

A young priest, Father William J. Linder, ministered to a parish isolated by violence. During five days of unrest, he walked the streets and public housing projects, transporting injured residents to hospitals and distributing food. After the violence subsided, the New Community Corporation (NCC), which Linder founded, launched an interracial dialogue called Operation Understanding. The operation paired interracial Newark residents for discussions in the suburbs exploring race relations and the problems of the inner city. Less than a year later, a Walk for Understanding brought 50,000 suburbanites and residents out on Palm Sunday for a peaceful interracial rally in Central

Ward. From this alliance, a fund-raising drive allowed NCC to construct its first housing development.

The Central Ward of Newark, New Jersey's largest city, had experienced problems similar to those in other metropolitan areas: decline of industry, white flight, and civil unrest. Neighborhoods were in ruins and the residents who remained—who had no other place to go—needed jobs, housing, and services. Because politicians demonstrated little interest in financing reconstruction, Newark's grass-roots activists banded together to provide affordable, quality housing.

"There really was a sense that people were going to take control of the community," Father Linder recalls. "My own thinking was that we needed to get a development corporation committed to low-income neighborhoods. The disorders forced us to get together and start implementing."

What NCC implemented has been unrivaled among community development corporations (CDCs). NCC hoped new housing would spur the Central Ward's revitalization and promote interest, pride, and responsibility among community members involved in the development process. This process would depend on a community of people sharing and caring for one another while working to design new housing.

The first proposal was to transform a forty-five-acre tract encompassing fourteen city blocks in the heart of Central Ward into a model of safe, new housing. NCC's first (modest) step was to purchase two acres. The organization then had to obtain approval of the housing plans from state and federal authorities, secure financing for construction, soothe racial tensions, and cultivate skills among its members to enable them to develop housing. Members of the fledgling CDC soon realized how difficult it was to obtain seed money to purchase and clear just two acres of land and to obtain permanent mortgages from financial institutions. At the time, lenders did not believe a community-based development corporation was a good risk. NCC combated this impression by demonstrating board-member continuity, hiring outside housing consultants and a minority-owned New York City architectural firm, and employing one of the state's largest accounting firms. These steps helped inspire trust among lenders and establish the credibility needed to secure mortgages.

Through NCC's efforts, thousands of new units

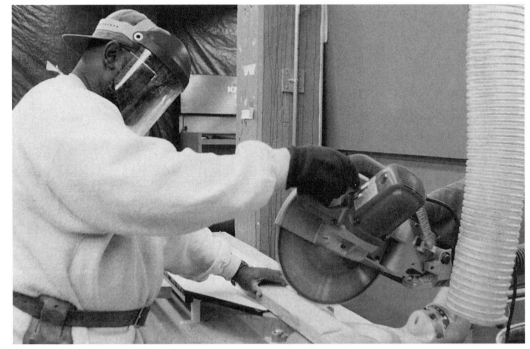

Photo left. *NCC Technologies, Inc. trains inner-city workers to build housing components in Newark and surrounding area.*

Photo below. *Pathmark Supermarket will celebrate its 10th anniversary in Newark's Central Ward in July 2000. Profits from the supermarket are donated to New Community.*

of housing have been built in the Central Ward and throughout New Jersey, beginning with New Community Homes, occupied in 1975. Progress continued in 1996 with the construction of seventy-four units at the Salem Lafayette housing complex in Jersey City. From an organization with only $13,000 in seed money from the New Jersey Department of Community Affairs, NCC has grown into a corporate structure with net assets of $300 million. In 1986, the Prudential Insurance Company of America deeded its massive Douglas Harrison apartment complex to NCC for one dollar. NCC currently owns and operates 7,500 units of low-income housing in Newark, Jersey City, and Englewood. Among its properties are facilities for extended care and transitional housing for homeless families.

NCC's grass-roots organizing principles have remained, as has its deep commitment to the Central Ward, now transformed from a desolate wasteland into a stable, productive neighborhood.

Denver Lower Downtown Housing
City of Denver
Office of the Mayor, City and County
Building, Room 350
Denver, CO 80202

Contact: Steve Gordon,
City Planner
303.640.4780

Downtown housing developments paired with historic preservation programs bolster the residential population in central Denver. Before the city of Denver decided to enter the downtown housing market, banks refused to risk money for residential construction in what they considered a downtown ghost town. Yet, the city had little to lose and much to gain by promoting a return to downtown.

Denver city leaders floated a bond issue and invested the money in streetscaping and sidewalk improvements downtown. Their investment preserved the character of downtown Denver through street design and landscaping, and helped city officials attract new residents to the center city. Developers, heartened by the city's investment, converted a few buildings—the first a warehouse—to loft condominiums, a relatively new type of housing in the neighborhood.

The city made a second round of commitments to the residential area by providing low-cost construction loans and even investing in projects. People who were eager to live, work, and enjoy the entertainment options of downtown snapped up the loft-condominiums. From the initial city-backed projects came many more projects—that had become a sound investment for developers thanks to the initial investment.

As is true of many reinvestment and redevelopment projects, once the government and private investors succeed in building and selling residences, the banks provided construction loans for further work. Conversion, through historic preservation, has been the major avenue

of development. Construction projects for new housing, however, are underway, including a 160-unit condominium project. Recognizing that strong communities are often economically diverse, the Housing Authority has enacted a policy to insure that thirty-one of these units are delegated to low-income buyers.

Residents are attracted to the lofts with high, airy ceilings and unique, historic details. To keep the streets active and full of life—which makes them safe at night—most buildings retain ground-floor retail space. Developers, city officials, and community members show a strong interest in developing the historic housing district. Parking structures are carefully and cleverly designed so that older buildings are not razed. To add to and complement historic Denver's architectural style, design standards for new buildings are carefully scrutinized and must comply with the existing architecture. The City also has rezoned several parcels to encourage a mixture of uses in the old warehouse district. The historic character of the area was preserved through design codes, while flexible zoning enabled the elusive mix of residential and commercial that allows diverse urban districts to come to life.

Residents flocking to downtown lofts have matched the energy and enthusiasm of the city, demonstrated through its investment in infrastructure. This energy fuels still more development. In the early nineties, Denver acquired a major league baseball franchise, and sports enthusiasts, inspired by the downtown residential and commercial renaissance, decided to relocate the new Coors Field downtown. The new stadium attracted moderate- to high-priced restaurants, sports bars, music clubs, and group pubs. Because more people live downtown, now full of restaurants and entertainment venues, more office buildings are being constructed by developers responding to people's desire to work in a "fun" environment. These elements generate more success and appeal, creating a vibrant Lower Downtown Denver.

Manna, Inc.
828 Evarts Street, NE
Washington, DC 20018
www.mannadc.org

Contact: Jim Dickerson,
Founder and Chairman
202.232.2844

To revitalize the U.S. Capital's traditional African-American neighborhoods, Manna combines historic preservation with human-capacity building. Founded in 1982, the nonprofit Manna-owned housing projects stretch throughout Washington, D.C. The organization builds new houses and finances historic preservation projects for low-income home buyers. The new and renovated homes anchor communities and provide solid foundations for families and communities to grow and develop. Manna also takes advantage of the HUD Scattered Sites project and will redevelop fifteen buildings with a total of twenty vacant single-family homes located in Columbia Heights and Shaw.

To further promote community development in Shaw, Manna CDC sponsored the Shaw Heritage Tour with the D.C. Chamber of Commerce and the D.C. Heritage Tourism Coalition. The D.C. Heritage Tourism Coalition, implementing its vision of improving the city's image, serves as a catalyst to link heritage resources and community development. The Chamber, Manna, Shaw, and D.C. Heritage Tourism all preserve historic buildings and boost economic development.

Quality affordable housing in historic buildings is key to the groups' stewardship. Manna offers assistance and training to families before and after they purchase their homes. They provide essential advice on the complicated process of achieving home ownership for low-income home buyers, as well as on how to maintain their new homes. In Shaw, the added challenge is historic preservation. Manna provides information and helps to access historic preservation loans, grants, and tax deductions for Shaw home owners. Manna also renovated the Whitelaw Hotel, built in 1919 by African-American developer John Whitelaw Lewis. The Whitelaw Hotel was the first, and only, first-class accommodation for African-American entertainers and visitors to Washington, D.C. Its location, one block south of the up-and-coming U Street corridor and the historic Lincoln Theatre, puts it in the center, physically and historically, of the area's heritage and contemporary revitalization. Duke Ellington, Cab Calloway, Joe Lewis, civil rights leaders Charles Houston, A. Philip Johnson, and Thurgood Marshall all attended the lavish events at the Whitelaw. The Whitelaw's original Italianate design fell victim to the riots of 1968 and a fire in 1981. Manna restored it to its original glory, and the Whitelaw now serves as a landmark for the flourishing historic Shaw District.

Neighborhood Housing Services

Santa Fe Affordable Housing Roundtable
1570 Pacheco St., Suite A-1
Santa Fe, NM 87505

Contact: Mike Loftin,
Executive Director
505.983.6214

Santa Fe's Neighborhood Housing Services helps low- and middle-income individuals and families experience the rewards of home ownership. The city's popularity as a destination for affluent home owners created steep housing costs, but service-sector jobs offered low wages. These economics forced many to move out of the city, often to substandard rural housing in villages and outlying cities.

The Neighborhood Housing Services (NHS) of Santa Fe, a community-wide partnership, attempts to remedy the shortage of affordable housing in the city by creating a coalition of government, private investors, and nonprofit organizations. The NHS helped to create the Santa Fe Affordable Housing Roundtable in 1992. The Roundtable brings together city and county officials with nonprofit housing and service providers to develop new approaches to affordable housing and to find new funding sources.

NHS also obtained a Pew Partnership for Civic Change grant, intended to improve life in small cities through community development. The grant program represents an attempt by Pew to help nonprofit organizations solve urban problems in the future. In Santa Fe, at least, one answer is home ownership and home improvement for low-income families. The Pew grants allowed NHS to help 450 families purchase, and an additional 150 families to renovate, their homes. These grants, it is estimated, pumped $40 million into the local economy during the last four years by attracting contractors and small businesses to the region.

Many grants paid for individual home improvements, but the program is touted as "more than bricks and mortar." This housing helps build and stabilize the community. The Pew Partnership considers these investments in affordable housing as encouragement for people to realize their dreams and fulfill their responsibilities as citizens. The opportunity to purchase a home helps individuals and families build a healthy, economically diverse community. To maximize families' benefits, NHS also provides a home-buyer training class, which has graduated 1,931 people.

The city helped the Roundtable organize and finance its programs and provided technical assistance and low-cost land. As a result, hundreds became home owners and discovered that home purchasing and home improvement are more than just financial transactions. They are vehicles people can use to invest, engage, and improve their community.

New York HELP

HELP USA
30 East 33rd Street
New York, NY 10016
www.helpusa.org

Contact: Claudia Stepke,
Director of External Affairs
212.444.1916

HELP USA combats the underlying causes of homelessness, helping people become and remain self-reliant. Widespread home ownership forms part of the vision of contemporary communities; homelessness remains in any realistic view of downtowns.

New York City's several branches of HELP USA have established quality programs to address its root causes. As a startling statistic demonstrates, "it costs New York City $75 a night to place a family in a room in a welfare hotel with no hope for breaking the cycle of dependency, while it costs just $55 a night to place a family in an apartment in one of HELP USA's clean and safe facilities with on-site services designed to help residents become economically independent."

HELP USA is the nation's largest builder and operator of transitional housing. It has operated in New York City since 1986 and by July 1998, had moved 2,233 families into permanent housing. HELP USA provides on-site human services for homeless families recognizing that homelessness is not merely the result of lack of housing. Services vary from site to site, but most provide on-site day care, recreational services, parenting and life skills education, case management, maintenance, medical care, and education linkages that address the complexity of causes for homelessness. In New York City, special linkages with the New York Hospital, H. G. Birch services, and HELP R.O.A.D.S., provide advocacy, community education, hotline services, and individual and group counseling for domestic violence survivors.

The group also links homeless clients with the East Brooklyn Employment Services for employment screening, job-readiness assessment, training, and job placement.

This tremendous effort combats the staggering numbers of homeless families. A consistent focus on root causes, the commitment to quality affordable housing, and the willingness to go beyond traditional shelter services set the efforts of New York City's HELP USA branches apart.

Jefferson at North End
JPI
600 East Las Colinas Boulevard
Irving, TX 75039
www.jpi.com/props/northend

Contact: Carol Peddy,
Regional Manager
972.556.3789

Dallas is finding brownfield redevelopment a valuable means of urban revitalization. Cities across the United States are developing their brownfields, reweaving these abandoned industrial spaces into the urban fabric.

Delvelopers turned a classic, eleven-acre brownfield in central Dallas into a luxury apartment building. The site had seen an assortment of industry over the years—gas stations, battery manufacturers, metal companies, scrap yards, chemical companies, and furniture makers—all of which took their toll on the land. "Teamwork truly made Jefferson at the North End possible," asserted J. Frank Miller, the chairman and CEO of JPI, the project's developer. He was referring to the cooperation between city officials, state agencies, and the U.S. Environmental Protection Agency (EPA) that was necessary to realize the project.

Dallas city officials made a commitment of city and county tax abatements and road improvements over ten years

that improved the streets and traffic flow around the area. The Texas Voluntary Cleanup Program, created by the legislature to encourage brownfield rehabilitation, played its part by offering incentives to developers that propose remediation programs. The Texas Voluntary Cleanup Program (VCP) does not sanitize redevelopment issues. Rather, it encourages a realistic view of risk and assists owners and developers to create risk-based plans for contamination cleanup. Far too often brownfields are considered too far-gone, too contaminated, and too expensive to revitalize. By approaching the challenge with a determination to conquer the problem, and thereby achieve revitalization of abandoned sites, the VCP is combating these seemingly insurmountable obstacles to brownfield redevelopment. In the case of Jefferson at the North End, VCP provided a full release of liability for future owners and lenders through the Texas Natural Resource Conservation Commission.

Cleanup, which began in 1996, involved the removal of 37,630 cubic yards of contaminated soil, resulting in 1,882 truckloads of soil hauled from the site. After the soil removal, hundreds of samples were taken and analyzed to determine that Conservation Commission-approved cleanup goals had been met and that lead levels had been reduced to below established "naturally occurring" levels. Once this was accomplished, the City's provision of infrastructure was crucial because utility and infrastructure records for the area were incomplete. Exploration was done to find used and abandoned underground utilities. However, during this, and throughout the construction process, unexpected underground systems continually popped up. In one instance, this proved a historic boon when the City's oldest brick streets were uncovered. JPI brought in skilled craftsmen to chip away the concrete covering the bricks and restore them to their original condition, enabling them to be used in the new development as deco-

rative paving and pedestrian crosswalks.

Bringing the site up to standard cost close to $2 million. But the benefit resonates throughout the downtown. The site is now a 540-unit luxury apartment community. The units vary from penthouses to modest apartments. The complex is designed to foster a neighborhood atmosphere with internal streets and pedestrian walkways to encourage foot traffic. More than housing 500 people, and repopulating the downtown with suburban returnees, the project has brought the land value up to $75 million, while construction and continuing operations have added close to 250 jobs to Dallas. The Jefferson at North End project inspired still more development: a sports arena anchoring a mixed-use development featuring entertainment, retail, and office space. The project serves as an example to Dallas and the nation of the value of contamination cleanup.

Project Open Doors
Mercantile Bank
150 Northland Shopping Center
St. Louis, MO 63136
www.mercantile.com/personalbanking/html/opendoors.html

Contact: Terri McDaniel,
Community Lender
314.381.2258

Since its inception in November 1997, Project Open Doors has helped 650 residents purchase their own homes. Cities around the nation are recognizing home ownership as a key component of downtown revitalization. In St. Louis, the Mercantile Bank has joined several community organizations to offer incentives for low-income homebuyers. Since its inception in November 1997, Project Open Doors has helped 650 residents achieve the purchase their own homes. Their success stems from loosening traditional loan restrictions and providing greater financial assistance. Families with incomes lower than $40,800 a year can qualify for loans from Mercantile Bank for as much as 100 percent of a home's purchase value, with down-payments as low as $250 to $500. An applicant can qualify for a loan if his or her income exceeds the $40,800 ceiling by agreeing to purchase a home in a federally designated low- or moderate-income census tract. In addition, the bank waives the Private Mortgage Insurance. Rather than paying for the insurance, loan recipients are required to contribute $25 a month to an interest-bearing reserve account, to be used only for unexpected repairs.

To ensure that loan applicants are sufficiently prepared for the complexities of home-ownership, Mercantile Bank and local community organizations offer training classes in contract negotiations, loan applications, and home maintenance and repair. Participating organizations include the Catholic Commission on Housing, Peterson Housing and Reinvestment, Neighborhood Housing Services, the St. Louis Reinvestment Corporation, and the Neighborhood Council. The bank also relies on these organizations to identify potential borrowers and select neighborhoods for investments.

Neighborhoods to Standards
Mayor's Office
City of Houston
611 Walker Street
Houston, TX 77002

Contact: Judy Butler,
Coordinator
713.247.2666

Economic-development planning, neighborhood planning, and promotion of homeownership are all part of Houston city leaders' search for a secure future.
As part of a program called Imagine

Houston, Houston's leaders are promoting homeownership, making it the possible dream. Economically driven population shifts reduced downtown housing in Houston. While a downturn in the housing market in the 1980s enabled many to buy homes that were previously unaffordable, the shift led to disinvestment, abandonment, and demolition of housing in eastern and southern neighborhoods. The Homes for Houston, a block-by-block revitalization effort, enables low-income families to purchase new homes, and renovate and rehabilitate existing houses. Homes for Houston forms partnerships with individuals, communities, civic organization leaders, Community Development Corporations, churches, schools, and businesses committed to affordable housing.

Another element of neighborhood revitalization, the Parks to Standards Program, supplies city green space. Planners hope to upgrade all 277 Houston parks to a uniform condition, encompassing security, safety, and accessibility. The careful coordination of design and engineering, bidding, construction administration, standard city operating procedures, and special interest-group requests has minimized setbacks and delays. Parks to Standards also encourages significant contributions from residents.

In addition to homeownership promotion, and park revitalization, the city is concentrating on economic development planning in neighborhoods. Because reviving Houston's neighborhoods tops the planning agenda, the Houston planning department continually works with citizens, businesses, developers and builders to revitalize and stabilize their neighborhoods. A 1997 federal grant allowed Houston's East End Development Project to leverage city staff time to assist neighborhood groups in using small innovation grants to develop creative solutions to their neighborhood's economic development problems.

With the aim of helping neighborhoods

help themselves, the Houston planning department has held several symposiums and workshops to provide neighborhood groups with training. Some symposiums' topics include: affordable housing, economic development, accessing basic city services, senior citizen services, and flooding.

The commitment by Houston's city leaders and city planning staff to promoting and maintaining true partnerships with residents has proven an effective way to achieve the combined goals of economic development, neighborhood revitalization, and homeownership.

The Economic Engine:
Regions Fueled by Vital City Centers

4 | Harnessing Global Forces to Provide Jobs

More than a decade ago, seven governors from the Midwest and South appeared on "The Phil Donahue Show." They wanted to prove they would do anything to capture the holy grail of economic development: the plant General Motors was planning for its then-new Saturn line of cars. One by one, the governors extolled the virtues of their states—dedicated workers, low taxes, and an outstanding quality of life.

The successful economic development and job creation strategies of the twenty-first century will permit American communities to focus on their core assets: people and places.

Tennessee eventually won, and its taxpayers had to pay $26,000 in economic incentives for every job Saturn brought to their state, Phil Donahue notwithstanding.

Saturn has, by all accounts, been a net plus to Tennessee. Nevertheless, this story of the eighties reveals a great deal about how much America has changed. It is not hard to imagine a gaggle of governors going on "The Jerry Springer Show" today. It is hard to imagine them talking about economic development. Not only has the hot topic of talk shows changed, but the nature of economic development also has changed.

The last fifteen years has witnessed an overhauling of the economic structure of America's communities. Industries have moved to shorter business cycles and individual companies are no longer tied to specific geographical locations. These changes step up competition among our communities—indeed, among communities all over the world—for jobs and economic growth. Globalization and technology also have changed the rules of the economic development game profoundly.

The approach that led the seven governors to appear with Phil Donahue does not always work anymore. Large companies have proved more than willing to quickly abandon major capital assets, such as plants designed to last for decades, under the dictates of global economics. Large businesses no longer drive economic growth. In a global economy, the network of economic assets within each region—people, relationships, and physical facilities—drives growth. The rules of the game have changed. The successful economic development and job creation strategies of the twenty-first century will permit American communities to focus on their core assets: people and places.

The Global Information Economy: Fast-Paced and Footloose

Twenty years ago, when most American communities crafted economic development strategies in earnest, they operated in a far different world than they do today. In those days, the entire American economy was bloated and sluggish—and communities had to undertake aggressive efforts to promote economic growth. The twin perils of stagnation and inflation—which together gave rise to the term stagflation—were slowly eroding the American economy. Communities lost economic ground because of antiquated industrial plants, higher wages and costs, and a stagnant or declining market for their products.

Today, stagflation is behind us. And, although many American communities are still at risk economically, the underlying economic structure depends as much on flexibility and innovation as on stability and resources. The changes provide boundless opportunities for cities and towns that understand the new foundation. Instead of a moribund national economy suffering from inefficient plants and high costs, America now faces the challenge of a new global economy—one that generates vast wealth, but is also fast-paced, footloose, and fickle.

This remarkable economic change has come about because of globalization and technological advances. The rise of the information economy—driven largely by telecommunications and the Internet—has greatly accelerated the pace of economic activity, as well as the productivity of individual workers. Because the Internet makes the business world increasingly placeless, companies can search the globe continuously for the strongest

consumer markets, the cheapest labor markets, and the best sources of raw material.

Indeed, today's global economy has far more in common with the ruthless world marketplace that emerged a century ago than with the strong but steady nationalistic economy Americans knew in the fifties and sixties. In the years between the Civil War and the First World War, the emergence of the telephone and telegraph, a worldwide system linking railroads, and some fast oceanliners created a global economy operating on a much larger scale and at much faster speed than anything the world previously had known. The result, not surprisingly, was the rapid creation of enormous wealth and an increasing gap between the *haves* and the *have-nots*, as new locations and new laborers became part of the massive economic system.

Not surprisingly, this period also was a tumultuous time for American communities seeking economic prosperity. Thousands of towns had been created in the United States in the nineteenth

century, as founders tried to cash in on the expansion of the American population and the American economy. With the quantum economic leaps of the Gilded Age, a harsh reality emerged. Those communities lucky enough to be hooked into the global economy—through railroads, ports, telecommunications, and connections with

High-tech companies that abound in North San Jose, CA, and the light rail system give this area a competitive edge in the global market place of the new information-technology age.

The Gateway Arch in St. Louis, Missouri. St. Louis, a great industrial-age city, like New York and Chicago, is now a center for high-tech companies.

industrial powerhouses—thrived. Those who had none of these advantages were left behind. Indeed, many communities rose and fell in only a few short years—going from boomtowns to ghost towns as economic conditions changed.

Today's technological advances have similar consequences for American communities. The sudden emergence of a global information economy driven by the World Wide Web has created exploding economic opportunity all over the world. Information technology creates new economic activity, and the Web, in particular, is creating business connections and relations that simply didn't exist before. It is now possible for a company to identify markets on a worldwide basis and, at virtually no cost, allow its global customers to learn about and purchase its products.

The resulting creation of wealth has been nothing less than astonishing. Massachusetts Institute of Technology economist Lester Thurow recently pointed out that the number of billionaires in the world increased some fifteenfold between the early eighties and the late nineties.

We are discovering that a global economy quickly creating vast amounts of wealth also is likely to be ruthless, driven by an endless search for efficiency. An American company may discover a global market at virtually no cost

because of the Web. But the same factors also mean that communities—no matter how large or well-established—are likely to face intense competition from everywhere else on the globe. In 1965, for example, IBM faced 2,500 competitors in all markets; by 1992, it faced 50,000 competitors.

Competition can also be unpredictable. The recent spate of mergers among computer, telecommunications, and entertainment companies reveals that few companies focus on single businesses, and any company from any sector of the economy may become a competitor to an established firm.

Not surprisingly, in this cutthroat global marketplace, companies increasingly find that they compete, not only with the industries all over the world, but also with the clock, and even with themselves. The new product cycle grows ever shorter, especially in the information-technology industry. Companies must innovate, grow, and expand quickly, or they will die. Furthermore, they must scan the globe constantly for the most inexpensive labor, the most creative workers, the most favorable regulatory system, and the cheapest capital. It is not only technology companies, which are operating in a fast-paced, high-growth sector of the economy, that face global competition. Companies in mature sectors—including traditional manufacturing—also must gain a competitive advantage through better use of information technology and global connections.

Many successful and fast-growing companies need not make a major investment in place-based capital assets in order to thrive. When the Web auction company eBay went public in 1998, the market valued this company—which has almost no physical assets—at almost $2 billion, or twice the value of the esteemed, centuries-old auction house, Sotheby's.

Many other companies do not base their business model on material assets. Although they may need physical assets, they can rent them cheaply across the globe, picking them up or dropping them as conditions change. The biggest high-tech manufacturing firms—companies like Intel, for example—recognize that although they must make massive capital investments, the plants they build may only be competitive for a short period of time. The new-product cycle has been reduced to a few months—meaning assembly plants become obsolete almost as soon as they are built.

Twenty-first Century Competitive Tools: Regional Knowledge Networks, Vibrant Central Cities

The emergence of the global information economy has completely changed the relations between businesses and communities, and, therefore, radically altered the ingredients of a community's competitive advantage in the business world.

In the industrial age, local economic advantages were tied almost entirely to geography. Communities close to raw materials, markets, or transportation routes prospered. Indeed, many communities existed for no other reason than proximity. Mining companies built cities, such as Butte and Scranton, on the mountain of raw materials whose extraction provided their wealth. America's great industrial-age cities—New York and Chicago—thrived when railroads replaced water transportation. Nevertheless, the components of a community's success were more fixed and more predictable. Proximity to raw materials or transportation usually brought industrial factories, which, in turn, brought workers, which, in turn, created both labor and consumer markets. In other words, the barriers to entry for a community seeking economic growth were high. Communities incurred great expense trying to improve their relative advantage in the larger economy.

Today, the barriers have fallen. Because the global economy changes quickly, traditional competitive geographical advantages are no longer important. Increasingly sophisticated transportation services—overnight shipping by air, seagoing container ships, and intensely competitive parcel and bulk delivery firms—transport raw materials and finished goods quickly and easily no matter where they originate. No investment—not even capital investments in the billions of dollars—locks investors to a place. Companies are not tied to particular geographical locations.

Rather, companies are drawn to, and retained by, specific communities because the quality of life can attract and retain productive workers, especially in the knowledge field. Companies also seek communities where the knowledge-based economic infrastructure—the educational attainment of the workforce, quality of universities, and availability of civic and cultural amenities—can sustain the business.

During the twenty-first century, no city, community, or metropolis anywhere in the world will enjoy advantages based solely on geography. All communities must constantly build, exploit, and reexamine their assets. Competitive advantage is now found solely in the combination of people and place and the networking among people and institutions within proximity of one another. This, for example, is the reason why Silicon Valley—one of the most expensive and crowded regions in the United States—still retains a competitive advantage over virtually all other locations in the world in high-tech industry. The Valley's information-technology networks remain so rich they add a value that no other region can match.

The New Rules of Economic Development

Factories once dominated the small city of Auburn, located among the scenic hills and farms of upstate New York's Finger Lakes district. A half-dozen industrial plants—most of them owned by local business barons—lined the banks of the Owasco River, and over time, immigrant neighborhoods grew up at the factory gates, making Auburn the prototype of an industrial village. Classic industrial-age principles guided Auburn's success. Founded near access to waterpower, it thrived, in large part, because of its proximity to the big northeastern markets and to major transportation routes (including the Erie Canal and the main line of the New York Central Railroad).

Almost a half-century ago, however, the big factories departed for the Southern United States (they later moved to the Pacific Rim). In succeeding decades, the city entered a long, apparently irreversible, decline toward economic oblivion.

Yet, today, Auburn has stabilized, and a new industrial sector has emerged. Old factories have been demolished and rebuilt to meet fresh needs. New plants have been constructed in a city-owned industrial park on the edge of town. With eighteen percent of the city's employment, manufacturing is still the economic base of the city, and the community is learning the rules of economic development required to maintain its strength and vibrancy in the twenty-first century: networking, people, and place.

As with so many residents of other factory towns, many people in Auburn insisted that when the big factories left, the town would wither. Yet, they soon discovered that multiple factors made Auburn thrive: a network of entrepreneurs and engineers in plastics and other industries not only in Auburn, but in nearby towns, and a capable

The City Hall in Auburn, NY. Auburn, located in the Finger Lakes region of New York State, relies on its civic institutions, good labor force, and business networking to retain and attract small manufacturing companies to the area.

workforce that wanted to retain the community's long-established tradition of factory employment.

A cluster of small fiber-optic companies now flourishes throughout the Finger Lakes with Silicon Valley-style mutual effectiveness—largely because entrepreneurs remained in the region, kept in touch, and built small companies from the ashes of the older, larger plants. The once-stable factory workforce has begun to reassemble, as distant family members have returned from the South and West to work in the new industries back home. This evolution depended, among other things, on collaboration between the city and the local community college to highlight the products manufactured in Auburn. Although urban renewal and highway construction ravaged some central-city neighborhoods, it remains an attractive and manageable community with many local attractions, such as a thriving minor-league baseball team and outdoor recreation opportunities.

Auburn and other similar small communities still face economic perils. City officials will campaign to attract a single manufacturing company, when necessary. But factories, companies, and even industrial sectors will come and go, often in the space of a few years—that is the nature of the new global economy. Auburn's successful economic development stems not from attracting or retaining an individual plant, but from nurturing the infrastructure of economic success—entrepreneurs, business and marketing networks, universities and other civic institutions, a good labor force, and a sense of pride in the town that will retain and enhance its reputation as a good place to live.

Community Business Networks

Building business and community networks requires a far more subtle and sophisticated strategy than the traditional economic development approach—buying jobs with subsidies to individual businesses. But using such a strategy successfully requires more than shifting gears. It requires a rethinking of economic development from top to bottom.

In particular, the new rules of economic development require American communities in the twenty-first century to document and analyze their assets, understand how to combine those assets in innovative ways to complement the global, information-driven economy, and implement their

strategies to maximize the return on public-private financial investment in economic development.

Communities have long understood they must retain a strong perception of their economic assets. Only lately have they recognized the full breadth of those assets. Such assets are not limited to skills in the labor force, existing physical plants, and hard infrastructure, such as roads and sewer service.

Local assets also include business networks, entrepreneurial and financial experts, and unique labor pools. The variety of community assets has made *cluster analysis* one of the most powerful tools in the new world of economic development. Using statistical techniques, economic wizards identify which business and labor sectors are *clustered* in a given community—providing local leaders with a better understanding of their assets and opportunities. Cluster analysis often uncovers whole economic sectors not readily apparent at first glance and identifies how a community's economic networks can be strengthened and reinforced to generate more business opportunities.

Once the community's assets are identified, communities must devise a strategy to combine fragments into a rational network. The rapidly growing and rapidly changing global economy has created economic opportunities literally everywhere—in all geographical areas, in all industries, and in combinations that have never existed.

As the Auburn experience indicates, for example, manufacturing offers more opportunity today than anybody would have predicted a decade ago. Because manufacturing is a basic industry, it provides far more economic benefit to the typical town than the service businesses they are likely to woo following plant closures. According to the Congressional Research Service, every manufacturing job creates 2.5 spin-off jobs in the local economy—almost double the figure for service jobs.

Manufacturing job growth is in small, not large, companies, however. According to the National Association of Manufacturers, net employment at large manufacturing companies (more than 500 employees) dropped by 2.4 million between 1967 and 1992. Net employment at smaller companies grew by 1.7 million, almost offsetting the loss. The future lies in the network of small manufacturers, not in the big plants. For these small manufacturers, investing in the education of skilled workers and nurturing the networks is far more important in the long run than giving a tax rebate to a big factory.

A city's development strategy must be built on the foundation of innovative relations and connections among local institutions that may not traditionally be considered economic players. Education is an obvious example. If manufacturing workers must become knowledge-workers to operate the modern plant, then the notion of a *skilled worker* changes—and the manufacturing sector's connection to the local community college becomes more important.

This need for innovative partnerships is more evident in other emerging economic sectors, such as place-based entertainment and tourism. Many communities—even those in decline—have many local attractions—historic sites, museums, charming downtowns, or recreational opportunities at lakes and beaches. Only by linking these assets—and building an economic development strategy around all of them—can communities ensure their economic success.

Similarly, communities will not be economically successful in the twenty-first century unless they understand—and exploit—their surrounding regions. Many smaller or more remote communities with a four-year university may seem to be at a disadvantage, for example. But communities often recognize that the university in a neighboring town or city actually serves their community—and, by networking with university officials, they can strengthen both their town and the region.

The final implementation step in making communities economically successful in the twenty-first century is forging partnerships and regional connections. In economic development, implementation usually means determining how to invest a limited number of public dollars to provide maximum economic benefit to the community.

A cluster analysis would do little good if, in the end, the community simply chose only to offer the tax incentives provided a single manufacturer as before. Once communities understand and can link their assets to global opportunities in a sophisticated way, emergent development strategies will be tailored to take maximum advantage of those assets and opportunities.

It is always tempting for a community to take most of its business loan funds and earmark them for one big project. But small, not large, companies will fuel this country's economic success in the future. Small businesses of all kinds—service, man-

ufacturing, and others—create far more jobs than big ones. Indeed many of the biggest success stories from poor neighborhoods stem from economic development agencies granting microloans to neighborhood businesses.

Many successful communities in the twenty-first century will conclude their economic development funds are best spent not on the businesses themselves, but on the raw material of economic success—people, places, and networks. Education and job-training programs help communities maintain competitiveness in a fast-changing global marketplace. Reviving older neighborhoods and small downtowns often provides opportunity for businesses to thrive in previously written-off locations. Identifying and maintaining links among businesses and business owners may generate whole new areas of business opportunity that no individual company would—or could—pursue on its own.

Conclusion: Succeeding in the Twenty-first Century

Of all the civic activities undertaken by American communities and their civic leaders, economic development is at once the most alluring and the most risky. In today's cutthroat global economy, economic forces beyond a community's control can threaten its success. By undertaking economic development, a community can gain some control over the chaotic environment in which it must operate. For politicians, nothing seems like a better photo opportunity than bringing in a big-name company and cutting the ribbon on its plant or store.

Yet, such steps provide no guarantee of success. Smart economic developers have always recognized they are hostage to large economic forces; you can do everything possible to help an important local business stay competitive, but you cannot control the markets. In today's fast-paced global economy, a community cannot purchase jobs through economic development. The most anyone can hope to do is temporarily rent those positions.

That is why wheedling on talk shows to acquire an automobile plant just will not cut it anymore. No individual plant or store or business can guarantee long-term economic success to a community. Only by investing in the economic infrastructure— its people, its places, and its networks—can the American community hope to remain competitive during the twenty-first century.

In today's fast-paced global economy, a community cannot purchase jobs through economic development. The most anyone can hope to do is temporarily rent those positions.

Mayor Glenda Hood Drives
Economic Growth, By Air

LEADERSHIP
PROFILE

Think globally, act locally is a popular saying among civic activists. Glenda Hood, the mayor of Orlando, Florida, views her role as the executive of an international city, and has linked her constituents with businesses around the globe. At the same time, she runs a livable city back home.

Hood, a two-time Republican mayor of one of America's fastest growing cities, has witnessed remarkable growth in Orlando, a quiet agricultural town that catapulted into an international tourist destination more than twenty-five years ago when Disney World opened.

The Universal Studios launch a few years later added to the area's allure. Balancing two very different agendas, Hood has fought to support the quality of life in Orlando while trying to garner economic benefits for residents. Hood senses the economic potential of the region's international profile, and has flown to China, Russia, Japan, and South America, to forge international trade alliances for greater Orlando.

The story of Hood's outreach to Curitiba, a city in the State of Parana, Brazil, exemplifies her willingness to promote Orlando in far-off places. Writing on behalf of the Metro Orlando International Affairs Commission, which she helped found in 1995, Mayor Hood invited Mayor Jaime Lerner of Curitiba to consider establishing a sister-city relationship.

Hood and a group of Orlando business leaders flew to the Brazilian city, famed for its progressive city planning and mass-transit facilities, for a pre-planning mission that included making key local contacts and laying groundwork for an official trade mission. In March 1996, Hood met with a Brazilian delegation for a briefing on that country's business outlook and economic conditions. Mayor Hood led a delegation of ten business leaders to Curitiba, where they signed a sister-city agreement with local officials. The agreement is one of several that Orlando has signed with cities globally, including Cape Town, South Africa; Urayasu, Japan; and Orenburg, Russia.

One of the trade delegates on the Curitiba mission was Calvin Peck, managing partner of the

Orlando office of VOA Associates Inc., a Chicago-based design-build firm. While the company already had a presence in several South American cities, Peck said, the Orlando trade delegation was useful to his company.

"Obviously, when you go on a trade mission, you are able to meet with people that otherwise you might not get in front of," he said. The Curitiba mission, as it turned out, would bear fruit for Peck's firm. In November 1998, VOA signed an agreement with local officials to build a $125 million Curitiba International Trade Center. Peck praises Hood as a trade promoter.

Hood understood a "large international presence out there could tap into the city of Orlando, as it were, from the business side," he said. "We receive a lot of visitors here every year from around the world, and some of these people come back and buy residences or buy businesses."

If the city could take advantage of the awareness created by local attractions like Universal Studios and Disney World, Orlando could deepen and diversify its business base, rather than depending on the local entertainment juggernauts, according to Peck. Local companies, experts in entertainment and hospitality, could find new work through the sister-city programs and trade delegations.

Hood does not limit herself to expanding international trade opportunities, however. She also works to maintain the quality of urban life.

"One of her legacies, in addition to international trade, is the community development and residential development that has taken place in Orlando," Peck said. He also cited the mayor's commitment to redeveloping the city's downtown area, as well as her attempts in neighborhood preservation near the urban core.

A ten-year veteran of the city's planning commission, she has attempted to take a long-term view in a city consumed by the rapid changes of the present. She has conceived, and largely implemented, a comprehensive strategy for the city that involves annexation, growth control, neighborhood preservation, and mass transit. She also has planned for a new cultural district and new parks.

Hood is a planner wrestling a daunting urban-growth challenge. Orlando has been described as an economic miracle, but miracles can bring mixed blessings. Since 1971, when Disney World opened, the population has more than doubled to

185,000 people. About forty million tourists stream through the city each year. Hoteliers operate 100,000 rooms.

"I think we're neck-and-neck with Las Vegas," Hood said.

Cities that dream of theme parks as the panacea for weak local economies envy Orlando for its crush of tourist traffic. Although the revenue from tourism is rich, the visitor traffic is also punishing. The city's major roads and highways—notably Interstate 4 and International Drive, which feed into the theme park district south of downtown Orlando—damage the air quality in a region long noted for clean air. The city's infrastructure has also taken a battering.

"To tell the truth, when Disney opened their doors in seventy-one, it was a wonderful opportunity for this community to play catch-up," Hood said. Before Disney World, "we had pretty much a season[al] type of tourist community, in which people from the North would come south for the winter." With Disney World, however, "our season started to develop to a year-round season, and there was increased impact on infrastructure."

The State of Florida did not always acknowledge the impact of the tourist onslaught in Orlando; the city continues to receive money for roads and bridges from the state based on its full-time population, not on the hundreds of thousands of visitors who might be in town at any moment. Similarly, during the city's long wrangle over a light-rail, Hood insisted that city residents, not just tourists, should benefit from the system; the original proposed route had stopped far short of downtown Orlando.

Hood is a native of the region; her paternal great-grandfather settled in nearby Melonville (now Sanford). A century ago, Orlando's farmers specialized in citrus and cotton, which a railroad helped link to the rest of the country. Marketing itself as "The Phenomenal City," Orlando tapped into the growing trade of tourists migrating south from colder climates for the winter. Eventually, the seasonal presence of northerners and midwesterners influenced the city's urban design: Downtown Orlando resembles a midwestern city, with a well-defined central square.

During the first two decades of the century, Orlando followed the example of Chicago and other northern cities by embracing the principles of the City Beautiful movement, including a public park system, plentiful planting of trees along major boulevards, and classical architecture.

"We are very fortunate the way some of the buildings were designed and the way some of the neighborhoods were laid out," she said.

Hood attended public school and studied Spanish literature in college—a background that has aided her in communicating with the city's expanding Latino population. Her interest in politics took root when she spent a year in Costa Rica studying international business and Latin American history.

"I was able to look at our government's structure through other people's eyes, and it made me realize that I wanted to become well-informed and to become involved in decision making," Hood said.

Returning to Orlando after college, she started a small business as a translator and as a public-relations executive while chairing committees for local chambers of commerce and citizen advisory boards. In 1982, she joined the Municipal Planning Board.

"I became quite intrigued by planning," Hood said. "I always considered myself a very organized person, and as someone who plans. City planning fascinated me."

Hood was elected to the Orlando City Council in 1982, and became mayor a decade later.

Without Hood's advocacy, downtown Orlando might well have been overlooked during the city's theme-park-related economic boom. The city went through its suburbanization period in the 1970s, which coincided with the first incursion of the big theme parks.

Today, the downtown experiences more new office and hotel construction than ever before, Hood says. She also wants to promote culture: She has supported the creation of both an arts district and a theater district.

"People have come to understand that the arts and the cultural elements of our community are an economic-development tool," Hood said. "The arts are a need-to-have, rather than a nice-to-have."

Hood subscribes to the 1,000-points-of-light theory and provides neighborhood organizations with an infusion of city funds to boost volunteerism. She has created a program of $5,000 neighborhood grants that neighborhoods apply to a variety of uses, such as landscaping, plaques marking historic places, and emergency-response training. After Orlando's schools performed

Glenda Hood, Mayor of Orlando, FL, works to maintain the quality of life and to advance economic development in Orlando.

Church Street Station, a downtown shopping and entertainment mall, has helped revive the city center of Orlando, FL, attracting businesses and tourists.

disappointingly in a state survey of reading and writing skills, Hood kicked off a program of volunteer tutors.

"I have challenged people in those neighborhoods to mentor young people," said Hood. In the next twelve months, she added, "I expect to have 1,000 volunteers helping in these schools to help raise the reading, math, and writing skills." Those efforts are not intended to help only school children. "You have to have a strong school to have a strong neighborhood that is desirable for people to live in."

Hood also has big plans for increasing parkland in a city already rich in open space. "Green space is a very good growth-management tool for us," she said.

During the City Beautiful period, city officials acquired many lakes and surrounding lands. The city maintains these properties, though it has made few improvements. Hood proposes developing active parks on the lakefront land. To create new open space in the city, Hood has pushed through a $30 million program to create four new cornerstone parks while putting aside $10 million for future open-space development.

To accommodate growth, Hood prefers expansion to infill—replacing vacant or abandoned housing with new neighborhoods. She said she is proud of her record of annexation: In 1998 alone, the city grew by almost five square miles. At the same time, she is also a supporter of downzoning to preserve the density and character of existing neighborhoods. Hood has worked to restore the old red-brick pavements of neighborhood streets

that had been hidden under layers of asphalt. The road restoration reflects New Urbanist values, beautifying neighborhoods and slowing traffic.

"It's an amenity that is creating some of the highest-value housing in the region now," she said.

As a manager, Hood describes herself as hands-on and detail-oriented. She can also seem almost grandmotherly at times.

"I refer to city employees as my 'city family,' and I refer to citizens as my 'extended family,'" she said. She also describes herself as a demanding administrator who asks senior managers to relate all their actions to core values.

"We know what our core values are in transportation, in the redevelopment of our downtown area, in growth management, in efficiencies in government, [and] maintaining quality in economic development," Hood says. "All of those things are related."

Richard Fleming's Bold Visions
Reflect His Mentors' Wisdom

LEADERSHIP
PROFILE

Dallas and St. Louis fought head-to-head for eighteen months to attract MasterCard International's Global Technology and Operation Center, a prize that meant thousands of jobs to the chosen community.

The stakes were particularly high in greater St. Louis, where MasterCard already employed 1,400 people. The winning community would employ a total 2,000 people; the losing community would forfeit all.

St. Louis prevailed largely because Richard Fleming, president of the St. Louis Regional Commerce and Growth Association, understood how to pool an entire region's resources to build an effective recruiting platform.

As president and chief executive officer of the St. Louis Regional Commerce and Growth Association, Fleming and his civic partners decided to woo MasterCard by obtaining a number of incentives, including $12 million from *Build Missouri,* a state incentive program, as well as local subsidies for infrastructure. Countering a pitch from Dallas, which had also pledged a large incentive package, Fleming and his colleagues argued that MasterCard would be best served by choosing an area with a strong labor pool, both in quantity and quality. Fleming pointed out that MasterCard was pleased with the high productivity of its existing employees in St. Louis, but risked losing many of those employees if the company moved to Texas.

MasterCard eventually selected the 1,500-acre Winghaven master-planned community in O'Fallon, a city in suburban St. Louis, for its new $155 million global operations headquarters. Although Dallas had offered a generous incentive package, MasterCard chose greater St. Louis, Fleming says, largely because "the region was able to respond on a unified basis to a customer, and do a deal as a region, not just a lot of individual jurisdictions."

Fleming, a man of strong views, unafraid of the limelight, says he is one of a handful of economic-development professionals who work to boost the fortunes of broad regions, sometimes encompassing multiple counties and cities, rather than those of individual jurisdictions.

"We have very consciously tried to foster a departure from the zero-sum approach to economic development in a metropolitan area," he says. "In too many cases, economic developers (of neighboring cities) spend a lot of their time negatively marketing each other."

Thinking broadly is second nature to Fleming, a central role in nearly every important urban development trend of the past three decades—turning historic structures into commercial malls and fusing public and private resources and values. He counts among his mentors the late James Rouse, founder of The Rouse Company, and Edmund Bacon, the uncompromising former planning director of Philadelphia.

Born and raised in Baltimore, Fleming attended Loyola College, a Jesuit institution where he developed public-speaking abilities and competitiveness as a debating team member. After graduating in the late 1960s, he went to work for Rouse, where he helped plan Columbia, Maryland, the well-known new town in suburban Baltimore, and early stages of the Fanueil Hall retail development center in central Boston. Fanueil Hall became the prototype for projects throughout the country that capitalized on both historic buildings and the pleasures of being a pedestrian in an attractive urban area.

Fleming describes James Rouse as his first major influence. When a Rouse tennis partner broke his wrist, the young Fleming filled in and joined long discussions with the powerful developer. Fleming says he admired Rouse's combination of idealism and business savvy.

"Most people don't realize that he was extremely astute as a businessman as well as a mis-

Richard C. D. Fleming, President and CEO of the St. Louis Regional Commerce and Growth Association, actively promotes regional cooperation for economic development in a twelve-county area.

Richard Fleming at the podium with Jerry McElhatton, president and CEO of MasterCard International's Global Tehnology and Information Center.

sionary of cities," Fleming says. "He was brilliant with numbers."

Fleming, who had originally planned to attend law school, instead turned to urban issues. After leaving Rouse's shop, he earned concurrent master's degrees at the University of Pennsylvania: one in public finance from The Wharton School and the second in urban planning from the School of Fine Arts. Among his instructors was Edmund Bacon, then the executive director of the Philadelphia Planning Commission (a post he held from 1949 to 1970), and one of the most influential planners of his generation. Bacon introduced Fleming to the then-novel concept of a public-private partnership.

After Wharton, Fleming became the master planner of Peachtree City, a 15,000-acre planned community just outside Atlanta. Subsequently, he was recruited as the vice president of Central Atlanta Progress, which was headed by the man Fleming described as his third great mentor, the late Dan Sweat.

"Sweat and I had a wonderful opportunity to fundamentally reshape what a downtown organization did," Fleming recalls.

Rather than narrowly promote businesses, Fleming says, he and Sweat "identified a public-purpose dimension" and extended the group's leadership to the quality of urban design, the desirability of historic preservation and mixed-use development, and the need to reintroduce residential units downtown. They struggled to prevent white flight and create viable center-city neighborhoods.

Central Atlanta Progress also was influential in

building business support for the city's light-rail system, as well as the development of Hartsfield International Airport—the first of Fleming's three airport projects.

In his spare time, Fleming also campaigned for Jimmy Carter in 1976. Carter appointed Fleming deputy assistant secretary at the U.S. Department of Housing and Urban Development (HUD), administering the $3 billion Community Development Block Grant Program (CDBG).

Fleming takes particular pride in being what he describes as a "principal architect" of HUD's $1.2 billion Urban Development Action Grant Program (UDAG). The new program attempted to remedy the loss of the Urban Renewal program under the Nixon Administration.

"We wanted to make economic development a more eligible activity for federal block grants," he says. "UDAG complemented this purpose."

By the time Denver recruited Fleming to the Downtown Denver Partnership in the early-1980s, he had "learned to deal with a lot of urban-development issues."

By the mid 1980s, Denver was suffering a prolonged depression. The boom-and-bust town lost more than 100,000 jobs from 1985 to 1986. Fleming saw the economic crisis as creating the sense of urgency that could bring together formerly feuding municipalities.

"There's no substitute for a burning platform to get a community to do what it ordinarily would not be able to do," he says. "The collapse of the local economy in the mid- to late-1980s created such a crisis that there was a receptivity of local governments, and local economic developers, to pool their efforts on a region-wide basis."

The hurdles were significant given the historic rivalry between Denver and its growing suburbs. Neighboring Aurora, for example, had once tried to discourage companies from locating in Denver by belaboring its poor air quality.

"As if the air pollution wasn't going to cross the jurisdictional line between Aurora and Denver," Fleming observes wryly.

In Denver, Fleming headed two organizations. He was the founding president of the Downtown Denver Partnership, and later president of the Greater Denver Chamber of Commerce. Charged with revitalizing the Denver economy, the groups promoted the creation of a new pedestrian-only 16th Street Transit Mall, the Colorado Convention Center, and the new Denver International Airport. They also recruited a major league baseball franchise to the city.

The centerpiece of his regional initiative was the Metro Denver Network, a new organization within the Chamber that represented six contiguous counties, as well as each of the major cities in that region, including Aurora, Lakewood, and Boulder.

That cooperative approach was virtually mandated by political geography: Hobbled by state limits on annexation, and ringed by suburbs with strong economic and civic aspirations of their own, Denver could not simply try to grow its way to prosperity.

"The predicate was that if we fashioned a way in which we could position Denver on a regional basis, without regard to where those [economic] opportunities would be physically located, we would have a far greater success rate, and that over time we would have a net benefit for all the individual players," Fleming says.

The cooperative approach paid off for the Metro Denver Network. During Fleming's fourteen years in the city, businesses in the region added 240,000 jobs.

In 1994, Fleming was recruited as president and CEO of the St. Louis Regional Commerce and Growth Association. Serving as the chamber of commerce for a twelve-county region, the organization has a membership of 4,000 companies. As Fleming had done in Denver, in St. Louis he accepted a dual role by adding the presidency of the Greater St. Louis Economic Development Council.

Unlike Denver, St. Louis suffered the doldrums, not an economic crisis.

"In this case, the region had a long history of flat growth," Fleming says. The similarity between the two assignments, he adds, was "the need to bring the region together."

He created the Greater St. Louis Economic Development Network, a framework for mutual cooperation among the region's cities, real estate firms, and local economic-development officials. The MasterCard International relocation was a coup for that group. They also wooed Boatmen's Bancshares (now Bank of America), which selected St. Louis for its retail loan-servicing operations, keeping 150 jobs that may have otherwise fled the region and adding another 300. Fleming dissuaded Boatmen's from leaving town, in part, by helping the company expand into an affordable office sublease near its existing downtown headquarters.

Another St. Louis-area program is Technology Gateway Alliance, which seeks to help high-tech entrepreneurs with capital formation, workforce development, and technology transfers. The Gateway also markets St. Louis as *America's Center for Technology*. Fleming acknowledged that the city "historically has not been seen as a high-tech center," yet about 1,000 high-tech companies are based in the area. Industry clusters include information technology, plant sciences, and biotechnology.

Regionally, Fleming is once again frying big fish: He is promoting the $3 billion expansion of Lambert International Airport, in part to accommodate the major expansion of TWA and Southwest Airlines at the airfield. To provide an additional link between St. Louis and Lambert, Fleming's organization spearheaded a $1 million election campaign to win voter approval of the $550 million Page Bridge across the Missouri River.

Unlike some economic-development professionals, Fleming has a powerful ego, another trait he may have picked up from Ed Bacon, who acquired a reputation in Philadelphia as a forceful and authoritarian leader. Fleming believes that economic developers should propose strong ideas, even if they cause controversy.

"My working philosophy is something similar to what a Jesuit father once said to me in Loyola College: 'Sometimes it is better to ask for forgiveness than to ask for permission,' " Fleming says. "My observation is that economic organizations, and the individuals who lead them, often spend too much time asking for permission. In too many cases, they are overly reticent when they need to be bold."

Creating Globally
Competitive Communities

LEADERSHIP
PROFILE

"The twenty-first century belongs to jurisdictions that put export-driven manufacturing at the core of balanced economic growth to maximize their quality of life." So averred the influential publication Industry Week in its May 20, 1996 issue. Two days later, the Manufacturing Institute—the educational and research affiliate of the National Association of Manufacturers (NAM)—and Partners for Livable Communities released the findings of a year-long study of how manufacturers and local government officials, working together, can create livable and globally competitive communities.

Increasingly, leaders in the private and public sectors realize community life, trade, and economic development are mutually reinforcing. Localities become globally competitive not only by meeting the needs of employers, but also by enhancing their workers' lives.

The NAM/Partners report defined the ideal globally competitive community. None may exist today, but each city and region can learn from the criteria of greatest concern to the 400 civic and business leaders polled.

A globally competitive community:

1. Introduces each new generation to the work ethic, underscoring the importance of responsibility, initiative, team participation, and pride in workmanship. Across the nation, manufacturers bemoan the deteriorating work ethic among new, young employees.

2. Augments basic school curricula and electives with workplace-focused coursework that helps students move from the classroom to the job ready to contribute to the local economy and eager to pursue ongoing career preparation.

3. Adopts a comprehensive strategy of balanced growth from high-performance economic development, emphasizing wealth creation through modern manufacturing and the service industries that support it.

4. Commits to becoming outward looking and export oriented. It collaborates with industry to introduce advanced technologies and advises smaller employers how to adjust to change. Studies have shown that exporting companies create jobs almost twenty percent faster than comparable nonexporting firms, are more stable, witness greater worker productivity, and pay their employees better.

5. Knows its strengths and how to leverage them to build logical economic clusters.

6. Levels the playing field for existing smaller companies and start-ups, declaring them as eligible as large companies for expansion incentives that are consistent with their potential to create new jobs over time.

7. Strives to avoid adversarial relations when implementing environmental and other regulations, understanding that mature, public-private partnerships foster a climate of constructive communication, common objectives, and trust.

8. Encourages the cleanup of—and productive new uses for—abandoned and polluted brownfields so that all local resources pull their economic weight and residents of older urban neighborhoods can access gainful employment near their homes.

9. Upgrades its transportation and transit infrastructures and expands information highway linkage, so all citizens have access to decentralized modern manufacturing employment and mobility for learning, safety, and health.

10. Urges utilities to sell power to industry at competitive rates, to broaden incentives for energy conservation, and to improve the quality of power for sophisticated, computerized manufacturing technologies.

11. Levies taxes, fees, and permit charges with an appropriate balance between legitimate community needs for revenue and the employers' need to invest profits continuously in technologies that boost productivity and worker pay.

12. Pursues and monitors, with local business support, an inclusive vision of quality of life so citizens of all ages and incomes can participate in the educational, recreational, civic, and cultural aspects of community life.

13. Encourages local and regional sources of capital to assist economic development by making expansion loans to innovative smaller manufacturers and other qualified applicants who are poised for more growth.

14. Cosponsors promotional initiatives to build support for economic growth, entrepreneurship, and careers in manufacturing. It lays the groundwork for *aftercare* attention to the newer employers attracted to the area.

Alpine Diamond:
Building an Economy
Across National Borders

LEADERSHIP
PROFILE

With the decline in power of the nation-states of the European Union, citizens in France, Italy, and Switzerland are likely to define their neighbors regionally. Cultural and economic links between shopkeepers in Lyon and Turin may outweigh links to more far-flung parts of the two countries. Andre Soulier, a French member of the European Parliament, describes the new primacy of regions:

> "The rise of a global economy, accelerated by advances in travel and telecommunications, has unleashed forces beyond the control of any nation-state. And the call for political power in a uniting Europe [recently enlarged to include former members of the Eastern bloc] to be brought closer to the people makes regions the most natural constituency." (*The Washington Post,* October 15, 1995)

One European region undergoing a transborder transformation is the Alpine Diamond—the Rhône-Alpes in France, the Italian Piedmont, and the canton of Geneva in southwest Switzerland. Here, where three nations meet and local history books depict long-standing cultural and economic relations, the Alpine Diamond is building a regional giant intended to compete successfully on the world economy. An informal think tank with no institutional structure, the Alpine Diamond unites individuals from the three countries to develop and structure local initiatives and ventures.

Government and civic organization members of each Alpine Diamond city—Lyon, Turin, and Geneva—believe it beneficial to coordinate planning for environmental protection, job creation, transportation, energy, and business growth. The Alpine Diamond's initial goal for the Geneva-Turin-Lyon axis set up in 1985-86 was to promote a stronger image of the three cities abroad in order to attract businesses and tourists. At the same time, the policy study group sought, through meetings and publication of a report, to increase awareness among local actors of an Alpine territory. The group's priorities focus on preserving the shared cultural heritage, advancing university research, and building transportation and communications infrastructure. Book fairs, opera coproductions, exhibitions, recitals, and planning for a single museum ticket illustrate regional cultural programs. Academics jointly plan university research, student exchanges, joint seminars, and computerized library resource networks. Area civic organizations are lobbying to create a high-speed

transalpine rail service to hasten the trip from Lyon to Turin.

Claude Haegi, president of the Geneva government, foresees a time when Europe of the Regions will include a dynamic, culturally vibrant diamond stretching across the Piedmont, Rhône-Alpes, and Swiss canton borders. Alpine Diamond projects are helping to make Haegi's prediction come true and return the region to the glory days of the sixteenth century when it was a cultural and economic powerhouse.

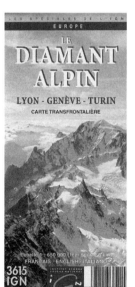

(Above) *The Lyon Part-Dieu Station of France's high-speed train system, the TGV. The Alpine Diamond of Lyon, France; Geneva Switzerland; and Turin, Italy promotes regional cooperation across national borders on issues ranging from transportation to economic development.*

HandMade in America, Inc.
67 North Market Street, PO Box 2089
Asheville, NC 28802
www.wnccrafts.org

Contact: Rebecca Anderson,
Executive Director
704.252.0121

HandMade in America, Inc. capitalizes on the community's extensive network of artisans in Western North Carolina by using their crafts to stimulate economic growth and revitalization. In the hilly western region of North Carolina, residents' adoption of the homily, "Make do with what you have," has given birth to a varied and skilled craft culture that provides jobs, and attracts tourists bearing wallets.

The genesis for HandMade in America was a six-month regional planning session, involving 350 citizens who outlined steps to make Western North Carolina a national center for handmade objects such as baskets and pottery. A twenty-year action plan evolved with the following goals:

- To develop community strategies for growth.
- To establish an academic base.
- To develop a communication plan.
- To create economic strategies emphasizing the artisan industry and cultural and heritage tourism.
- To enhance opportunities for object makers.
- To encourage the public, private, and nonprofit sectors to develop independent and interdependent methods for developing the handmade industry.

The citizen-planners also worked out strategies aimed at creating sustainable economic opportunities while maintaining their rural quality of life.

Western North Carolina is dotted with watersheds, land reserves, and mountains. Historically, a large percentage of absentee landowners and the nearby Appalachian Range created barriers to development. To encourage and capitalize on tourism, HandMade in America, Inc. published a guidebook called, *The Craft Heritage Trails of Western North Carolina.* The book directs readers along seven *trails* and highlights craft studios, galleries, restaurants, and historic inns. Many stopovers are towns that benefited from the Small Town Revitalization Project, an urban renewal project sponsored by the Appalachian Regional Commission and HandMade in America, Inc. Residents of six towns meet regularly to exchange ideas and plan city improvement projects, such as an intertown river walk, downtown revitalization, landscaping, and economic development.

A recent study by the Center for Business Research at the Appalachian State University found that handmade objects and craftspeople contribute approximately $122 million each year to the region's economy. Faced with this statistic, it was not hard to convince the North Carolina Department of Commerce and a nonprofit organization called Self-Help to join HandMade in America, Inc. in extending loans to craftspeople. The resulting fund provides loans of $1,000 to $50,000 for equipment, studio construction and expansion, materials and inventory, as well as for land, shops, and galleries. The investments have proven fruitful, allowing small craft businesses, characteristically undercapitalized, to achieve a secure spot in the marketplace.

These projects have increased tourism and craft-related revenues. Increased tourism has further expanded the demand for skilled craftspeople, a demand HandMade in America, Inc. meets through its many training programs. The Mayland Community College and the Penland School of Crafts jointly manage an entrepreneur program providing crafts and business training to adults. Students acquire skills such as basket weaving, woodcraft, and pottery while learning how to market their products.

HandMade in America, Inc. also works to safeguard the region's cultural heritage. The A+ Schools project encourages the use of crafts in schools. Basket-weaving techniques are used to teach math skills, and natural dye processes are applied to chemistry lessons. This merging of learning and crafts preserves traditional skills for future generations while encouraging vocational interest in crafts at an early age.

Seattle Jobs Initiative
720 Eighth Ave. South, Suite 120
Seattle, WA 98104

Contact: Dianna Hanna
Acting Director
206.628.6975

In 1998, the Seattle Jobs Initiative (SJI) launched a business-office occupations-sector project linking low-income Seattle residents with living-wage jobs in business and finance. Residents access training through seven ethnically and geographically diverse community-based organizations (CBOs). The training is a partnership between Seattle Jobs Initiative and Seattle Vocational Institute.

The training developed as part of the Seattle Jobs Initiative sector strategy that designs training to meet employers' hiring needs in growth sectors of the economy. Labor market research showed an unmet demand for entry-level workers with computer literacy and office skills. Major employers, such as Washington Mutual, Starbucks, and Safeco Insurance, set skill standards for the training and each has hired graduates from the program.

SJI has endured many challenges. Low-income residents often cannot afford to attend daytime training. The SJI now offers part-time evening courses. SJI also started job-search groups to provide peer support after graduation and reduce pre-employment attrition. To boost graduates' job retention, SJI plans to offer seminars on problem solving, life management, and upward mobility.

After completing fourteen weeks of intensive training, office occupations graduates earn an average starting wage of $9.26 per hour. After a year, seventy-one percent of the graduates are still on the job. The SJI provides the following free services for low-income Seattle residents, ages eighteen and older:

1. Career and skills assessment, work place readiness training;
2. Intensive, real-world training for jobs that pay at least $8 per hour, plus benefits;
3. Human services support (e.g., child care, transportation) integrated with job-training placement and retention;
4. Interviewing and job-search assistance;
5. Job placement;
6. Two years of on-the-job retention support; and
7. Skills-upgrade training.

Greater Jamaica Development Corporation
90-04 161 Street
Jamaica, NY 11432

Contact: Brian Williams,
Director of Public Affairs
718.291.0282

The Greater Jamaica Development Corporation is generating jobs by revitalizing a deteriorated central business zone in the Queen's borough of New York City. Greater Jamaica Development Corporation is trying to upgrade a rundown neighborhood to create a dynamic multipurpose center for business, transportation, government, as well as stimulate cultural and higher education opportunities.

Historically an active commercial, governmental, and cultural center in the sixties, the area witnessed a steady erosion of its economic base. Rapidly

changing demographics also heightened private sector uncertainties about the community's development potential and helped drain the downtown vibrancy.

Nevertheless, three decades of dedicated planning and strategic development efforts have made a tremendous difference. The corporation played a major role in securing over $1 billion in public and private investments in Jamaica, including two federal government service centers, a college, transportation hubs, and a new Queens Civil Court building. The Corporation and its private and public partners also delivered incentives to small business and rehabilitated thousands of apartments in addition to encouraging the development of amenities, services, and cultural programs to enrich the community.

The centerpiece of redevelopment is the Jamaica Market, an award-winning site and bright symbol of the borough's economic rebirth. The market attracted commitments from the Queens borough president, the city's Department of Business Services, and the New York City Economic Development Corporation. Formerly a weed- and rodent-infested vacant lot, the central market now houses thirty restaurants and shops in a circuit around the arcade. The market also operates a conference room that can be used for receptions and luncheons.

Local residents' entrepreneurial spirit and energy are also credited as the source of much of the area's success. Those who chose to stay have invested in the area's homes and businesses. Home ownership has been strongly aided by Queens Borough President Claire Shulman who sited many public projects in Jamaica center and who fought to create incentives for home ownership. The start-up of new business ventures generated increased employment opportunities, upgraded living standards, and enriched the quality of community life in Jamaica. Similarly, the corporation encourages business development with its revolving loan fund, enabling entrepreneurs to expand and

develop without onerous interest rates.

To generate more jobs, an organization called the Regional Plan Association also designated the Jamaica rail station, the site for a major intermodal transportation center and a hotel. The organization also has approved a plan for a rail connection to John F. Kennedy International Airport. The planners believe the airport rail link will make Jamaica a stronger magnet for domestic and international enterprises. By linking the downtown with the airport, planners hope to fortify Jamaica's ties to the global marketplace and increase residents' job opportunities. More jobs and better links to the global economy help Jamaicans build a stable future.

Greater St. Louis Economic Development Network
St. Louis Regional Commerce & Growth Association
One Metropolitan Square
Suite 1300
St. Louis, MO 63102

Contact: Gary C. Broome,
Director of Communications
314.444.1171

The Greater St. Louis Economic Development Network was established in 1995 as a framework to efficiently coordinate different economic development organizations in the St. Louis region.
This collaborative venture includes more than sixty regional economic development professionals representing the twelve-county greater St. Louis region including local jurisdictions. A shared e-mail system and regular meetings allow utilities, real estate firms, political jurisdictions, and local economic developers to communicate and jointly respond to and initiate prospects.

The Network aims to:

• Eliminate duplication of efforts;

- Maximize resources by focusing activities;
- Present a unified image to prospective businesses looking to relocate in the region;
- Provide all organizations with consistent data via the web site and Internet; and
- Improve communications among the organizations.

Acción El Paso/Texas

Montwood National Bank Building
7744 North Loop Road
El Paso, TX 79915

Contact: Diana DerKoorkanian
Outreach Marketing Coordinator
915.779.3727

El Paso residents have, since 1996, reaped the rewards of an influential South American export—*microlending.* Microlending can fill program-funding gaps. Acción El Paso grants small loans to stimulate enterprise development by people with low- to moderate-incomes who may not qualify for a bank loan. In 1961, Joe Blatchford founded Acción International to provide an average of about $500 in loans to start-up South American businesses. *Acción* set up its first U.S. affiliate, *Acción* New York, in Brooklyn in 1991. Five years later, *Acción* El Paso opened.

Acción El Paso is an atypical loan institution with atypical clients. Loan officers work out of free space in local bank branches and pitch their services to seamstresses, vendors, and artisans. By approving loans based on character rather than collateral, *Acción* violates many rules of banking. Yet, the organization has been very successful. The *Acción* network reports an average ninety-seven percent annual payback rate; only three percent of borrowers default. This tremendous rate of return is achieved by keeping the loan size small and the interest rate moderate to high (usually around sixteen percent).

In addition to loaning money, all *Acción* affiliates, including *Acción* El Paso, also advise borrowers on how to create a budget and business plan, establish a good credit history, and manage money. Loans often are made to groups and peer pressure provides added incentive for repaying the loans. Group members also provide financial and advisory support when other members experienced business downturns.

In El Paso, *Acción* has funded a myriad of enterprises, including a flavored popcorn business, for example, and a meat distribution service. Entrepreneurs can work full or part time, formally or informally. The program offers loans between $250 and $25,000 for working capital, the purchase of equipment, and other business purposes. Many clients apply who have either a poor or no credit rating and no collateral. *Acción* provides their last chance. Initial loans are small, but increase in size with timely repayment, providing committed entrepreneurs a source of capital and business assistance until they can access bank credit. After obtaining two loans, *Acción* El Paso clients increase their take-home pay by thirty-eight percent.

Acción El Paso is designed to promote the economic self-reliance of individuals and families. The program operates on a *hand-up* rather than *hand-out* principle. By creating jobs and increasing families' overall income, *Acción* has helped revitalize El Paso's neighborhoods.

Johnson Development Corporation

9100 Wilshire Boulevard
Suite 1060, West Tower
Beverly Hills, CA 90212
www.magicjohnsontheatres.com

Contact: Kenneth Lombard,
President
310.247.2033

The Johnson Development Corporation (JDC) develops entertainment complexes, restaurants and retail centers, provides jobs, and employs local minority contractors within underserved communities.
JDC was formed in 1994 by Earvin "Magic" Johnson, former NBA basketball player, to serve as a business stimulus, foster local economic growth, and create financial empowerment in underserved inner-city minority neighborhoods. In 1995, JDC and Sony Theatres formed a partnership to develop, build, and operate large multiplex movie theaters specifically targeted for underserved minority neighborhoods.

Under the name "Magic Johnson Theatres," the first theater was opened in June 1995 in Baldwin Hills Crenshaw Plaza Mall, the heart of a minority community in Los Angeles. The partnership theater is one of the top-grossing theater complexes in the country. By 1998, three more theaters had opened in Atlanta, Houston, and Detroit. Six more theaters in underserved communities are planned to open this year. Magic Johnson Theatres (MJT) estimates the total investment in the new theaters at $30 million.

The following facts verify that developing inner-city theaters was a wise investment decision by the Johnson Development Corporation, as well as a plus for the neighborhoods in which they are located.

- Superior performance of the Los Angeles theater: 30,000 customers a week.

- In April 1996, MJT posted the highest weekend box office receipts in the country for such black-themed pictures as "Waiting to Exhale," and the "Dead Presidents."
- Each theater lifts community morale and creates more than 100 permanent jobs.
- Additional corporate ventures, between JDC and Starbucks Coffee and JDC and TGI Friday's, have been developed.
- MJT has further optimized its retail advantage in the community by hiring from the community.
- Eleven thousand local students recently were given passes for a free movie and lunch.
- Programs for community groups are held in the theater's community hall.
- Movie stars drop by at premieres. Sports personalities are scheduled to read children's stories.

The presence of the theater has been the main driver for reversing the economic decline of the Baldwin Hills neighborhood. For example, first-floor tenants of the Baldwin Hills Crenshaw Plaza Mall reported an increase in business activity from twenty-five percent to fifty percent; overall business in the mall increased from thirty percent to fifty percent, and mall revenues increased in the first year from five percent to fifty percent, depending on the retail establishment. In addition, MJT served as an anchor and attracted other retailers by demonstrating the strong purchasing power of neighborhood residents. JDC's successful projects are a call to other developers that economic development projects in inner-city neighborhoods are good business.

John Bowne High School Agriculture Program
63-25 Main Street
Flushing, NY 11367

Contact: Steve Perry,
Assistant Principal
718.263.5555

As traditional careers in agriculture dwindle, new careers, like aquaculture, emerge. One agriculture program helps students discover their way through the maze of old and new fields. In the Queens borough of New York City, an agriculture program at John Bowne High School continues to thrive after its founding in 1917. Originally established as a program mainly geared towards horticulture, John Bowne's agriculture department offerings have multiplied into an array of fields—aquaculture, landscape construction and design, floral design, zoo keeping, botany, horticulture and entomology—that prepare students for the workplace. The extensive breadth and range of courses offered to students in grades nine through twelve make the agriculture department one of the largest and most competitive in the state.

John Bowne is not a specialized school; instead the agriculture department is an educational option. Students interested in agriculture must apply to the program in eighth or ninth grade. The program is also offered to special education and English as a Second Language (ESL) students. While the agriculture department is not a separate school, the students in the program usually take their non-agriculture classes together. This allows participants to know their fellow students and the teachers in their academic track intimately.

In the first two years of the program, students do not declare a major but take general agriculture classes in addition to basic college preparatory courses. During the eleventh and twelfth grades, students specialize in either the plant or animal sciences. In addition, students must commit two summers to agricultural work. The first summer, as a rising tenth grader, students devote half the day to classes in agricultural areas and the remaining half to working on the school farm and maintaining their own plot of land. The students take home the crops grown from their plots, and school crops are sold in a produce stand. The second summer, as a rising eleventh grader, students choose the type of job they would like, whether in the city or on a farm. Many times, students end up continuing to work into the school year. Most students opt to work in the city, and finding a summer job is not difficult.

Steven Perry, the assistant principal, who began at John Bowne as a student, vouches for the positive effects on the students. About ninety percent of the graduates of this program are accepted into colleges of agriculture. Bowen states that, "The agriculture department is not an agriculture/vocational school. We are academically inclined but we believe in hands-on experience. For students to make money in agricultural fields, they need the education." With this philosophy, the agriculture department at John Bowne develops enthusiastic students ready for immediate immersion into both today's workplace and higher education institutions.

The Boundless Twenty-First Century City

From Charlotte to Chicago, Salt Lake City to Seattle, *regionalism* has emerged as the guiding principle for communities seeking better services and a better lifestyle. Cities within the same regions pool resources to resolve long-standing disputes, attack common problems, and boost their competitiveness in the emerging global marketplace. Regional cooperation will be a major issue for American communities well into the twenty-first century.

Regionalism has existed, as a concept, at least since the twenties, when large urban-suburban metropolises emerged as a driving national-growth force. But the concept has gained a new currency. Business leaders preach the gospel of regionalism as an antidote to the limitations imposed by local political and economic structures. Environmentalists now understand that conservation strategies focusing on individual species are ineffective unless they take into account the complex biological relations operating throughout an entire ecosystem. Social activists have recognized that equity issues are best addressed on a regional scale, where wealthy and poor communities can begin to recognize their commonality.

These factors have converged in a new movement toward regionalism, not just in the United States, but elsewhere. Long-standing political and economic boundaries are quickly falling away and leaders from the public and private sectors cross old lines to create new productive alliances and plan transportation, environmental management, economic development, and social stability.

Regional Alliances Build Strong Cities

"Regions," notes Rochester Mayor William Johnson, "are the smallest scale at which it is

possible to capture most of the key labor and revenue flows and meaningfully resolve problems in an integrated fashion. At the same time, the region may be the largest geographical unit that people can grasp and around which they can come together."

Mayor Johnson's words help explain why studying regions has become an important way of looking at many problems. The overarching reason why regionalism has moved back into public policy discussions is the globalization of the economy.

"The economic region is the basic building block of the economy," policy analysts William Barnes and Larry Ledebur report in their recent book, *The New Regional Economies*. Furthermore, they add, "The fulcrum of the local economic region is the metropolitan area, not the city or any governmental jurisdiction."

When goods and services are traded all over the globe, New York does not compete with New Jersey or Dallas with Fort Worth. Instead, the New York-New Jersey region not only competes with the Dallas-Fort Worth region, but also with the greater-London, greater-Hong Kong, San Diego-Tijuana, Seattle-Vancouver, and other regional economic blocs.

As the economy has become international, it also has changed. For many companies, proximity has become important. In his recent book, *The Regional World*, economic geographer Michael Storper of the University of California at Los Angeles (UCLA) asserts that the vertical disintegration of companies—the splintering of large business structures—makes international and intercompany relations more important.

The economy is far from the only reason why the region has emerged as a focus of public policy. The evolution of transit and transportation planning, new ecological information, and perceptions of inequities between city and suburban dwellers underpin new regional development policies.

(Above) *Denver International Airport, a new and technologically advanced air center, gives Denver and its surrounding region an advantage in global competition for trade and jobs.* (Left) *Post Alley in Pike Place Market in Seattle, WA.*

Regional Leadership

Perhaps the biggest breakthrough in the new regionalism movement is that organizations and institutions can make changes by lobbying in regions. For most people, a region often seems too large and too hard to conceptualize. Yet, communities are demonstrating a growing awareness that actions can affect a whole region. "We can't view metropolitan regions as being things we are unable to control," says Michael Gallis, a Charlotte-based consultant specializing in regional analysis. "We have to understand how to control and direct the regional dynamic."

The most precious commodity in any local or regional civic activity is leadership. Yet, a broad group of new players has emerged to lead the charge—bringing new leadership to politics and obtaining innovative leadership from the institutional sector and the world of business.

One reason that past efforts to fuse regions often failed was that government agencies alone led these efforts. Occasionally, powerful regional agencies have been created—the California Coastal Commission, the Adirondack Park Agency, and Portland, Oregon's Metro Council—but they are the exception rather than the rule. More

Transportation and Other Urban Systems. Transportation, water delivery, waste disposal, utilities, and telecommunications have operated at the regional level for more than a century. Indeed, it would be hard to envision a society that could function effectively if these systems did not operate on a regional scale. In recent years, as population and employment have decentralized, the regional issues associated with urban systems—

especially transportation—have gained importance. Increasingly, no one entity can maintain urban systems on a regional basis; rather, maintenance requires the coordinated effort of many different municipal governments, special districts, and similar organizations. Reforms in federal transportation policy during the nineties make the region more important. The 1991 Intermodal Surface Transportation Efficiency Act (ISTEA) and 1998 Transportation Equity Act for the 21st Century (TEA-21) gave considerable power to regional planning agencies to approve or deny local transportation projects based on their ability to help blend, rather than fragment, regions.

Efficient transportation systems require the regional cooperation of jurisdictions.

The Environment. As the scientific understanding of ecosystems has grown more sophisticated in the past thirty years, efforts have shifted from preserving a single species and establishing isolated preserves with arbitrary boundaries to conserving broad regions to protect multiple species and habitat types. The science of ecology—concerned with the interconnectedness of species and habitats—was first conceived in the late nineteenth century. For the next 100 years, however, the discipline concerned itself primarily with counting and describing the plants and animals. With the exception of air quality management, where the regional nature of the problem has been obvious for decades, most environmental policy focused on narrow species and land parcels. In the last decade, however, this fragmented view of the environment has changed. Increasingly, environmental policy concentrates on environmental problems, such as watersheds and ecosystems, which are regional in scale just as transportation and economic issues are regional. The regional approach has galvanized both government bureaucracies and citizen activist groups that rapidly have embraced the regional approach to organize policy discussions and implementation. Regionalism is especially evident in the area of water quality, where increasing concern over urban storm-water runoff has led to a regional approach in many metropolitan areas.

Social Equity. As suburbs expand and central-city populations contract, regions have become more socially fragmented. This phenomenon has raised important new concerns about equity. It is not just that the poor are being left behind in inner-city neighborhoods. In the suburbs, political fragmentation and economic stratification related to income levels and property values have segregated groups of people and their jobs. Small neighborhoods and spheres of influence—some rich, some poor, some who cope well with urban problems, some who do not—give little sense of the regional *whole*. With fragmentation, many political analysts have reexamined the dynamics of urban growth to discover that social equity can be achieved only at the regional level. "Any attack on urban social and economic problems," wrote David Rusk, the former mayor of Albuquerque, in *Cities Without Suburbs*, "must treat suburb and city as indivisible parts of a whole." Similarly, the work of Myron Orfield, a Minnesota state legislator and head of the Metropolitan Areas Research Corporation, highlights the extreme disparity between social need and fiscal capability among the jurisdictions in the typical U.S. metropolitan area. A century ago, these problems were resolved by the creation of large municipalities—such as greater-New York, which grew in 1898 with the addition of Brooklyn, Queens, and Staten Island. Today, policymakers show an increasing recognition that the disparity between rich and poor can be meaningfully attacked only at the regional level.

commonly, regional-planning efforts have been organized around regional councils of governments (COGs)—federations of cities and counties.

Following these governmental models has always proved difficult. Most citizens—to say nothing of local elected officials—resist the creation of regional

agencies with strong regulatory power. Opposition from local government representatives, for example, helped quash a legislative attempt to create a Southern California regional planning and regulatory agency in the early-1990s, despite strong support from state leaders. Local elected officials find it difficult to look beyond their own constituencies and take on regional challenges.

Government efforts still play a role in this new regional movement, and, in many cases, a very important one. Some regional issues are so pervasive they require significant government involvement. In Georgia, for example, when Atlanta-area elected officials recognized a need for bold action to curb urban sprawl, air pollution, and traffic congestion, they established the far-reaching Georgia Regional Transportation Authority in 1998.

In Southern California, the U.S. Fish & Wildlife Service stimulated a regional planning effort by using its regulatory power to protect rare plant and animal species threatened with extinction.

More often, however, political leadership emerges when elected officials recognize that to succeed in their own communities, they must form a relation with entire regions. Former Seattle Mayor Charles Royer recalled recently that the concept of regionalism first struck home with him when he organized an annual leadership conference for business and civic leaders in Seattle. It has expanded farther beyond Seattle's boundaries every year.

"We knew we had really gotten it right," Royer says, "when we decided we should hold our Leadership Conference not in Seattle, but in Boise, Idaho, because when we are talking about economic development in Seattle, Boise creates a lot of the reason that we have a port. We started thinking about our region as Oregon, Washington, Alaska, Montana, Idaho, Wyoming, and two Canadian provinces."

Many times elected officials will promote regionalism despite considerable political risk. Maryland's *Smart Growth* effort reflects, almost entirely, the courageous leadership of Governor Parris Glendening. Today's regional effort in Memphis owes its creation to the political leadership of many: Mayor Jim Rout of Shelby County, Tennessee, and the governors of Tennessee, Mississippi, and Arkansas, who worked with Rout to create the Governors' Alliance for Regional Excellence.

The New Regional Leaders: Corporate Chiefs

One of the most important reasons for the revival of regionalism has been business executives' unprecedented interest in regional issues. Operating in national or global markets, contending with regional labor and housing markets, and concerned about large-scale transportation and commuting patterns, corporate executives may have an easier time seeing past political boundaries and long-standing interjurisdictional hostilities.

Last spring, Hugh McColl, chairman and chief executive officer of Bank of America, welcomed the leaders of the shopping center industry to a conference in his hometown of Charlotte with a remarkable speech calling for more regional cooperation. "As cities grow, and transportation and communications enable communities to interact more and more," he said, "the need for regional growth strategies becomes greater than ever."

It is no wonder that business executives are leading the way. Increasingly, they apparently believe that the fragmented and often bickering nature of local governments impedes their ability to get the job done. "Businesses do not operate in political space, they operate in economic space," says Michael Gallis. "The private sector has to do business and the politics is driving them crazy."

Business executives have organized regional associations and moved regional issues forward where public bodies have failed. In St. Louis, for example, the Greater St. Louis Growth and Commerce Association now covers fifteen counties in two states and frequently takes on a regional leadership role that no elected official is capable of filling. In California's Silicon Valley, major computer companies have long provided enlightened leadership for the region, but the recent creation of Joint Venture Silicon Valley provides the most important example so far. By convening industry leaders, local government officials, and education and nonprofit leaders, Joint Venture produced Silicon Valley 2010, a strong framework for future regional action. Already, Joint Venture has worked with major corporations in the region to create a funding pool to promote affordable housing in one of the nation's most prosperous and expensive regions. Most recently, the group organized the creation of a $20 million Housing Trust Fund for Silicon Valley, soliciting donations from major computer companies, home builders, and public agencies.

One other group joins the business community in leading regions: the institutional sector. Two kinds of institutions promote regionalism: those with a regional mission and those organized by a series of local players who recognize they must

"As cities grow, and transportation and communitiies enable communications to interact more and more, the need for regional growth strategies becomes greater than ever."

—HUGH MCCOLL
CHAIRMAN AND
CEO, BANK OF
AMERICA

work regionally. Both types of institutions have existed in many regions for a long time. They have amplified their regional mission.

Hospitals and universities, for example, do not simply serve clientele within a geographic area defined by arbitrary local boundaries. They also shape the region and allow it to function. They concentrate services and employment as assets to the entire region and help build transportation and communication nodes.

Foundations especially play a major role in regional efforts. Many foundations have provided financial support for regional planning in the past. The Russell Sage Foundation financed the first regional plan created in the United States during the twenties: New York's Regional Plan Association. Now foundations create regional visions and strategies in their community bases. Perhaps the best-known commitment came from the Lyndhurst Foundation, which helped to kick-start the visioning process in Chattanooga more than fifteen years ago—a key component in Chattanooga's well-known revival. Now other foundations are also taking up this challenge, including the Turner Foundation in Atlanta—which has helped highlight the sprawl issue—and the John D. and Catherine T. MacArthur Foundation, which has taken a special interest in the Chicago region.

In addition, community foundations also get involved in regional efforts. In the past, these philanthropies have played passive roles, serving as vehicles for programs. Now some foundations work aggressively with communities to bring focus to regional agendas. For example, the Greater Kansas City Community Foundation—which manages more than 800 different endowment funds—has stimulated the creation of innovative local youth programs by pursuing partnerships with community organizations, business leaders, and other civic entities.

Civic groups and similar organizations also are identifying regional issues and using their combined muscle to create solutions.

One of the most inspired efforts in the nation is the work of Detroit's Metropolitan Organizing Strategy Enabling Strength (MOSES), a faith-based organization that includes two hospitals, one university, and fifty-three churches representing six different denominations. MOSES has opened up a dialogue among congregations in Detroit and the suburbs, helping those congrega-

tions share their many mutual problems, including low attendance, fiscal decline, and the loss of the church community.

These concerns led MOSES into a dialogue about metropolitan growth patterns and suburban sprawl. The organization financed the work of the Metropolitan Areas Research Foundation to analyze regional inequities and fragmented land-use patterns in the Detroit region. In 1998, the group held a rally with Detroit Mayor Dennis Archer—whose innovative approach to regional coalition building has been admired throughout the nation—at which MOSES members read a Declaration of Interdependence among the city and suburbs.

Getting Things Done: Role Players and Coalitions

The new players promoting regionalism represent only part of the concept's success. In many cases, regions succeed in large part because existing players work together in unusual new alliances.

Both new and veteran players recognize how regions work and what roles different organizations and institutions can play. Only by understanding their roles can organizations work together in innovative ways to bring about change.

Consultant Michael Gallis says the effort of raising regional consciousness forces institutions and organizations to think about who they are and what they do. He compares regionalism to a successful athletic team. "The reason teams succeed is not because they have the best players," he says. "Teams succeed because different players play different roles really well."

To help regional players understand their roles, Gallis often produces resource books explaining to government agencies, businesses, and citizen groups the structure of regional operations. For example, in his resource book for Cincinnati—written as part of a regionalism project for the Greater Cincinnati Chamber of Commerce—Gallis defines rings of development ranging from downtown Cincinnati; examines the transportation corridors that provide regional orientation and structure; and identifies the many systems—economic development, infrastructure, culture, and history—that shape the metropolis.

Once people and organizations understand the broader context, they can find their place. They can view themselves as one component of an organism working toward a common goal, rather than as individuals operating alone toward their own goals. When they realize their common regional identity, the concept of boundaries begins to fall away. United regional players promote cooperation among organizations and institutions that formerly appeared to have nothing in common—or, worse, who formerly held to long-standing hostilities.

To build regions, institutions must recognize their role in the structure and combine forces with other groups to achieve specific regional goals.

The leaders may be different in different locales. In a relatively young and fast-moving region, the leaders are likely to be successful businesses—such as the computer industry in Silicon Valley. In a more mature region with a strong institutional structure, such as Philadelphia, educational institutions, such as the University of Pennsylvania, and philanthropic organizations, such as the William Penn Foundation, lead the region. In Memphis, leadership has fallen to local and state elected officials who see advantages in working together.

Just as important as the leaders, however, are the other organizations and institutions who work with leaders to get things done. In St. Louis, more than 200 companies and institutions—including the Federal Reserve Bank of St. Louis and St. Louis University—have formed the Technology Gateway Alliance that will promote technological advancement in the region. The Alliance already has documented that airline-hub cities such as St. Louis are more likely to attract high-tech industry.

In California, where rapid growth and innovation remain part of the regional culture, organizations have joined to solve problems in ways that would have been unimaginable only a few years ago.

Fresno, one of the fastest-growing urban regions in the country, would not seem the natural center for an alliance among farmers, developers, and environmentalists, for example. One of the most important agricultural areas in the world surrounds the city, and agricultural land must be sacrificed to make room for urban growth. Nevertheless, recognizing that Fresno's future requires both agricultural production and the urban markets and an infrastructure that supports it, a new coalition has sponsored the Growth Alternatives Alliance to preserve farmland and maintain urban growth. The coalition includes the Fresno Chamber of Commerce, the Fresno Farm Bureau, and the Building Industry of the San Joaquin Valley.

Even more remarkable, in many ways, is the effort to preserve habitat for endangered species in Placer County, California—a fast-growing area near Sacramento that extends from California's Central Valley to the Sierra Nevada Mountains. Placer County officials who wanted to plan wildlife preserves got help from an unexpected source: the Sierra Business Council, which represents 500 businesses in the Sierra Nevada foothills. The council published a study, called "Planning for Prosperity," that showed the importance of environmental and quality-of-life issues to regional growth. With foundation support, the council and county created a joint plan to protect potentially endangered species.

Perhaps the most remarkable coalition joins the dozens of organizations, businesses, and government officials to create Envision Utah, a joint public/private/institutional regional-planning effort to accommodate growth in Salt Lake City. Concern about urban expansion and sprawl led to a coalition of dozens of groups—including the Save Our Canyon Commission, Utah's major banks, the state's Martin Luther King Commission, the state superintendent of public instruction, the Mormon Church, major newspapers and television stations, and even a justice of the Utah Supreme Court. The coalition and its technical experts conceived a new vision for the region's future to accommodate an additional million people while preserving agricultural land and open space.

Regional Coordination Shapes Future Communities

The region now defines the potent political jurisdiction for America's communities. Early in the twentieth century, many small- and medium-sized communities could view themselves as isolated and independent—separated from the rest of the world. At the millennium, however, no American community can afford to view itself as an island. Even small communities in rural areas have come to recognize that regional approaches are required to maintain economic competitiveness and ecological health. In the twenty-first century, the notion of communities in combination with one another—rather than cities or towns in isolation—will define the American urban and suburban landscape.

The Sierra Business Council, which represents 500 businesses in the Sierra Nevada foothills, created a plan with Placer County, CA, to create regional wildlife preserves.

New Federal Leadership:
Preventing Sprawl and Reviving Regions

The relentless decentralization of commercial and residential life in the United States has generated a new interest in metropolitan policies that address cities and suburbs as interdependent units. Rapid employment and population growth creates wealth in the outer suburbs, while central cities and inner suburbs shoulder the responsibility of caring for the nation's poor.

The federal government's leadership has contributed to suburban growth through transportation policies that favor the car and ease families into the suburbs. Housing policies that concentrate the poor in homogenous settlements and tax incentives that encourage the ownership of single-family dwellings on extensive parcels of land also encourage middle class and affluent families to relocate to semi-rural communities.

Because the federal government helped facilitate the decentralization of U.S. cities, it can now help reverse the trend. By reexamining and transforming the federal policies that helped create sprawl, the government can lead communities in their efforts to slow the inexorable growth of suburbs. New federal leadership can encourage states to build transit systems and streamline metropolitan public housing administration. New federal tax policies can help shift the costs of metropolitan development to suburban homeowners.

Suburbs Siphon Jobs from Cities

As the brief history of metropolitan growth patterns noted in Chapter II, central cities are disproportionately responsible for dependent populations and for additional costs for schools, police, welfare, and social services. Residents and businesses that remain in cities are taxed heavily to resolve these problems. They migrate to suburbs to reduce their costs. From 1989 to 1996, 7.4 million upper- and middle-income households left cities for suburbs while only 3.5 million moved from suburb to city.

According to John Kasarda, a researcher at the University of North Carolina, by 1999, most jobs had moved to the suburbs and exurbs.

"Manufacturing employment is now over seventy percent suburban; that of wholesaling and retailing is just under seventy percent. Even the last bastion of central-city employment dominance—business services—succumbed to the powerful suburban pull."

Federal policies that aid growth at the cities' expense contribute to the attractiveness of the suburbs. For decades, only urban residents and politicians suffered the negative effects of decentralization. Now suburban dwellers bear some of the costs development policies once allowed them to shift onto others. They face congested roads, overcrowded schools, deteriorating air and water quality, and the loss of open space. U.S. traffic congestion is worsening, increasing by more than twenty-two percent from 1982 to 1994, as minor suburban roadways have become conduits for thousands of people traveling to and from new office complexes, malls, and subdivisions.

Sprawl increases congestion by raising the number and length of automobile trips. The expansive style of new developments also raises the costs of building new and maintaining existing infrastructure. Roads and utilities for compact subdivisions cost seventy-five and eighty percent, respectively, of what sprawl development costs. Finally, sprawl jeopardizes environmentally sensitive lands, such as wetlands, estuaries, and flood plains. One study estimated that sprawl-style development in New Jersey, Kentucky, and Michigan would consume almost one-fifth more sensitive environmental land than more compact types of development. Other studies of Orlando, San Diego, the San Francisco Bay area, and the Chesapeake Bay region of Maryland have reached similar conclusions.

Many urban problems are actually urban and suburban—metropolitan—problems. Hyper-growth in the suburbs and under-investment in cities cause problems for both. Emigration from cities causes pressure in suburbs. Overheated suburban growth draws resources from the cities, where a stable population could strengthen neighborhoods and maintain the tax bases. In the service of sprawl, market forces and individual preferences have contributed to urban decline and suburban growth.

The Federal Role

Major federal spending programs, tax incentives, and regulations also have helped make cities and some older suburbs unattractive while rendering newer suburbs perhaps too attractive for their own good.

Housing policies contribute to the concentration of poverty in city centers. The U.S. Department of Housing and Urban Development recently concluded the combination of federal admission rules, which until recently gave first priority to the poorest households, and the location of public housing developments has led to "the physical, social and racial isolation of public housing in many cities, cutting off residents from jobs, basic services, and a wide range of social contacts." Nearly fifty-four percent of public housing residents live in neighborhoods with a thirty percent or higher poverty rate.

Vouchers could reduce the concentration of poor in the inner city, but the fragmented housing program administration offers recipients too little information about their housing choices. In the Detroit metropolitan area, for example, thirty-one public housing agencies administer separate Section 8 voucher programs.

While some government policies have height-

ened the concentration of the poor, others have helped disperse the more affluent. Construction of the interstate highway system encouraged suburban development, enabling families and businesses to locate far from urban centers while accessing the benefits of the central city. Highway spending has favored suburbs in general and suburbs with large employment concentrations in particular.

In 1991, Congress attempted to reduce the role of national transportation in creating sprawl. The Intermodal Surface Transportation Efficiency Act (ISTEA) allowed highway funds to be rededicated to transit projects, and included new funds for either highways or transit. However, few states have taken much advantage of their new flexibility and powers.

States spent forty-one percent of their flexible funds in fiscal year 1997 on reconstruction and repair of existing roads and fifty-nine percent on new road construction. Few states exercised their new flexibility, in part because of an intersection of federal and state laws that prevented them. In 1998, Congress reauthorized the transportation law, renamed it the Transportation Equity Act for the 21st Century (TEA-21), and increased authorized spending by forty-one percent. Nevertheless, states and metropolitan areas continue to use the

Portland, Oregon's answer to managing growth was the creation of the Urban Growth Boundary (UGB) program to contain development and preserve open space.

new funding for expensive road-building projects in the outer suburbs, which may again undermine older, established urban economies and accelerate the decline of inner suburbs.

Tax provisions that promote homeownership, such as the ability to deduct mortgage interest and property taxes from federal income taxes also powerfully influence where people live and businesses locate. These provisions, which lowered federal revenues $58 billion in 1998, appear spatially neutral, as high-rise condominiums in central cities are as eligible for these tax breaks as are suburban single-family houses. In practice, however, tax breaks favor suburban communities, because the value of tax deductions is greatest to people who face the highest tax rates and who itemize deductions. They are likely to live in the suburbs. Upper-income households also purchase more new goods than do low-income households, and this pattern extends to housing: New housing is scarce in older cities and abundant in suburbs.

Tax incentives also are applied to the combination of land and buildings that make up owner-occupied suburban residences. Vacant suburbs supply opportunities for construction of low-taxed housing and land. The interaction of tax policies, spending habits, and land development patterns have favored the movement of upper-income households to the suburbs.

As economists Joseph Gyourko and Richard Voith point out, the U.S. tax system may be the most influential factor in the decision for families to locate to the suburbs.

"The decentralized, stratified urban form of America's cities could be the result of people reacting to a price system profoundly affected by tax policy as opposed to a reflection of intrinsic American preferences for low density, stratified communities."

Federal Government Sprawl Prevention: an Unrealized Obligation

The federal government plays a crucial role in setting the rules of the development game with its housing and transportation polices; in determining the geography of governance through the administration of social programs; and in leveling the playing field between cities and suburbs by providing information about the location of federal spending.

The federal Department of Transportation (DOT) can help curb sprawl through its administration of TEA-21. Without guidance from DOT, most state and metropolitan transportation bureaucracies are likely to use TEA-21's funds for road building. However, DOT will re-certify every metropolitan planning organization in the country over the next few years, and can encourage states to balance new road building projects with infrastructure repair; ensure they comply with civil rights laws in their operations and investments; and provide the public with information about state investment decisions.

The federal government also can assist state policymakers by providing them assessments of the spatial effects of large-road expansion projects, including their effects on older communities. The public, particularly the residents of older communities, should know what the full impact of new highway projects would be. But the federal government also should ensure that suburban dwellers understand the advantages and disadvantages of new roads and their influence on the quality of suburban life.

Housing policies now encourage a greater mix of incomes in public and assisted housing developments, which reduces the chances that poverty will concentrate. Some 100,000 public housing units will be demolished by 2003 and replaced with smaller housing developments interspersed in other neighborhoods and housing vouchers. Congress has appropriated funds in fiscal year 2000 for 60,000 new vouchers.

The federal government could streamline the voucher program by centralizing its administration in metropolitan, rather than local government, and requiring a single, consistent set of rules in each metropolitan region. A streamlined regional agency could reduce the concentration of poverty directly caused by federal housing programs while at the same time reducing program administration costs.

The federal government also could provide support for expanded metropolitan governance in areas like workforce and economic development programs. The current parochial administration of these programs hinders low-income families from connecting to opportunities in other jurisdictions.

Where metropolitan governance is impractical, the federal government could encourage cross-jurisdictional collaboration, by giving governments that apply for block grants or special funds extra points if they demonstrate plans for metropolitan collaboration.

Metropolitan governance efforts will not make a difference if other federal inducements to sprawl remain in place. The federal government should provide metropolitan areas with a clear spatial analysis of how federal resources are allocated and routinely examine the spatial impacts of major spending programs, tax expenditures, and regulations. Are central cities and inner suburbs treated fairly in the allocation of federal resources, particularly those that create wealth? Do federal regulations tilt the playing field against redevelopment or investment in cities?

The federal government's answer to these questions and correcting the appropriate policies will go far toward promoting fairer metropolitan growth patterns in the future.

Prevent Sprawl and Revive Entire Regions

Reducing the needless costs of sprawl and restoring the vitality of older cities will not happen easily even with federal leadership. Some people and businesses benefit from sprawl and enjoy the lifestyle it allows. Deficient city schools, crime, and bad services impede urban restoration. A metropolitan approach by the federal government is not an urban panacea, but it can help mayors, community groups, and civic and corporate leaders reverse decades of core city decline. The metropolitan agenda taps into a widespread feeling that our growth patterns cannot be sustained. It offers an alternative way of growing and holds the promise of a true urban revival, greater equity, and improved quality of life in both city and suburbs.

Developing a mix of housing close to the center city places residents closer to jobs and reduces the pressure to expand highways.

Parris Glendening: Bold Leadership and *Smart Growth*

Smart Growth has vaulted to significance as an issue in the U.S. presidential debate and now many government leaders talk about its core principles—using financial incentives to manage growth and combat sprawl. Parris N. Glendening, the governor of Maryland, talks of those principles with particular pride. And rightly so. The former college professor coined the term shortly after arriving in Annapolis in 1995—and the Maryland *Smart Growth* program has since become a model for the entire nation.

The Maryland initiative sets state land and development priorities and backs them with financial and infrastructure incentives. Residents and business owners marvel at its simplicity despite the complicated political machinations required for its passage. Other states fan tensions among developers and environmentalists by emphasizing regulations. The California Coastal Commission and Portland Oregon's Urban Growth Boundary requirements, like many other statewide and regional planning initiatives, empower the state to strong-arm local governments and developers. The restrictions earn the wrath of builders and property owners and often cause a legal backlash.

Glendening's Smart Growth state planners strong-arm no one.

"The key to our success in Maryland was our decision 'to step out of the box,'" he says. "We did not develop a new layer of review or a new set of regulations. Rather we decided to use our budget as a \$15 billion incentive for *Smart Growth*. And we have begun to use our tax laws as a disincentive to sprawl."

First passed in 1997, the *Smart Growth and Neighborhood Conservation* program channels state infrastructure money into priority funding areas, including existing cities and rural population centers, as well as some greenfield areas suitable for new development. The *Rural Legacy* program channels the state's funding of land acquisition to designated conservation areas. The three other primary components of the program include *Voluntary Cleanup and Brownfields*, *Live Near Your Work*, and the *Job Creation Tax Credit*.

If any governor should know how to use a state government's powers to stop sprawl, it is Parris Glendening. The 57-year-old Democrat grew up poor in southern Florida and earned a Ph.D. in political science and urban administration at Florida State University. He spent twenty-seven years teaching government and politics at the University of Maryland. He served three terms as the county executive of Prince George's County and wrote a widely used textbook called *Pragmatic Federalism: An Intergovernment View of American Government*.

As Glendening matured politically, population growth shifted from the North to the Southeast and new city builders occupied the rural landscape, building sprawling subdivisions, endless interstate highways, and strip malls. Traveling from north to south Florida as a college student, he took roads that crawled through the once-pristine backcountry to save money rather than the quicker turnpike toll highway.

"I saw the Everglades being filled in," he recalls, "and I instinctively knew that we were doing something wrong."

As a Hyattsville, Maryland, city council member, he watched in frustration as sprawling developments on the edge of town undermined the city's revitalization efforts.

Narrowly elected as governor in 1994 to succeed the legendary William Donald Schaefer, Glendening and his staff immediately plotted how to marshal the state's power to curb sprawl. It was an uphill political battle, and Glendening knew that it involved considerable political risk. Viewing the passage of an antisprawl package as a marketing problem, he sat down with aides to devise a way to communicate the message.

"Somebody said, 'Let's call it smart development,'" he recalls. "I said, 'No, we can't use the word development. So, what if we call it *Smart Growth*? That way, we can say our opponents are for dumb growth.'"

The term caught on, allowing Glendening to promote a package of *Smart Growth* initiatives as a single statute rather than allowing opponents to attack it one bill at a time. Opposition confronted him every step of the way. Home builders so stridently opposed his proposal that Glendening had to recruit testimony from builders willing to buck the construction industry party line at legislative hearings.

"I had to use every bit of political leverage I had to get it through," he says.

Even after the passage of the *Smart Growth* initiative, Glendening questioned whether good policy would necessarily lead to good politics. He had won narrowly over Republican Ellen R. Sauerbrey in 1994, and expected another close battle. In fact, Glendening won an unexpectedly decisive victory in 1998—in part, apparently, because of the popularity of the *Smart Growth* initiative. He says environmental issues associated with *Smart Growth* swung six percent of the electorate—an enormous measure of support for a single initiative.

Glendening's electoral victory in 1998 lent vigor to the *Smart Growth* effort. More land has been conserved since its enactment than has been consumed by new urban growth. In 1998, for example, the state preserved 22,000 acres while developers converted 13,000 to new construction. His administration also has made strides in conforming new school construction to the priorities of *Smart Growth*. The governor recently announced that the state spends eighty-four percent of all school construction money in built urban areas, compared with only forty-two percent devoted to cities when he took office.

Glendening now spends a good deal of his time traveling throughout the nation—and even overseas—spreading the *Smart Growth* message. The publicity he and Maryland has received surprise him.

"I did not realize we would wind up leading the country," he says.

Both the rhetoric and the policy approach associated with *Smart Growth* have spread across the nation to such unlikely places as Georgia, Tennessee, and Utah—states that try to combat sprawl. Republican Governor Mike Leavitt leads Utah's campaign to promote *Smart Growth* solutions.

"This is not a Democratic or Republican issue," Glendening says.

(Above) *Maryland's Governor, Parris Glendening, created the Smart Growth initiative to combat urban sprawl and manage growth throughout the state. Smart Growth has become a national model for other communities.*

Jim Rout's Vision Recognizes
No Boundaries

"When I look out my office window in downtown Memphis," says Jim Rout, the Mayor of Shelby County, Tennessee, "I can see the bridge over the Mississippi River that connects to Arkansas. If I jump in my car, I can be in Mississippi in fifteen minutes—maybe twelve."

That is how the fifty-seven-year-old Rout explains why, after more than twenty years in elected office, he recently decided to take the initiative in creating a new regional coalition—including not only Memphis and its suburbs in Tennessee, but also a wide range of political leaders and institutions in Arkansas and Mississippi.

Mayor Jim Rout, of Shelby County, Tennessee, speaks at the groundbreaking of a new county library. Mayor Rout promotes regional cooperation across state borders, as a competitive edge for Shelby County, Memphis and the entire Mid-South region. He spearheaded the Governors' Alliance for Regional Excellence.

Together, the Mid-South region, as it has come to be known, includes some four million people (and a $50-billion-per-year economy) in places that are as diverse as the emerging entertainment and gaming center of Tunica, Mississippi; the college town of Jonesboro, Arkansas; and the booming suburban industrial areas of Memphis.

At Rout's instigation, the three state chief executives have formed the Governors' Alliance for Regional Excellence. They have convened a thirty-six-member task force from the region, and commissioned North Carolina regionalism expert Michael Gallis to identify and explain the geographical and economic structure of the region. Rout also hosted *Crossing The Line*—a major national conference on regionalism in the fall of 1999, that focused on the Mid-South.

Already, Rout says, the regional effort has paid off in relationship building. Medical centers from around the region are talking about joint projects, and tourism operators are discussing how to piggyback on other state initiatives. Halfway through his second term, Rout says, his goal is for the Mid-South region to become "the leading laboratory for regionalism in the United States."

Like most regionalism efforts, Rout's bid to strengthen regional cooperation began with the unintended consequences of other political events. In 1997, the Tennessee Legislature passed a bill—known as the tiny towns law—designed to permit incorporation by the small town of Hickory Wythe, in Fayette County, just east of Memphis.

The law simplified incorporation for small towns and prompted controversy. It proved partic-

ularly contentious in suburban Memphis, where the possibility of incorporation was exciting to local residents in unincorporated areas—and threatening to elected officials in Memphis and other existing cities, who were afraid they would get hemmed in geographically because they would no longer be able to annex new property.

Although the Tennessee Supreme Court eventually declared the tiny towns law unconstitutional, it caused Jim Rout to rethink many long-standing assumptions about how he and other elected officials in the Memphis area should approach their jobs. The tiny towns law, he told the Memphis Chamber of Commerce in 1998, has created friction and division.

"We have endured the most turbulent, divisive period in recent decades," Rout said. "Nothing struck me more deeply during this controversy than how fragile our community still is. All of us have been proud of the progress that we have made in recent years. Most of us had assumed that the cooperation and communication that characterized these achievements had become a fundamental part of our community.

In the wake of the tiny towns law, Rout made regionalism the centerpiece of his 1998 reelection campaign.

"What it pointed out to me," he recalls, "was we had to look beyond traditional notions of city limits, county boundaries, and even state lines." During his reelection campaign, he challenged Shelby County and the entire Mid-South area to begin thinking regionally. "If we continue to define the controversial issues before us in terms of 'we versus they' or as 'city versus suburbs,' we will have forever limited the possibilities for growth and economic development that now appear so bright," he said during the campaign. "If we are to compete in a global economy, we must not just have a quality *city or county* infrastructure. We must have a quality *regional* infrastructure...an infrastructure that links our businesses up quickly, cheaply, and efficiently to the global marketplace."

If anybody in Memphis had a mandate to take a regional approach, it was Rout. The job of mayor, to which he had been elected in 1994, had been created in 1974 specifically because the previous county government had suffered from poor coordination and overlapping responsibilities among elected county officials. Rout himself had seen both problems and opportunities created by regional growth during his sixteen years as a member of the county board of commissioners, when he represented a district that included many of the region's biggest economic drivers—including Elvis Presley's Graceland home, the Memphis International Airport, and the booming industrial area around the Federal Express headquarters. In addition, thanks to a long career in business—both as a manager at Xerox Corporation and founder and president of a health-care company—Rout saw that businesses increasingly operated at a regional level and thrived on regional cooperation among governmental and civic leaders.

After he was overwhelmingly reelected as mayor, Rout set about to make his dream of regional cooperation into a reality. Recognizing that he had to reach across even state lines, he arranged to meet with the governors of all three states that are part of the Mid-South region—Don Sundquist of Tennessee, Kirk Fordice of Mississippi, and Mike Huckabee of Arkansas. In the past, elected officials had ignored pleas for regional cooperation, partly because they focused on regionalizing governmental activity. Rout was well known as a political leader with a business perspective, and, like all three governors, he was a Republican. "I was lucky in that I knew the three governors very well," Rout said. "In fact, Don Sundquist and I had once been in business together. So we said, 'let's get forty-five minutes on each of their calendars at their statehouses.' We took the same message to each of them."

The message was that the entire region needs to work together to promote economic growth, and it hit a responsive chord in all three statehouses. In May of 1999, Rout and the Memphis Chamber of Commerce organized a press conference with the three governors at The Peabody Hotel in Memphis to unveil what they called the "Governors' Alliance for Regional Excellence." The mayor acknowledges it was unusual to get Fordice and Huckabee to agree to a media event out of their jurisdictions. Remarkable as it was for two of the governors to cross a state line for the press conference, their rhetoric was more remarkable still. Governor Huckabee said the Alliance provided an opportunity "to see economic development the likes of which we have never seen." Governor Fordice said the region "could be at the absolute center of the largest of worldwide markets if we ever get it together." And Governor Sundquist—as

the chief executive of Tennessee, the host of the press conference—added: "We all prosper if we have a strong Mid-South."

Rout believes the Alliance for Regional Excellence paid off within a matter of months simply because the government agencies and other institutions in the Mid-South region began communicating with each other in a new way. Major medical centers in Memphis and at Arkansas State University in Jonesboro began to discuss ways to work together. Regional economic development officials and real estate brokers began to swap information about leads and available properties. And tourism leaders from across the region—who use Memphis International Airport—are looking at ways to enhance the regional economy by working in concert with one another.

For example, the tourist industry in Memphis previously had been threatened by the rise of the gaming and entertainment industry in Tunica, Mississippi. Nine major casinos and hotels, all offering top-name entertainment, had been constructed only twenty miles from Memphis. Nevertheless, by working together, the tourism officials saw a new opportunity.

"We had lunch with the convention and visitors bureau in Tunica and Memphis," Rout says. "We agreed to start talking to the bus tour operations so they can spend three days in Memphis at one end of the trip and three days in Tunica on the other."

Tunica is one of Rout's favorite examples to explain why he believes his commitment to regional cooperation will pay off handsomely for everybody in the end.

"If we don't always get caught up as to whether we're Arkansas or Tennessee or Mississippi, we're going to see this region become a good performer," he says. "It's just networking. You think you know what the guy over there is doing, but you don't really know what it is you could do together."

Jim Rout, mayor of Shelby County, TN.

Wellington Webb Builds a
City from Within

LEADERSHIP
PROFILE

Most big-city mayors have rattled a tin cup in Washington seeking financial help from the federal government to solve the supposedly intractable problems of their cities.

That is why it is so remarkable to hear Wellington Webb, mayor of Denver, compare the federal government to an Air Force "dropping laws on cities without looking at the collateral damage." Recently elected to his third term, Webb is president of the U.S. Conference of Mayors—traditionally the vehicle for big-city lobbying inside the Beltway. Yet, Webb will likely be a cautious campaigner for federal aid.

"Webb sees federal policies as more of a hindrance than a help," says Fred Segal, an urban expert at Cooper-Union College.

Webb considers the mayor a city's chief executive officer (CEO) and he has focused on downtown revitalization, the opening of America's first new major airport in a quarter-century, and boosting international trade. Quality-of-life issues—including art and culture, open space, sports franchises, and children—represent Webb's main priorities.

When first elected mayor of Denver in 1991, Webb had a tough act to follow. His predecessor, Federico Peña, elected in the eighties during the depths of Denver's oil-related depression, had worked with city leaders to revive the downtown, construct a new airport, and follow other civic priorities.

Nevertheless, Webb—the first African American elected to the post in this multicultural city—has proven to be both popular and innovative through three terms. He supervised the final days of construction of the Denver International Airport and the conclusion of the downtown revival. Webb now oversees the redevelopment of the 5,000-acre Stapleton Airport, one of the most promising infill development sites in the country.

Webb often has spoken eloquently of the need to revive older cities in a sustainable way, promoting economic development and restoring a sense of place. Indeed, Webb is an unabashed supporter of what he calls the great American city.

"As study after study establishes the interdependence between the vitality of the central city and the economic success of entire regions, it is clear that the agenda of the cities is an essential part of our nation's agenda," he declared in his 1998 address to the James W. Rouse Forum on the American City in Washington.

Indeed, Webb often sounds unfashionably down-to-earth when describing the importance of quality of life in urban neighborhoods and downtowns.

"Whether you like it or not, people's perceptions of the city are based on the downtown," he says. "When your Aunt Sally visits, if you take her downtown, it's because you're proud of it. If you don't take her downtown, she wants to know why."

Webb grew up in Denver and has been a public servant most of his adult life. He was a Colorado state legislator, a regional director of the U.S. Department of Health and Human Services, and a member of Governor Dick Lamm's cabinet before his election as Denver city auditor in 1987. After Peña stepped down, Webb garnered eighty-one percent of the vote in 1989, a margin that made him one of the most popular mayors with his constituency.

Webb has presided over an unprecedented economic boom in Denver, brought about, in part, by the opening of the Denver International Airport (DIA). Because it provides the Rocky Mountain region with direct flights to other continents, DIA has stimulated foreign trade and foreign investment in the Denver area.

"The air is our ocean," Webb muses. "It allows us to move back and forth, east and west...that is our port."

Regional economic growth must be coupled with a livable urban environment for Denver to succeed as a place to live and a place to invest, according to Webb. He promotes public safety, open space, fiscal stability, and kids and schools. He has led an expansion of the city's open space by fifty percent—from 4,000 acres to 6,000 acres.

On education, Webb has argued forcefully for cooperation between the city and Denver's independent school district. The city also has provided more than $20 million to fund police officers in school, early education programs, and summer youth employment programs. The city also took over and energized the Head Start program.

"Mayors must have a closer connection to schools," he says.

Webb also has made a major commitment to

Denver's downtown and its older city neighborhoods. Under his administration, the city made sweeping changes in downtown zoning regulations to encourage the construction of more housing and change the parking system to maintain the downtown's stock of existing buildings. During his administration, fifty-one vacant downtown buildings have been renovated, including more than 2,000 residential units, 1,200 hotel rooms, and 400,000 square feet of commercial space.

In keeping with his courageous assertion that cities and neighborhoods belong to the people who use them, he rejected a recent proposal to license the name of Mile High Stadium—home of the Denver Broncos football team—to a corporation. His vision of a vigorous downtown includes professional sports teams and he has vigorously supported their expansion. But he still balked at the idea of renaming the stadium.

"There are too many memories of the Broncos and the field to casually dismiss 'Mile High Stadium' for the highest bidder," he said.

Mayor of Denver and Denver County, Wellington Webb advances the interdependence between the vitality of the central city and the economic success of entire regions. (Above) Denver as seen from City Park.

St. Louis Regional Clean Air Partnership

1 Metropolitan Square
St. Louis, MO 63102
www.cleanair-stlouis.com

Contact: Gary C. Broome,
Director of Communications
314.444.1171

The St. Louis Regional Clean Air Partnership is a coalition of business, industry, legislative, health, and community organizations formed to develop and implement a plan to encourage voluntary volatile organic compound (VOC) emission reductions particularly during periods conducive to high levels of ozone formation.

The partnership, established in 1995, promotes a variety of programs encouraging voluntary emission reductions, particularly on days when ozone levels exceed the federal ozone standard. This effort complements existing mandated emission reduction measures and seeks to shave the peak ozone levels.

Four work groups coordinate partnership activities: Public Relations, Information Outreach, Community, and Work Trip Reduction Development. Some partnership programs are relatively long-range in scope, such as pollution prevention workshops to influence industrial practices. Other programs target actions that should be taken during periods when ozone reaches high levels.

The partnership has trained over 300 people as "Clean Air Coordinators" and "Employee Transportation Coordinators." Clean Air Coordinators are employees of companies assigned to provide information to and obtain information from the public. When the partnership forecasts a Red or Orange Quality Day, these coordinators receive an alert. The coordinators then post notices, send e-mails, and make public announcements to fellow employees alerting them of impending poor air

quality and asking people to take steps to limit or mitigate pollution. Industrial partners cooperate by voluntarily complying with congestion mitigation efforts.

The partnership provides free e-mail health alerts to concerned residents as well as air quality forecasts for local news programs. It has earned the Environmental Protection Agency's Region 7 pollution prevention award.

Crested Butte Land Trust

P.O. Box 224
Crested Butte, CO 81224

Contact: Glo Winningham,
President
970.349.1206

The Crested Butte Land Trust public-private partners saved or helped save 1,000 acres of land from development.
Historically, western states relied on their natural resources, however, those states extracted, rather than preserved or conserved, those resources. The Crested Butte Land Trust in Colorado is an example of the growing awareness that preservation need be a vital component of any community's strategic planning. Inspired by the efforts of a local builder named Norm Barden, the Land Trust was formed in 1991 with the intention of "preserving the present for the future."

Mountains and wetlands, forests and rivers surround Crested Butte. To protect views of the mountain, in 1992 the Trust made its first purchase: a 10.7-acre parcel of land along the picturesque Slate River. The Trust's acquisitions have expanded tremendously. In 1997, $1.2 million in public and private money financed the purchase of the Robinson parcel, a total of 154 acres of undeveloped land. The Trust recently saw the culmination of their efforts to preserve an area of wetlands and springs known as the Lower Loop. The Loop transaction

required three separate purchases of two parcels and a right-of-way easement, bringing the total price of this purchase to almost $1.8 million.

The success of the Trust is due, in part, to its reliance on multiple funding sources, such as the Town of Crested Butte, the Gunnison County Land Preservation Board, the Great Outdoors Company, and the Crested Butte Mountain Resort. Private donations make up the shortfall; the Trust matches every dollar in private donations with $4 in government funds and foundation grants.

Another innovative funding source is the Trust's partnership with approximately 100 local area businesses in the *1% for Open Space* program. Each business has agreed to add an additional 1 percent tax to every customer's bill. The contribution is voluntary and customers can ask that it not be added. In fact, many do. However, most participating businesses have made up the difference out of their own pockets. In the words of Trust President Glo Winningham: "We've had to be innovative. Each different project has called for creative solutions to raise funds. The overwhelming support of our community and visitors has made this possible."

The Trust also has embraced different methods of land conservation, from outright preservation to conservation easements, in which the owners retain title to the land but agree not to develop it. In 1991, the Town of Crested Butte passed a 1.5 percent real estate transfer tax for the purchase of open space. Six years later, Gunnison County created a similar tax. In addition, 500 members of the Trust are active in trail maintenance and fund-raising. Recently two members asked that money be donated to the Trust in lieu of wedding gifts, helping to raise over $5,000.

Once home to ranchers and coal miners, the Crested Butte region has become a haven for skiers, hikers, bicyclists, anglers, and rafters. In a sense, it is as dependent upon its natural resources as it has ever been, and thanks to the efforts of the Land Trust, the area's environmental assets will be preserved for generations to come.

Sustainable Communities Demonstration Project
City of Orlando
400 S. Orange Avenue
Orlando, FL 32801
www.ci.orlando.fl.us

Contact: Kevin Tyjeski,
Chief Planner
407.246.3387

The goal of the Sustainable Communities Demonstration Project is to encourage innovative development strategies that enhance the minimum-growth planning criteria set out in local comprehensive planning. The 1996 Florida Legislature enacted the Sustainable Communities Demonstration Project to restore key ecosystems, achieve a cleaner and healthier environment, limit urban sprawl, protect wildlife and natural areas, advance the efficient use of land and other resources, and create quality communities and jobs. In January 1997, the City of Orlando was chosen as one of five Florida communities to participate in the program.

The creation of a sustainable community for present and future citizens of Orlando depends on the ability to understand where today's growth patterns may lead in the future. Sustainability means improving the quality of human life within the carrying capacity of supporting ecosystems. Sustainable development places equal, integrated emphasis on three key elements—economic prosperity, environmental quality, and community well-being. Following a sustainable development approach affords the City of Orlando the

opportunity to lift barriers between economic ambitions, environmental values, and community-betterment goals.

The Sustainable Community designation will enable Orlando to have significantly more autonomy from state and regional review of growth-management-plan amendments and actions. In addition, the executive office of the Governor and other state agencies will give extra consideration to the needs of the sustainable communities and provide specialized assistance, including expedited and prioritized development funding. In exchange, the City of Orlando has committed to the following initiatives:

- **Public participation:** Through public workshops, advisory committees, roundtable discussions, leadership training, and a sustainability web page, the City will increase public participation in the sustainability effort.
- **Major sustainability projects:** The City will incorporate sustainability practices into four major planning projects that address open-space preservation, historic preservation, downtown revitalization, and the reuse of a military base.
- **Other commitments:** The City will develop plans for a light-rail system, and will work with the State of Florida to build a demonstration house featuring sustainability principles.

Orlando's Sustainable Communities has brought measurable results in just two years. A Primary Conservation Network (PCN) assembles significant wetland areas into a corridor system, providing more land than required under state law for wetland preservation, upland buffers, and wildlife corridors. The PCN is designed to preserve wetland and upland areas as well as provide green space, passive recreation opportunities, and buffers between urban and rural, indus-

trial and residential, land uses.

Through the Sustainable Communities program, Orlando has created an alternative to the Development of Regional Impact review process. This proposed alternative system closely integrates plans for large-scale development activities with plans for surrounding areas. The Sustainable Communities program affords Orlando city officials and residents hours of training in sustainability issues.

Portland Metro 2040 Growth Concept
600 NE Grand Avenue
Portland, OR 97223
www.metro-region.org

Contact: Karen Blauer,
Public Affairs Officer
503.797.1790

Formed by voter initiative, Metro provides regional services to guide growth and create livable communities in the Portland metropolitan region. In 1979, Portland citizens initiated this unique, directly elected Metro government to serve 1.3 million people in the twenty-four suburban cities.

One of the most difficult tasks any region faces is the sensible management of resources to meet the demands of a growing population. Some urban-planning experts agree that Portland's answer to managing growth—creating an Urban Growth Boundary (UGB) to contain development over the next twenty years—provides an example for other communities. Metro faces the challenges of preserving rural areas, farms, and forests, while also providing living space. Metro has solved these problems with innovative land-use plans. City officials, home builders, and developers are all brought in early to plan the best, most effective use of urban space. The resulting "urban reserve plans" illustrate the future assignments of schools, parks, transit and urban services, and affordable housing. The plans lay out roads, designate open space, and site school buildings and affordable housing, all in compliance with the Metro development code. All these plans serve to limit sprawl, foster public transportation, and preserve inner-city residences.

Management of UGBs requires great flexibility and communication between concerned parties; land needs regularly must be reassessed. Incorporating new lands into the UGB is never as simple as it sounds. The 2040 Growth Concept describes where and how the UGB should be expanded as it defines density, reflects projected growth patterns, and maintains a measure of open space.

To meet these requirements, the Growth Concept creates guidelines for mixed-use urban centers inside the UGB. These higher density centers of employment and housing are served by public transportation; and compact planned development, retail, cultural, and recreational outlets surround them. Plans emphasize building compact communities to enhance walking from home to work or to shopping and entertainment centers, maximizing efficient access to goods and services.

San Diego Dialogue
Extended Studies and Public Programs
University of California, San Diego
9500 Gilman Drive 0176N
La Jolla, CA 92093-0176
www.sddialogue.org

Contact: Dr. Charles E. Nathanson,
Executive Director
619.534.8638

The San Diego Dialogue, a center devoted to public policy research and education, unifies the San Diego/ Tiajuana, Mexico region. A region need not stop at the border.

San Diego Dialogue is a community-based public policy center at the University of California, San Diego that provides policy research and education on future growth and development problems affecting the San Diego Bay region of Southern California and the Baja California region of Mexico. From its founding in 1991, the Dialogue's work has been to develop a common civic knowledge, encourage effective decision making, and build consensus for the pattern of the region's future development.

Drawing support from 100 leaders of regional industries, government, media, academic institutions, and nonprofit organizations, the Dialogue defines regional concerns and priorities. It focuses primarily on regional integration, equity, diversity, urban development, and globalization. The Mexican border bisects the region. The Dialogue considers the boundary a challenge to solve through analysis of the border administration, as well as consideration of the comparative advantages of a region within two nations. Experts speculate the area may become one of the continent's first binational cities. The Dialogue also promotes regional diversity and social-equity policies to turn potential multinational misunderstandings into opportunities. The emphasis on globalization reflects an appreciation of the area's economic future: The Dialogue attempts to build a diverse employment base tailored to trends in technology employment.

The Dialogue's two signature programs are *Fronterizo*, a public forum of nearly 500 business, government, and academic leaders from both sides of the border that meet to discuss cross-border issues, and the Regional Economic Breakfast Series, a public program that addresses key trends and issues affecting the regional economy. The Dialogue also hosts other community forums, workshops, and roundtables. The Dialogue has been praised for its role in addressing the

region's problems. With reports on regional resources and its monthly *San Diego Dialogue Report*, it provides professional networking opportunities and the latest information regarding the binational region's events and personalities. Working as an information hub and a catalyst for issues and ideas, the San Diego Dialogue demonstrates how academic research need not be arcane. Instead, it can complement and enhance the work of civic and business leaders by defining and shaping the future.

Framework for Action 2025
Northeast Ohio Areawide
Coordinating Agency
1299 Superior Avenue
Cleveland, OH 44114-3204
www.hoaca.org

Contact: Howard R. Maier,
Executive Director
216.241.2414 x380

"Framework for Action 2025: An Action Plan for Improving Northeast Ohio's Transportation System" aims to advance the region's economic competitiveness by developing sustainable neighborhoods and businesses. The plan outlines steps to enhance the natural environment and ecology of the region by improving air, land, and water quality, and by identifying and preserving existing critical natural resources and environmentally sensitive areas. Framework for Action 2025 is among the few transportation plans in the country that, in addition to addressing transportation infrastructure needs, also works towards environmental preservation, compact land use, and developing the urban core.

Framework 2025 is the brainchild of the Northeast Ohio Areawide Coordinating Agency (NOACA), created in 1968 to coordinate planning for the region as a whole by involving local governments and citizens in the planning process. In 1969, NOACA merged with the Cleveland Seven-County Transportation Land Use Study, expanding the agency's purview to include comprehensive transportation planning. This move enabled the organization to secure federal funding. Thirty years ago, NOACA developed "Framework for Action," the region's first comprehensive, regional transportation plan. Framework 2025 updates this original plan by incorporating development issues and environmental interests.

NOACA's governing board, comprised of mayors, county commissioners, and other elected officials, created this blueprint. The board invited the public to share ideas and voice concerns about the transportation process. By using surveys and focus groups, the board ensured that citizens were given every opportunity to express their opinions.

The cooperation and coordination of communities, government agencies, transit implementers, and the private sector are key to accomplishing the goals of Framework 2025. To guarantee public support, NOACA has developed "Working to Improve the NOACA Region" (WIN) agreements to document local government approval of long-term transportation investments. NOACA also is establishing measurable benchmarks for the plan's goals and will monitor progress toward meeting those goals. In addition, NOACA will host an annual "Working to Improve the NOACA Region" transportation summit to measure progress on the plan's application and revise and update strategies.

Sierra Business Council
P.O. Box 2428
Truckee, CA 96160

Contact: Elizabeth Carmel,
Director of Planning Services
530.582.4800

One of the strongest arguments for regional collaboration is that it enables the urban, suburban, and exurban areas to become more economically competitive in the global marketplace. It stands to reason then, that the private sector plays a strong role in stimulating and leading region-wide thinking and planning. In the Sierra Nevada, 450 business leaders, from the edge of the Mojave Desert to a region north of Lake Tahoe, have formed the Sierra Business Council, which is devoted to securing and enhancing the economic and environmental health of the region. Their efforts span twelve counties where population is expected to double in the next twenty years.

The Sierra Nevada region once based their economy on resource extraction. As tourism and outdoor recreation evolved as the primary moneymakers, business leaders noted that their economic health had become intertwined with the health of the environment and the appearance and accessibility of amenities, such as museums, parks, and recreation areas.

The Council conducted a financial, social, and environmental audit of the region's capital to create the Sierra Nevada Wealth Index, a compilation of forty-two indicators of the health of the region. The Index reported that the region, like much of the country, suffered the effects of urban sprawl. Cities and towns encroached upon green and open space, as city cores emptied and deteriorated. The report concluded that economic prosperity depended on preservation of the area's environmental assets.

In 1996, the Council published a growth blueprint, "Planning for Prosperity: Building Successful Communities in the Sierra Nevada," based on an analysis of growth plans for the twelve Sierra Nevada counties, a 1,000-person poll, interviews of planning directors, and consultations with business leaders. The report includes development principles, outlines steps for involving and serving business and the public, and provides a case study of Placer County that details the expected course of development, growth, and planning.

The Council aims to maintain natural beauty and environmental health, revitalize downtown cores, and stimulate community involvement. The Council is trying to prevent urban sprawl from suffocating the Sierra Nevadas by raising money for the Placer Legacy Project, a long-range comprehensive plan for protecting open space in Placer County. The Council also sponsors a five-month course on leadership aimed at expanding involvement in the public sector and strengthening individuals' ability to lead local initiatives to conserve mountainous landscape. As one council member explained, "Effective land-use planning is the best investment we can make in our financial security."

6 | The New Downtown: City as Living Room, Playground, Nightclub

On a warm Manhattan night, an unfamiliar whirring competes with the background hum of cars and subway. The sound gets louder as an unexpected ensemble comes into view: A swarm of young people on in-line skates careers through the intersection of Sixty-Sixth and Broadway, as if the street belonged to them. Cars stop.

"Though they stopped traffic—at one point they filled the uptown side of the First Avenue tunnel in front of the United Nations—and whooped and hollered through staid neighborhoods on the Upper East side, not even a cab driver screamed bloody murder back at them," *The New York Times* reported in 1997. "The exuberance of youth on a pretty summer night was catching."

Here is another surprising image: In the Little Italy neighborhood of Baltimore, 800 people gather to watch movies projected on the exterior wall of a warehouse. The project is the brainchild of local resident and restaurateur Mary Ann Cricchio, who decided to use *al fresco* cinema to persuade people to gather outdoors at night. She is hoping to emulate the street scene she experienced as a tourist in Palermo, Italy.

And another surprise: In downtown Los Angeles, possibly the least pedestrian-oriented area of any major city, the reopening of the Central Library has created something some observers thought impossible, a vital street scene in the heart of the city's high-rise financial district. The library is thick with patrons, who take advantage of subsidized parking in the office building next door. They can cool themselves under the olives and oaks of the West Lawn, which was formerly a parking lot for library staff. Library patrons can have a meal at the Pinot restaurant on the West Lawn; or they can cross Fifth Street, take the escalator up Bunker Hill, and visit the Museum of Contemporary Art; or they can hear a student recital at the new music school next to the museum.

These images offer an insight into the changing nature of the American downtown. Each anecdote describes people using the city in an unaccustomed way. The intersection of Sixty-Sixth Street and Broadway was not intended for roller-bladers; nor was the Baltimore warehouse intended as a movie screen, or the Los Angeles library parking lot, a park. In each case, the unfamiliar use of familiar urban space has released a captivating energy. People who use downtown now realize that the city is something that can be molded, manipulated, and redefined. Such experiences give the city residents a sense of ownership.

The feeling of ownership is an important, if subtle, aspect of urban vitality. Psychologists have taught us that when people do not feel the environment belongs to them, they will treat it disdainfully, with vandalism, graffiti, and neglect. Although vandalism and graffiti are reprehensible, they are also symptoms of something dysfunctional in the city: poor maintenance, isolation, lack of visual access, barrenness, and ugliness.

Fortunately, many city residents now experience an increasing sense of ownership of American downtowns. Downtown has become a meeting ground, a place of socialization. It is "the city as

playground," to borrow an expression from Josef Subiros, chief of staff to the mayor of Barcelona, Spain. This chapter defines downtown broadly, as all urban areas that provide places for crowds to gather, that offer destinations for those crowds, and are characterized by a mix of amenities, including shops, restaurants, street festivals, night clubs, newsstands, food vendors, coffee shops, and movie houses. The Hollywood area of Los Angeles, the North Beach area of San Francisco, the Manayunk district of Philadelphia, and the Lowertown area of St. Paul all fall under this expanded definition.

This new emphasis on the city as a social center, as a place of entertainment and cultural experiences, represents a change in the way Americans think about downtowns, as well as in the nature of downtowns themselves. Cities inevitably reflect cultural changes; cities, in fact, are the primary stage where cultural changes are acted out. The latest incarnation of the American downtown reflects the development of a postindustrial and information-based economy, as well as the dwindling importance of downtown areas as the primary locus of trade and industry.

Most American cities grew around primitive centers of trade, such as forts, missions, or trading posts, that later acquired harbors, railroad hubs, and highway crossroads. In the second phase of their evolution, downtowns capitalized on this proximity to transportation routes to become manufacturing centers and distribution hubs. After the Second World War, downtowns declined. Deserted by businesses and residents for new development on the urban fringe, downtowns became repositories of abandoned property and poverty.

The American downtown is now entering an era marked by increasing vitality based on social interaction. Since the 1970s, city governments have spearheaded this movement by constructing large-scale amenities, such as convention centers, art museums, interactive children's museums, libraries, sports stadiums, aquariums, plazas, and parks. Nonprofit agencies have helped attract a full-time downtown population by building new and reno-

(Above) *Bryant Park in New York City. (Center) Hundreds gather in front of Charleston, South Carolina's City Hall on historic Broad Street to celebrate the opening ceremonies of the Spoleto Festival USA. (Left) The Mint Museum in Charlotte, North Carolina.*

Consensus building. This may start with a public hearing, a community meeting, or a design workshop. Consensus begins with a broad-based effort to gather people's opinions about how to make their community better. Slowly, agreement emerges regarding particular issues: Certain buildings may be deemed eyesores that must be repaired. Other businesses or homes may be filled with trash, or have rusting cars out front. Important historic buildings may be moldering under layers of garish signs.

Team building. Successful projects rely on large teams, which include local activists, community-based nonprofit organizations, elected officials, city staff, lawyers, bond underwriters, lenders, contractors, and many others. In Cleveland, the city attracted the Rock and Roll Hall of Fame and Museum, and the striking I.M. Pei-designed building that houses it, through a public-private partnership of the City of Cleveland, Cuyahoga County, the State of Ohio, Cleveland-Cuyahoga Port Authority, private foundations, and local music-industry enterprises.

To build the Shreveport Riverfront Park, a new entertainment zone along the Red River's depressed industrialized corridor, the mayor of Shreveport, Louisiana, and the Downtown Development Authority lobbied state lawmakers. These municipal officials insisted the city needed family-oriented venues in addition to gambling, and obtained a $1.6 million tourism-development grant. The city has replenished its revenues with $182,000 in property taxes collected from the local Harrah's Casino. To develop the $1.55 million park on city-owned land, the officials included the Planning Commission, the Tourism Bureau, the Red River Revel Arts Festival, and two-dozen local residents in its design team.

Planning financial strategies The need to tap multiple sources of funding makes revitalization projects even more complex. Projects may rely on grants or equity contributions from private foundations, assistance from public agencies such as reduced property tax assessments, below-market construction loans, or financial assistance to home buyers. Cities also may obtain assistance from HUD programs such as HOME, state housing programs, urban development grants, and Federal Emergency Management Agency money in communities recovering from disaster.

vated housing for low-income households, elderly residents, and people with special needs. Speculative developers have transformed older buildings into loft housing and new storefronts. This gentrification could not take place so readily, of course, in cities that lost much of their older buildings to urban renewal, such as Los Angeles, Indianapolis, San Jose, and Charlotte. In many cases, those cities worked to re-create some of the amenities that had so carelessly been swept away only a few decades earlier. In one Minnesota city, for example, the government had condemned several blocks in the 1960s to make way for an enclosed regional mall that was built in the 1970s. The mall failed in the 1980s. In the 1990s, the city demolished the mall and rebuilt the original streets.

The Role of Partnerships in Downtown Renaissance

How are cities approaching the problem of redesigning their downtowns to create friendlier,

more habitable places? Which experiences are applicable to all cities?

A historian once remarked that the city is a collective work of art. Given the example of autocratic city builders—the Baron Haussman, Andre Le Notre, Robert Moses—it might seem difficult to imagine a democratic process at work in the creation of vital urban areas. Recent experience, however, has demonstrated that city making is indeed a collective enterprise, one that begins with establishing a shared vision and progresses to the creation of partnerships that bring money, skill, and political capital to the table.

The downtown revivals usually require enormous energy and organization. Often, individuals with strong ideas and strong personalities get much of the credit for building the momentum. Yet, by their nature, large-scale urban designs are collaborations among many people in many fields. Urban design, in this context, means the design of the framework of the city to provide the mix of uses—shops, churches, parks, newsstands, night

(Left and above) *A festival in front of Union Station in LoDo, the Lower Downtown district of Denver, Colorado.* (Far left) *The Northwest 23rd/Nob Hill shopping district in downtown Portland, Oregon.*

clubs, office buildings, and sidewalk vendors, among them—that can attract and sustain a stimulating flow of pedestrians.

The first step involves local politics, which eventually must broaden to encompass regional, state, and even national politics to unlock resources that will make large-scale urban redevelopment possible.

Leadership also comes in different forms. Some people are catalytic personalities who inspire or inflame other city residents to action. Other people, often in government, are consensus builders and coalition builders. Still others are experts both in public finance and real estate finance.

The *charette* process, where architects and urban designers create sketches during public meetings with local stakeholders, is an increasingly popular method of creating consensus in urban design. In an ambitious application of the *charette*, the Los Angeles Community Redevelopment Agency created a large advisory group in the early 1990s to help create a new set of urban-design goals for downtown Los Angeles. The group included city staff, real estate developers, property owners, white-collar business leaders, representatives from the food-packing and toy-wholesale industries, and even representatives from the homeless population. A city-hired urban designer acted as the facilitator

NEW TRENDS MAKE DOWNTOWNS HABITABLE AND ATTRACTIVE

Creation of new parks and public spaces. Cities are increasingly recognizing the need for open space, especially for active parks, to make downtown areas attractive and to provide visual and spatial relief from dense urban commercial districts. Linear parks, such as riverfronts, are an especially attractive strategy to provide a continuous green margin. Other cities may choose to create a regional network of urban parks, or a series of pocket parks within easy walking distance.

Decentralization of downtown experiences. Downtown-style urbanism need not be confined to historic city centers. Some suburban areas are experimenting with creating dense, socially active streets where pedestrians can easily maneuver. In Brea, California, city officials have fashioned a new city center out of the intersection of the city's largest streets. The result will be a mixed-use district with a variety of office buildings, a multiplex cinema, shopping, and a variety of housing choices, all within walking distance. Other cities, such as Cathedral City, California, are building entirely new downtowns designed by New Urbanist architects and planners. Peter Calthorpe is the architect of Cathedral City's new downtown.

Creation of urban villages. Though the term may refer to a variety of designs, the urban village is an attempt to create a social center around neighborhood-serving stores and shops. When properly designed, urban villages may provide pedestrian-friendly streets, as well as retail and service businesses within walking distance, to people who previously relied entirely on their cars for shopping and entertainment.

Removing the malls from downtown to promote pedestrian movement. Other cities converted pedestrian-only malls into streets accommodating automobile traffic after the commercial failure of car-free shopping districts. Rather than build inward-looking malls and self-contained shopping centers, cities are asking developers to build new retail centers within the outline of existing city streets.

Development of entertainment centers. In this multiplex urbanism, movie theaters are the primary attraction for a retail complex that typically includes fast food, coffee bars, and major chain bookstores, as well as impulse retail, such as clothing and household goods. The challenge in entertainment districts, again, is to ensure that the retail uses reinforce the activity on existing streets, rather than creating a separate, self-enclosed environment that siphons foot traffic and retail trade away from the open street.

and prepared the new urban design recommendations based on the yearlong discussion.

Elected officials may be leaders in rebuilding downtown areas. Even so, close coordination is needed among local, state, and national officials to tap resources. State legislators are needed to lobby for state housing dollars, while congressional representatives must be cajoled to steer U.S. Department of Housing and Urban Development programs and federal urban-development grants toward the city. Before those resources can be unlocked, however, a convincing project with tangible community support must be in place. Making projects happen involves a long-term political and financial strategy as much as it involves urban design or architecture.

Getting Started: Stewards and Urban Visionaries

Although developers and public agencies initiate most urban construction, grassroots organizations can also launch projects. Often, these groups involve people with a sense of stewardship over threatened resources: urban parkland, riverfronts, wetlands, and historic buildings. In St. Louis, Missouri, local concern about the poor maintenance of the 1,200-acre Forest Park eventually led to fundraising efforts to preserve and maintain the immense park, which also encompasses arts programs and theaters.

The residents helped prompt a new master plan. The city has created a nonprofit group, Forest Park Forever, to administer park and cultural program upgrades.

The Friends of the Los Angeles River in California protested and filed lawsuits to build an awareness of the recreational and aesthetic value of the concrete-encased waterway that runs through the industrial areas of Los Angeles County. The Friends now cooperate with a former adversary, the Los Angeles County Flood Control Department, in the building of five small pilot parks on the banks of the river. The Friends learned what urban visionaries also discover: Successful downtown revitalizing hinges on a few simple policies.

To raise the $8.5 million needed to transform a flood plain and dumping ground into the eighty-five-acre Mill Race Park, residents of Columbus, Indiana, obtained funds from multiple sources. The city's Parks and Recreation Department contributed $944,000, while fund-raising brought $5.23 million in donations and sponsorships. The Build Indiana Fund, a state economic-development program, chipped in $72,000, and the federal Job Corps contributed $2.14 million in labor.

Small, low-income housing projects often have as many as eight different funding sources. Each may have its own ethical, political, or design agenda. Some of those who provide funds target specific populations, such as single mothers. Others finance projects in communities with a low median income. Still others want the architects to design projects free of waste. Very often, projects are redesigned repeatedly to accommodate these agendas, and it is helpful to find out about those agendas before launching the development.

Physical Design Expresses Public Policy

Developers often discuss downtown redevelopment projects exclusively in terms of real estate—the financial package and its cash-generating potential. The desire for quick-fix solutions to depressed downtowns has led some cities to pursue large-scale private attractions that promise but do not always deliver big tax revenues to local governments. One example is Arizona Center, an entertainment-oriented retail development in Phoenix next to the city's new Bank One Ballpark. Although the project is commercially successful, critics have said the inward-looking orientation of the ballpark, not unlike that of an enclosed mall, represents a missed opportunity to create more pedestrian activity. The successful Branson, Missouri, district of country-music theaters and dance halls has attracted millions of visitors, and has spawned many imitators. Among the Branson *wannabes* is the proposed RogersDale USA theme park in Murrieta, California, with 100,000-square-foot rodeo grounds, an 8,000-seat concert hall, and a Western Sidekicks Hall of Fame. In Sevierville, Tennessee, developers are promoting River Bluff Landing, which would have three theaters, an aquarium, two hotels, and a boardwalk.

Why are such projects questionable, at best? Good urban design and good economic development need a variety of small and large projects to promote an area's economic vitality. Very often,

(Above) *Discovery Place in downtown Charlotte, NC.* (Left) *The Charlotte Convention Center.* (Far left, top) *Pioneer Courthouse Square in Portland, Oregon.* (Far left, bottom) *Dragon boats at Portland's Rose Festival.*

city officials fall in love with a single megaproject and become overly reliant on the tax revenues that such projects promise. In turn, cities may feel obliged to throw good planning out the window in order to accommodate the demands of the megaproject. In the end, the city runs the danger of having a poorly designed downtown and a city hall dependent upon the fortunes of a single project. That is the reason why, at this point in the story, we criticize the tendency of some cities to seize *golden-goose* projects, rather than do proper planning and economic development.

John Hannigan, a professor of sociology at the University of Toronto, criticizes such projects as falsifying both history and the urban context by substituting authentic urbanism with overblown commercialism.

"Are we prepared to overlook the cultural diversity in the community in favor of prepackaged corporate entertainment destinations?" he writes in his 1998 book, *Fantasy City*. "Will there be room for leisure activities other than those which can be branded, licensed, franchised, rolled out on a global scale? And, finally, are we prepared to designate our inner cities no-go zones except for the heavily fortified themed attractions which welcome a constant flow of tourists embarked on leisure safaris into the depths of the postmodern metropolis?"

Hannigan's remarks allude to the desirable qualities of urban revitalization projects: They should keep downtowns public, diverse, and usable by their own residents. Other goals must be to design democratic downtowns with well-planned commercial districts, and to encourage economic vitality and investment. City officials must plan for many kinds of activities, including those that generate income and those that simply create ambience. Downtowns are complex organisms. They have many organs that need to function well to remain healthy: major streets, major employers, and regional cultural destinations. Downtowns also need open space—ideally networks of open space every several blocks.

Downtowns must be designed to incorporate a variety of scales: both the high-rise scale of major buildings and the human scale of neighborhoods and historic districts. Some streets should be heavily trafficked to encourage crowds; others should be designed as quiet corridors for local-resident traffic only.

Cities often stimulate downtown revitalization by regaining use of natural features, especially rivers and waterfronts. The San Antonio, Texas River Walk proved so successful that a number of cities have pursued similar combinations of linear parks and commercial development along river-banks, including San Jose, California; Pueblo, Colorado; and Chattanooga, Tennessee. Though some cities have only repeated a pattern successful everywhere with insufficient analysis of the local needs, others create a plan that respects the water-front and its biological and habitat value.

Other cities are removing or transforming unsightly and out-of-scale buildings, such as bland convention centers, power plants, and regional malls, to make downtowns more attractive and more pedestrian-friendly. One extraordinary trend is the removal of downtown freeways, made possible by the need to replace or modernize monumental structures. Ft. Worth, Texas and Boston have invigorated and expanded their downtown areas by removing portions of freeways. In San Francisco, the removal of the earthquake-damaged Embarcadero Freeway has opened the city's water-front to downtown office users and has encouraged restoration of several historic structures, including the city's landmark Ferry Building.

Bringing housing downtown is a strategy that both helps local merchants and provides uses for historic buildings, often not originally built as housing. The New Urbanism, a fashionable 1990s doctrine of redesigning today's cities to resemble those of earlier generations, has taught us that

essential services—transit, social services, and neighborhood-serving retail—need to be within easy walking distance of housing. Downtown living will never appeal to everyone, but it could appeal to a great many more people if it were in proximity to transportation and plentiful open space, such as parks ideal for jogging, basketball, soccer, and walking the dog.

The Future of Downtowns: The City of Affiliation

In progressive communities, downtowns are becoming habitable once again. A generation ago, major projects like convention centers and sports stadiums were the focus of downtown investment. Now, however, smaller human-scale development has become more important. The purpose of urban design at a human scale is to make streets more comfortable and more usable by pedestrians and harmonize different city functions. If the convention center symbolized downtown America in the 1980s and the sports stadium provided the symbol of the 1990s, the symbol of the next decade may be the apartment above the store.

America's downtowns—historically centers of commerce, government, and transportation—have become stages and backdrops for public activity. People come downtown for the stimulation of being surrounded by different kinds of people, ethnic restaurants, festivals and cultural events, clubs, and conventions. They seek chance meetings. Most important, people come downtown because downtown offers experiences and choices not available elsewhere. Our parents and grandparents labored to get out of downtown areas and out of cramped housing and dangerous conditions. Now the meaning of downtown has changed.

Psychologist John Bradshaw has described groups that he calls *families of affiliation*. People sometimes leave their dysfunctional families, where relationships are unsuccessful or dissatisfying, and make a new *family* based on friendships and mutual interests. Although it is easy to overextend this metaphor; it may be helpful to define the new downtown as a *community of affiliation*—a place where people meet others, make business plans, or launch political movements. As it evolves from a factory dormitory or a holding cell for immigrants, downtown again becomes a place for participation in civic life.

(Above) *Portland, Oregon's Saturday Market. (Left, above). A horse drawn carriage and vintage trolley in the Skidmore Fountain area of Portland. (Left, below). MAX light rail at Portland's Pioneer Courthouse.*

A New Image for the Smelting Capital of the World

LEADERSHIP PROFILE

In mythology, Hercules changed the course of a river to clean the Augean Stables. Pueblo, Colorado, has done Hercules one better: It has moved the same river twice.

Both relocations of the Arkansas River occurred at critical moments in the history of this arid city at the foot of the Rocky Mountains. The city first changed the river's course eighty years ago, after the catastrophic 1921 flood. Days of steady rain had caused local reservoirs to overflow, sending a wall of water through the city, drowning hundreds of people, and leaving hundreds more missing.

At the height of the flood, downtown Pueblo stood under eleven feet of water. To prevent a similar recurrence, the city created a new channel four blocks to the north, behind the city's rail depot.

Today, the Arkansas River is changing course again. A city-funded agency called the Historic Arkansas River Project is returning the river, or some of it, to its original path. Unlike the earlier relocation, the new project reflects economic well-being rather than disaster prevention.

Bringing the river downtown restores part of the historical border between the French and Spanish territory at the time of the Louisiana Purchase; the United States acquired the French territory north of the river while the southern half remained under Spanish control. The new river connects the Union Street Historic District with the rest of

downtown Pueblo. The newly reinstated river also becomes the backdrop for the Arkansas River Walk, a newly landscaped collection of walkways and businesses that officials hope will emulate the famous and successful River Walk in San Antonio, Texas, with waterfront restaurants and attractions.

Moving the river, even twice, has not been Pueblo's most notable achievement. More remarkable has been the feat of reinvigorating and diversifying the economy of a city that had relied on the steel industry for almost a century. In little more than fifteen years, the city has found a way to rebuild its industrial base on a new foundation of warehousing and distribution, high-tech manufacturing, and other types of clean industry.

Pueblo's community was forced by economic hardship to inventory its assets and redefine its

role in a national marketplace. By itself, the story of hardship seems unexceptional; many cities traditionally reliant on smokestack industries collapsed, as did American cities reliant on heavy manufacturing. Pueblo differs because it succeeded in rebuilding its economy while other industrial cities remained floundering.

Since 1981, when the Pueblo Economic Development Corporation (PEDCO) was created, the city has managed to recruit nearly forty companies, including a number of Fortune 500 firms, bringing about 9,000 new jobs. The corporation also helped retain many jobs jeopardized by employers' plans to pull up stakes. Median household income has risen from $41,000 in 1984 to $65,000 in 1995. During the same period, population rose from 107,000 to 137,000 people. "From 1982 to 1999, this community rebuilt itself," said James Spaccamonti, president of PEDCO.

Local officials say they hope a diversified business base will insulate Pueblo from the boom-and-bust cycle that has been a part of the city's history from its beginnings. Founded in 1842 as El Pueblo, a civilian fort and trading post, the original settlement, besieged by Ute Indians, later was abandoned to the tribe. Settlers trickled back into the area, however, and the town of Pueblo was founded; settlers salvaged the adobe bricks from the old fort to build their houses and barns. The Gold Rush brought many people to Pueblo, some of whom stayed to mine for coal. The presence of plentiful coal eventually attracted the giant smelters of gold, silver, copper, and other metals derived from mines throughout Colorado. Pueblo became an industrial center. By the 1870s, residents referred to their city as "The Smelting Capital of the World." One of the largest operations was Philadelphia Smelting and Refining, built by the Guggenheims in 1888.

By the 1870s, four adjoining towns had emerged; the skewed street grid of present-day Pueblo is a reminder of those original towns. The Denver and Rio Grande Railroad came to Pueblo in 1872, subsidized by a $100,000 bond measure approved by Pueblo voters two years earlier, which paid to lay the track between Pueblo and Denver, 100 miles to the north. The city grew quickly, and became the second largest in Colorado.

With their heavy demand for coal, steel mills were a natural fit for Pueblo. By the turn of the century, Pueblo had at least three sizeable mills. The largest

(Above) *A summer, outdoor concert held on Friday evenings at the Sangre de Cristo Arts and Conference Center in downtown Pueblo, Colorado.* (Left) *Victorian-style architecture enlivens downtown Pueblo.*

Pueblo, Colorado

was Colorado Fuel & Iron Company (C.F. & I.), that was owned by the Rockefellers. The steady demand for labor encouraged companies to import European workers. In the first decades of the century, no fewer than twenty-nine foreign-language newspapers were published in the city. In time, Pueblo would also become a major center for meat packing and printing.

In the early 1980s, the long reach of the global economy arrived in Pueblo. The Japanese steel industry, built after World War II, could produce steel at a lower cost than could its American competitors, and exported tons of product below U.S. market prices. C.F. & I. could not compete. In 1982, C.F. & I. laid off 5,000 employees; the company later went into bankruptcy. "I remember the day clearly," said Spaccamonti, then a staff planner for the city. "It was like the day Kennedy was shot."

The local economy went into shock. Construction of four housing subdivisions in the city promptly ceased. Residents began leaving the city at a rate of 1,000 per week. At the height of the local depression, the unemployment rate topped twenty percent. In many cases, according to Spaccamonti, men left the city while their families moved in with relatives. It probably did not help that Denver, the nearest major city, was going through a depression of its own at about the same time because of the collapse of the speculative oil-shale industry. Local residents still talk about the experience with emotion.

"We had put all our eggs into one basket, and foreign steel stole it," said Rod Slyhoff, president of the Pueblo Chamber of Commerce.

Pueblans Tally Their Urban Assets

Communities in trouble often hope for panaceas or quick fixes. Puebloans expressed hope momentarily when Anheuser-Busch considered building a new brewing plant in the city. But the giant brewery located elsewhere. Fairly or not, city government took some of the blame for losing Anheuser-Busch. "The government had resources, but couldn't talk the language that business people wanted to hear," said Spaccamonti. "Businesses want to hear about the business climate, about what's good for them."

The failure of talks with the big brewery helped convince Pueblo officials to set up a professional economic development office. The result was the Pueblo Economic Development Corporation, a private, nonprofit partnership of the city, the county, the local council of governments, the Pueblo Chamber, and about 300 local business people. The organization is funded by a half-cent sales tax.

PEDCO officials tallied the town's resources. Pueblo had never been a tourist center, like Aspen or Leadville. Nor was it close to places of natural beauty, as is nearby Colorado Springs, in the shadow of Pike's Peak. On the other hand, Pueblo had room to grow; the city is surrounded by open land suitable for home building and industrial development. There are five industrial parks in the region, including the 900-acre Airport Industrial Center and the 23,000-acre Pueblo Depot Industrial, an Army installation where the City of Pueblo has leased nearly 4 million square feet to industrial tenants. The city's general plan has designated the northern neighborhood for high-end housing development, while concentrating home building in the fast-growing community of West Pueblo, which lies outside the city boundaries in unincorporated Pueblo County.

The city also houses two institutions of higher learning, the University of Southern Colorado and Pueblo Community College, which could supply an educated work force for growing industries such as high-tech businesses. Companies in search of newly trained engineers can find them at the University of Colorado in Boulder and at the Colorado School of Mines in Golden. Local housing was attractive and cheap. The area offers easy access to mountain sports, though major ski resorts are about a half-hour farther away than they are from Denver.

The presence of colleges helped PEDCO provide an incentive to businesses: PEDCO would pay to train workers for specific companies at Pueblo Community College in advance of opening day, so employers could open plants with a fully trained workforce. PEDCO also helps match employees to employers with a *prescoring* system that evaluates whether an individual has the appropriate aptitude and personality type for particular tasks.

The city successfully helped recruit Ashland Chemical Corporation, a Fortune 25 company that originally intended to build a 50,000-square-foot facility in the airport area to produce "ultra-pure" chemicals for the computer-chip industry. "As we kept talking to them, and we learned more about their business, and they learned more about us, the size of the [proposed] plant grew to 100,000 square feet," said Spaccamonti, who indicated Ashland showed a particular interest in the quality of the area's transportation network, as well as in the supply of locally trained chemists. Ashland eventually built a 240,000-square-foot plant.

PEDCO also uses real-estate incentives to attract industry. The organization has built new industrial buildings and rehabilitated existing ones. Foundation Health Systems has occupied an entire historic building in downtown Pueblo that PEDCO had purchased, renovated, and sold. The region's economic development organization also offers incentives for businesses to buy their own buildings: "We will act as a bank," Spaccamonti said. PEDCO offers a no-money-down mortgage, with monthly payments. After ten years, the company can buy the building by paying off the remaining principle. This arrangement obviates the need for companies to obtain conventional bank financing, or to tie up a lot of cash in down payments.

History as Market Place

Historic preservation, in one sense, is a luxury that communities can afford when most of the workforce is employed and business confidence runs deep. The Union Street Historic District began the conversion from a red-light district to a gentrified shopping district in the early 1980s. The district is the city's greatest architectural treasure. Anchored by the Pueblo Depot building, a Romanesque edifice dating from 1879, the historic district is a collection of eighty-six historic buildings, including many designed in the flamboyant Western Commercial Victorian style. Rather than maintaining individual buildings, the district preserves an entire nineteenth century commercial district. Even in its current, gentrified state—buildings now filled with fast-food restaurants, book stores, boutiques, and antique shops, among others—the area remains an evocative remnant of the city's first great boom period. In another nod to the past, the city's history museum has moved, and the old building has been dismantled to facilitate the excavation of an old Ute trading post.

The revival of the Union Street District has also encouraged city officials to identify and adopt a regional style for new construction in and around the historic district. The city now recommends the use of brick facades and gabled roofs. To some degree, this style is embodied in the city's new convention center and the accompanying Marriott hotel.

The Historic Arkansas River Project is a finishing touch, like a ribbon tied around the historical district. Surprisingly, many Puebloans seem scarcely aware that a river once ran through the city. Technically, the new Historic Arkansas River Project does not actually reroute the entire river; the water flowing through town follows a diversion channel that siphons some water from the main river and runs it through town before returning it to the river's concrete-lined main course. Nevertheless, the modest fiction works: The River Walk is a carefully landscaped area with plentiful public art. The city plans an interpretive program along the riverfront with plaques marking historic sites and events. Eventually, the centerpiece of the River Walk will be the Plaza, where the city has provided several building pads for future restaurants and other attractions.

Although the Union Street Historic District has a strong appeal for people interested in the history of the West and the railroad, city officials are not relying on themed entertainment to rebuild the local economy.

"Pueblo has never been a tourist town. It has been a steel town," said Planning Director Jim Munch.

How did Pueblo manage to rebuild its economy, when so many of the nation's old industrial cities are still struggling?

"We did not invest exclusively in tourism and service industries at the expense of reinvesting in our industrial base," said Spaccamonti.

Spaccamonti and other economic development officials say Pueblo residents are good workers who do not take business for granted. "I know that everybody else says that, but in our case, it's true," he said. He cited the city's decade-long depression as proof. "You don't have to tell people in Pueblo, Colorado, that it's important for the town to grow and prosper," he said. "They have seen the hard times, and that humbles people. Every time we land a new company, that's just one more. If and when a recession comes, we are just that more stable, and people will not have to go through the devastating trauma again."

The Pittsburgh Cultural Trust
Revives a Rusted City

The O'Reilly Theater—which opened in December, 1999—will add one more reason for local Pittsburgh residents to join regional, national, and international visitors flocking to the former steel capital's inner city to feast on a smorgasbord of art offerings. The new theater reflects the late mayor Jack Heinz's vision of a renewed downtown and his belief that with government support, arts and business sectors could make the city center a magnet for income-generating cultural activity.

symbolized the city's economic vitality. Sidewalks filled with local and out-of-town audiences moving to and from art venues reveal the essence of today's new era.

With each new addition to the fourteen-block Cultural District, cultural and business development is changing the city skyline and invigorating homegrown arts and cultural organizations. The Consolidated Natural Gas Company (CNG) tower office building and the Benedum Center for the Performing Arts next door both benefited from a $17 million federal Urban Development Action Grant, demonstrating how urban and economic development money can promote both business and the arts.

His legacy to the city—the Pittsburgh Cultural Trust—is a model of civic renewal through development of the arts. Planners hoping to breathe new creative energy into their own urban centers scrutinize the leadership of the Trust's first executive director, Carol Brown. By enhancing cultural amenities and undertaking historic preservation, business development, and community outreach, the city has inspired a mood of civic optimism unparalleled since the decline of the steel industry. Twenty years ago, smoke billowing from mills

Opened in 1987, the Benedum Center attracts crowds to the third largest stage in the country with state-of-the-art equipment and technical capability. The large center allowed the Pittsburgh Ballet Theatre, Civic Light Opera, Pittsburgh Dance Council, and Pittsburgh Opera to expand their seasons and sell more tickets. Local businesses thrived during the wildly successful nine-week run of *Phantom of the Opera* that attracted people (and their wallets) from more than forty-four states. One downtown restaurateur credited the popular musical for a seventy-percent increase in his business.

But the Cultural District is intended for more than blockbuster performances and large venues. The Fulton Theater and the Wood Street Galleries (leased from the Port Authority of Allegheny County) provide spaces for more than thirty small and midsized arts organizations. The availability of downtown office space has helped invigorate and stabilize the city's smaller groups, many of them African American. The Cultural Trust also boasts an outreach program offering reduced and free admission to students, the elderly, and the poor so they might take advantage of the expanded offerings of the cultural corridor.

(Above) *Carol Brown, the executive director of The Pittsburgh Cultural Trust, in front of the Louise Bourgeois "eyeball" bench at Katz Plaza. The Trust is a model of civic renewal through the development of the arts.* (Left) *Theater marquees of the Byham Theater and Benedum Center for the Performing Arts located in the cultural district of Pittsburgh.*

The Trust also promotes arts activity in other neighborhoods. In cooperation with the Urban Redevelopment Authority, it has spearheaded a campaign to restore the facades of more than fifty buildings. As a result, handsome turn-of-the-century architectural jewels have reemerged from decades of concealment behind unsightly aluminum fronts. Many troublesome businesses, such as adult bookstores, have closed, and their newly renovated buildings are used for businesses that complement other enterprises. For example, Pittsburgh Filmmakers has taken temporary residence in a former adult film center. Streetscape improvements include brick sidewalks, tree plantings, and a *trompe l'oeil* mural by Richard Haas.

When the O'Reilly Theater debuts in December, the structure, designed by Michael Graves, will house the 650-seat Pittsburgh Public Theater. A new office building, central park, and parking

garage with entertainment and retail space at ground level flank the theater at the corner of Seventh and Penn Avenues. The Trust combines amenities with core businesses in an urban setting that includes features that office workers and visitors want: historic architecture; modern design; handsome streets; and places to park, eat, and spend money.

The Trust also plans a major reshaping of the northern boundary of the Cultural District. Landscape architect Michael Van Valkenburgh and artist Ann Hamilton will design a two-level waterfront park along the Allegheny River. Just as the Pittsburgh Cultural Trust has led the way in its use of the arts as part of an economic revitalization strategy, the creation of a pedestrian-friendly waterfront park is intended to spur other municipalities to transform their shorelines into civic amenities.

Downtown Amenities
Attract Urban Dwellers

LEADERSHIP
PROFILE

Fifteen years ago, when Partners for Livable Communities published *The Economics of Amenity: Community Futures and Quality of Life—A Policy Guide to Urban Economic Development*, the changing nature of the economy and the ineluctable force of suburbanization had emptied traditionally strong cities of jobs, which lowered the quality of life for residents and created pockets of concentrated urban poverty. The country has since tried to renew the city center, converting many downtowns to the vibrant hubs of intellectual life and commerce that predated World War II.

Downtown amenities attract businesses, residents, and tourists. (Above) "Dunlap Avenue Tree Guards," by Garth Edwards, in Phoenix, Arizona. (Right) The International Rose Test Garden in Portland, Oregon. (Opposite, above) The North Carolina Blumenthal Performing Arts Center in Charlotte. (Below) An outdoor concert in the Governor Tom McCall Waterfront Park in Portland, Oregon.

Leaders and planners now understand that cities have evolved through centuries because their unique amenities—historic structures, proximity to natural features, and cultural institutions—fulfill human needs.

Since its inception as a coalition of twenty-seven nonprofits, Partners has tracked the dissolution and renewal of the American city. Now with hundreds of business, nonprofit, and foundation members, Partners believes its strategy of reviving urban centers by building museums, theaters, zoos, aquariums, and art centers works better than ever. Amenity industries—parks, cultural corridors, and downtown arts communities—not only pay for themselves; they also can attract new residents and visitors, increasing tourist and tax revenues. Moreover, these amenities also attract the support and dollars of local residents who spend their disposable income near their homes, in enterprises that add to the quality of life, animate their streets and attract more commerce.

Today, more than ever before, with the rise of information technology, the quality of the urban center attracts economic enterprise more than do accessibility or raw materials. New technologically savvy firms are drawn to the quality environments (natural, social, and cultural) cities offer. Companies know they get the most from their workforce when they operate in settings that contrast with isolated suburban enclaves: concentrated downtown arts and entertainment districts; quality design in the built environment; diversity; and churches, clubs, and civic leagues. Moreover, the tight labor market, expected to last through the

early years of this century, gives workers greater influence over business relocation choices. Increasingly, talented, enthusiastic, and capable workers seek residence in the historical centers of the nation's cities, attracted by a concentration of amenities unparalleled outside the urban boundary.

The sum of amenities describes a region's image. When the city of Bilbao in northern Spain asked the Guggenheim Museum in New York City to locate its new exhibit hall in a decaying Bilbao commercial corridor, the design, by pioneering post-modernist Frank Gehry, attracted worldwide tourist attention. The museum has fast become the city's *brand name*, as recognizable as the Statue of Liberty in New York City and the Eiffel Tower in Paris. Gehry's design, a scattering of metallic

shapes circuiting an atrium, provides multiple benefits. An emblem of modernity to the outside world, it represents civic pride for Bilbao residents, and demonstrates that the city's historic center has both aesthetic and economic value.

Cities that invest in cultural and natural assets attract tourists and businesses. Partners calls this investment in parks, art, and performance centers, as defined and supported by community members themselves, an *amenity approach*.

Nine-Mile Run
City of Pittsburgh,
Department of City Planning
200 Ross Street
Pittsburgh, PA 15219

Contact: Eloise Hirsch,
Director
412.255.2200

The City of Pittsburgh is working to restore the Monongahela River valley and develop a new urban neighborhood.
Nine-Mile Run stream is a natural drainage basin and is one of the last visible streams of the original Pittsburgh watershed. Between 1922 and 1970, the Nine-Mile Run stream valley was used as a dumping ground for industrial slag from Pittsburgh-area steel mills. In 1995, the City of Pittsburgh commissioned a master-planning study of the 230-acre site, now owned by the Urban Redevelopment Authority. The project will result in 100 acres of public open space (to become the Frick Park Extension), and a new housing development on the top of a slag plateau, known as Summerset at Frick Park.

Summerset at Frick Park will transform today's abandoned slag heaps into a new traditional neighborhood. It will have tree-lined streets with sidewalks, raised front lawns, porches, and a variety of housing options. The proposed master plan for Summerset will be developed in three phases over several years. The goals for the open space are:

- To create public open space that is safe and healthy, and to return an industrial wasteland to its former state as a riparian corridor and green open space;
- To develop a remediation process that does not have adverse environmental impacts on other areas of the region;
- To reinforce the connection between Frick Park and the Monongahela River and serve a variety of users; and

- To return Nine-Mile Run stream into an amenity for the housing development, Frick Park, and the area's significant wildlife population.

The development of an entirely new urban neighborhood on a slag heap, the park extension, and the restoration of the Nine-Mile Run stream are designed to create new economic, ecological, and aesthetic models of the benefits of brownfield redevelopment. The project is funded by public and private sources, including the Environmental Protection Agency, the State of Pennsylvania Department of Conservation and Natural Resources, and the City of Pittsburgh. The project also benefits from the assistance of many partner organizations, such as the Western Pennsylvania Conservancy, The Pittsburgh Children's Museum, and the National City Community Development Corporation.

Lowertown
Lowertown Redevelopment Corporation
175 East 5th St., Galtier Plaza, Suite 750,
Box 104
St. Paul, MN 55101
www.lowertown.org

Contact: Weiming Lu,
President
651.227.9131

Lowertown is an urban village encompassing housing, entertainment, artists lofts, and businesses in a once declining St. Paul neighborhood. As president of the Lowertown Redevelopment Corporation in St. Paul, Minnesota, Weiming Lu has had plenty of experience coordinating a public/private venture.

"Everybody talks about public/private partnership—when it works very well, it is like a group of cyclists that ride together beautifully," Lu told the Second International Urban Design Forum in

Yokohama, Japan, in 1998. "But more often, because of fighting for territory or resources, it may end up a mess. It is a great challenge for any partnership: When the boundaries are undefined, the responsibility is not clear. How do you develop consensus, then marshal the resources to find a common goal, to get something done?" When former St. Paul mayor George Latimer set aside $10 million in 1979 for program-related investments, he laid the foundation for the Lowertown Redevelopment Corporation (LRC), a private organization with a public purpose. The eight-member board of directors, including civic leaders, the mayor, bankers, labor leaders, and neighborhood activists, undertook the Herculean renovation of the Lowertown district of St. Paul. Lowertown covers eighteen blocks, almost one-third of downtown St. Paul, and it had become a labyrinth of abandoned warehouses, factories, and run-down neighborhoods.

In the simplest terms, the corporation serves as a development bank, but this label does not begin to tell the whole story. The LRC portrays itself as a vehicle for public/private partnerships. For every dollar the LRC invests in a project, it attracts $5 to $35 in public and private money. Investment in the area has jumped from an average of $22 million to $210 million per decade. The tax base has increased from $850,000 in 1979 to almost $4 million in 1993. A walk through the area reveals thriving businesses and strong communities.

The LRC's commitment to investment in design, marketing, and gap financing has led to its successes. The corporation recognized the importance of fostering a sense of place. Old warehouses and factories were not torn down but transformed into housing units.

The LRC's investment depends on the provision of housing for people of all ages and economic backgrounds. Today, twenty-five percent of Lowertown's housing is dedicated to people with low and moderate incomes. The LRC also has invested in adding amenities to the neighborhoods of Lowertown, such as parks, farmer's markets, and a new police substation and swimming pool.

Lowertown boasts one of the highest concentrations of working artists in cities across the nation—500 at last count. The LRC has fostered Lowertown's creative atmosphere by giving special attention to artists' housing. Artists, in return, help with many LRC projects, such as the park design. The LRC also tries to attract high-tech and cyberspace industries to the area. Young entrepreneurs, lured by the redevelopment potential of abandoned warehouses, can receive gap financing with LRC making up the gap between public and private financing as an incentive to remain in St. Paul. "With infrastructure, amenities, and affordable housing, we have been able to attract new people," asserts Weiming Lu.

Lu offers three tips for municipal officials seeking to create *soft cities*—places where residents feel secure and enjoy easy access to amenities; where they feel invested in their communities and can perhaps, create a simpler life:

- The new *soft city* must incorporate a diverse residential neighborhood, a colony for artists, a cyber village, a sustainable community concerned with ecology and the conservation of energy, a distinctive sense of place, and an accessible city. These elements should be combined to, in the words of Weiming Lu, "…create an environment where creativity is cherished and entrepreneurship supported; where one can fill the needs for community and provide an outlet for a civic spirit."
- Create a synergy of development in which growth dynamics are clearly understood and projects are linked in planning and development. Said Lu: "A *soft city* doesn't depend upon a megaproject, but on a myriad of small and moderate sized projects."
- The *soft city* needs strong neighborhood leaders who know how to tap the inner energy of an area to build a viable neighborhood.

Peabody Place
Belz Enterprises
100 Peabody Place, Ste. 1400
Memphis, TN 38103
www.belz.com

Contact: John Dudas,
Public Relations
901.260.7244

The rehabilitation of the old Peabody Hotel by a private company spurred a downtown revival boosted by historic-preservation tax incentives and other government programs. In the early morning of April 4, 1968, Memphis, Tennessee entered the country's collective conscience as the "backwater delta" where Martin Luther King, Jr. was killed. Riots soon followed, lasting several days and destroying not only property, but also residents' sense of home and security. Memphis residents often date the city's decades-long decline to that April morning. In the following months and years, the downtown quickly emptied, as both residents and businesses fled to the suburbs. There is a saying in the South that "the delta begins in the lobby of the Peabody [hotel]." When the Peabody closed its doors in the 1970s, it seemed as though the doors had closed on Memphis as well. The city and surrounding region, like many across the country, reverted to a decaying and poverty-stricken urban core ringed by suburban sprawl.

Downtown revitalization has many parents, and in Memphis, one of the most persistent was a sentimental developer. Rumor has it that one of the patriarchs of the Belz Corporation, the largest developers in the region, proposed to his wife in the lobby of the Peabody Hotel. Driven by either nostalgia or a vision of economic profit, Belz acquired, renovated, and reopened the Peabody in the mid-1980s. The company then moved its headquarters downtown and required that all supporting businesses be located

within the city limits as well. These first steps became the basis for a business renaissance in the downtown corridor, spurred by tax-break incentives from the newly formed Center City Commission, created by the governments of Memphis and Shelby County.

The rapid rate of this resurgence could have led to a patchwork landscape of hastily constructed skyscrapers and industrial complexes with no unifying theme. To prevent this, the Center City Commission offered incentives encouraging developers to use existing buildings. A twenty-year cessation in development starting in the sixties left Memphis bereft of modern construction. The city still possessed most of its historic offices, shops, and buildings. "People left in such a hurry that they left some pretty wonderful buildings behind," explained Jeff Sanford, president of the Center City Commission. The Commission preserved and renovated these buildings, helping to create a unique urban design.

The success of the Peabody renovation led the Belz Company to consider a more ambitious project, the largest mixed-use urban development in the South. Proponents of smart growth have long advocated mixed-use neighborhoods where people can live above the shop. The Belz project, called Peabody Place, is an amplified version of this idea. The project will cover eight city blocks and include office space, residential apartments, restaurants, shops, and entertainment centers. The elements will be scattered through the city in different buildings connected by skyways, corridors, and trolley stations. One of the unique aspects of the project is its incorporation of historic buildings, embracing renovation over construction.

The Belz Company's efforts to restore and renew downtown Memphis appear to be paying off. Bucking national trends, people are now moving back into the city in record numbers.

Maya Lin Project
Frey Foundation
48 Fountain Street NW, Ste. 200
Grand Rapids, MI 49503-3023
www.freyfdn.org

Contact: Milton Rohwer,
President
616.451.0303

Drawing on its history as one of the first cities in the United States to install public art, Grand Rapids, Michigan, has hired Maya Lin to create sculptures to enhance community revitalization. In 1995, the trustees of the Frey Foundation capitalized upon Grand Rapid's impressive public art collection to explore new work as a catalyst for continued downtown improvements. Over 100 civic leaders participated in a brainstorming session that resulted in the selection of Monroe Mall as the site and sculptor Maya Lin as the artist.

Maya Lin, best known as the designer of the Vietnam War Memorial, participated in the project's preliminary planning. She proposed an experiential park—a design that is simultaneously a park and a work of art. This project includes redesigning the public amphitheater as a community gathering place. She envisions the ampitheater as a place for ethnic festivals and concerts, a place that will both shape and express the identity of Grand Rapids.

The park, scheduled for completion by the end of 2000, will feature sculptural elements that incorporate different stages of water. The central feature is the amphitheater that will become a refrigerated ice rink in the winter. Fiber optic stars are inlayed in the base, creating a night sky visible through ice. The design incorporates an accurate chart of the the stars and constellations of the winter night sky. The park's sculpted grass mounds represent Grand River rapids. Lin also designed a misting fountain at the park entrance and a gently cascading, tree-sheltered

reflecting pool. The park's focus on water reflects the heritage of Grand Rapids and provides a downtown identity.

Intended as the city's welcome center for visitors and residents, the park's objective is to draw people and encourage interaction. Lin envisions the amphitheater as an area combining architecture, art, and landscape into something entirely new, not as a conventional sculpture. Lin hopes that each visit will create a fresh experience and will enhance Grand Rapid's reputation as the first city to experiment with public art in its many forms. The sculptor worked hard to ensure that the park reflects not only her own vision, but also the community's dreams as well. Maya Lin's project representatives met with community members frequently.

The Frey Foundation is a major financial contributor to the Maya Lin project and the recent stages of the Monroe Mall renovation. In total, the foundation has donated $1 million and attracted an additional $2 million from the city as part of a private-sector challenge-grant program. The city's evident long-term commitment to the project attracted the Frey Foundation. In turn, the foundation's contributions encouraged the donation of more public funds. The Frey Foundation conditioned its funding on the provision of funds by the City of Grand Rapids/ Downtown Development Authority to complete the project. The foundation promised to match the city's contribution to an endowment established for project maintenance.

Port Discovery
The Children's Museum in Baltimore
35 Market Place
Baltimore, MD 21202

Contact: Dr. Beatrice Taylor,
Director of Education and Programs
410.864.2656

Downtown entertainment gets a vibrant,

youthful jump-start at Baltimore's Port Discovery, a kid-powered museum that helps children develop leadership skills. Encouraging youthful dreams may seem the responsibility of educational institutions, but rich, innovative programs offered at Port Discovery in Baltimore's revitalized downtown demonstrate new spaces and methods of learning.

Presented in an environment where young people can discover their talents and interests, Port Discovery's interactive activities allow kids to test and expand their ideas. Port Discovery aims to teach children the process, persistence, and responsibilities required to fulfill their dreams through education and positive role models.

One of the most important Discovery programs allows small groups of children to experience the museum in a unique and highly personalized way. The museum also incorporates a community library branch, enabling children to expand their current interests and explore new ones. Librarians, Internet access, and a rich variety of books and databases provide valuable free resources.

The surest way to end a program is to force it on unwilling or uninterested participants. Port Discovery depends on input from a Youth Advisory Council. The council reviews all programs and activities to ensure they are developmentally, educationally, culturally, and socially appropriate. The group also organizes Port Discovery's two annual community outreach projects: the Friendship Food Basket Gathering and the Bubbles and Ball Drive. Port Discovery staff note that the food baskets and ball drive enable the museum to contribute to its neighbors in the Jonestown area and enhance children's social awareness by developing their philanthropic and community-development skills.

The Youth Advisory Council was formed in advance of the opening of the museum. With two children from each suburban county and ten from Baltimore, the Council supervised the initial survey for use in designing the best programs for Port Discovery. With assistance from a national researcher, the children designed the survey and administered it to their peers. The results were surprising: Children wanted to spend more time with their families. The surveys allowed Port Discovery to craft exhibits and programs tailored to area children's interests, and Youth Council members gained valuable life skills, such as conflict resolution and public speaking.

Youth Council kids move on to the museum's programs, growing up with Port Discovery, through a series of volunteer opportunities. They can serve at the museum with assistance from their parents or an adult until they are sixteen and can solo. A few of the first Youth Council participants are eighteen and have advanced to paying jobs with Port Discovery.

Port Discovery's outreach programs are long established and well-supported. Regardless of their age or family income, all children are welcome at Port Discovery, where every child can find innovative and thought-provoking projects to engage the imagination.

Urban Village

Urban Village/CityLink Investment Corp.
2025 Congress Ave., Suite 110
San Diego, CA 92110

Contact: William Jones,
Director
619.220.7094 ext. 301

A community investment corporation provides financing to rebuild a blighted San Diego neighborhood. Redevelopment does not just happen, and putting together the right variables involves commitment from the community and investors. A dream does not hurt. With the vision of one man, and the spirit and hopes of a community, urban redevelopment becomes a reality.

William Jones had a big dream, a

dream that took City Heights in San Diego from its blighted past to a hopeful present. Building on a solid career in city government, where he learned the difficulty of encouraging private-sector investment in neighborhoods, and his years managing a commercial real estate portfolio, Jones returned to his San Diego home in 1993 to found, with Sol Price, the CityLink Investment Corporation. Jones intended to redevelop an inner-city neighborhood and create a more wholesome, livable urban community.

The success of the Urban Village project is not measured by the bottom-line. The benefits to the area's citizens and the demonstration of successful inner-city redevelopment together set a precedent for future redevelopment utilizing public/private partnerships. City support, private investment, and community involvement have resulted in a new police substation, gymnasium, swimming pool, elementary school, and shopping center. The center boasts a grocery store and pharmacy, adult education center, library, and child care program. San Diego residents are deeply involved; they have put in thousands of community service hours. Residents also take full advantage of the library services and training opportunities.

The Urban Village began simply with the construction of a police substation. Area residents previously had to contend with frequent robberies and shootings and a plethora of prostitutes and drug dealers. With an initial $100 million in public and private funds, the community hired an architect to design the Urban Village master plan, which the resident activists examined during a meeting that lasted well into the night. From the beginning, the Urban Village project captured the imagination, time, and contributions of neighborhood citizens. Their goals were basic. Neighbors wanted to park their cars without fear of harassment or vandalism. They wanted essential neighborhood amenities: a grocery store, a school within walking

distance of their homes, and a public swimming pool.

The tremendous energy, hope, determination, and optimism of the residents fueled further stages of the project. Community interest and energy also led to planning for a new adult education center and a gymnasium as a part of the police substation. The Rosa Parks Elementary School's new principal toured area schools, parks, and libraries with area children to help plan what amenities they would add to their new building. In its parent room, area mothers gather in the morning to provide sweat equity and perform tasks that teachers do not have time for—like cleaning the chalkboards— and also learn to use the same computers the children already have mastered.

The Urban Village is still being developed, and its primary investors are still hesitant to declare it a complete success. The project attempts to improve job opportunities and provide affordable housing and health care on par with other city neighborhoods. But planners do not want development to occur so quickly that real estate costs rise exponentially, driving out the very people the Village seeks to serve. The project provides an eloquent counter to rhetoric that inner-city residents will not work to save their own neighborhoods. Social experiments are never that simple. Taken as a whole, examined as a work-in-progress, the Urban Village serves as an inspiration and a guide for other reinvestment projects.

Peekskill Artist District
City of Peekskill
Department of Planning and Zoning
840 Main Street
Peekskill, NY 10566

Contact: Susan M. Colvin,
Zoning Coordinator
914.734.4211

Peekskill has created SoHo North for artists who want a change from the pace of New York City by relocating in Peekskill and helping to revitalize the center city. One hundred artists have brought a tremendous amount of new energy to the Peekskill Artist District. By encouraging artists to live and work downtown, Peekskill has increased the number of new businesses and the level of economic activity, transforming the city into a dynamo.

The City of Peekskill has made a commitment to attracting and keeping artistic and high-tech industries. Most newcomers consider city support the primary impetus for drawing and keeping artisan-residents. Artists who hear of the city's willingness to provide for them invite their colleagues to join them downtown. After years of effort, the city has been transformed into an urban colony where painters, sculptors, dancers, filmmakers, and others live and work in converted retail storage lofts.

The artists have a similarly diverse client base. One studio turns out designs for clients such as Disney, MTV, and McDonalds, while another produces fine art for collectors. Bookstores, cafes, restaurants, and an increased number of entertainment outlets attract still more people and businesses downtown.

In the early nineties, Peekskill city officials helped developers convert space suitable for lofts and studios by adjusting zoning codes, coordinating leases with owners and artists, and providing low-interest loans and advice on renovations. The city's role unified the loft designs and

ensured they would be affordable to working artisans.

The district has attracted computer graphics and multimedia businesses and is now home to several multimillion dollar consulting firms who draw their employees from the growing number of highly skilled residents.

Peekskill channels area students into the new businesses. A scholarship and internship program enables students to take college courses in multimedia computer arts while working as interns with one of the new high-tech businesses. These students then form a labor pool with diverse skills and talents for area arts and high-tech businesses.

The Peekskill Artist District provides both affordable housing and small business development and demonstrates the different components required for economic development and downtown revitalization.

BridgeClimb
5 Cumberland Street
Sydney, NSW 2000
Australia

Contact: Marketing Department
61.2.9240.1100

Sydney, Australia, has tried something a little different—a high-altitude stroll—to draw people to its downtown and take advantage of its magnificent skyline. Sydney's BridgeClimb enables people to take a guided walk across the Harbor Bridge. Allowing tourists to scale one of the world's largest steel arch bridges has proven tremendously popular. Bridge Climb, which opened in 1998, now accommodates up to 600 visitors each day. Demand is high for the high-level bridge tour, and reservations often are needed a week in advance. The city carefully screens for alcohol and depression and uses a metal detector to make sure no one goes on the bridge for anything

other than a glorious view of the Pacific Ocean, Sydney Opera House, or the Sydney Olympic Park. Walkers empty their pockets and step into a pocketless one-piece suit for their climb. Nothing is allowed to fall onto twelve lanes of cars hundreds of feet below or onto the harbor ships even lower.

To keep the participants safe, each climber is harnessed into a hybrid safety belt tethered to a steel safety cable running the length of the walk. A guide provides continuous narration during the tour that includes climbing a ladder between lanes of traffic and viewing the dusty footprints left by bridge painters who work without harnesses. The guide, through a two-way radio clipped to participants' safety belts, narrates the history of the bridge's construction. High winds would prevent visitors from hearing a guide speaking without the aid of a radio.

Like other Sydney businesses, the city is expected to garner extra profits from the BridgeClimb when international visitors flood the area for the scheduled 2000 Summer Olympic Games. No other attraction offers the visitor such thrills. Afterwards, downtown Sydney can offer climbers much needed relaxation and refreshment.

Flower City Looking Good Gardening Program
Department of Parks, Recreation, and Human Services
City of Rochester
Rochester, NY 14614

Contact: Jim Farr,
Assistant Manager
716.428.6866 or 726.428.6755

After the devastation of an ice storm that took out 20,000 urban trees, many more than 100 years old, volunteers reforested the streets of Rochester, New York. The City of Rochester's Flower City Looking Good gardening initiative has enjoyed tremendous success. Residents seeking ways to bolster flagging spirits and beautify defoliated streets started the Reforest Rochester Trust Fund and the Flower City Looking Good programs in 1991, following one of the area's worst ice storms. Flower City Looking Good engaged thousands in the replanting. The trust fund was intended only as the mechanism for the city's continuing urban forest restoration, but the program expanded. City staff now hopes to renew memories of Rochester's heyday at the turn-of-the-century as a center for horticultural activities by emphasizing Rochester's image as the Flower City.

From a vision of a few staff members, assisted by several dedicated volunteers, the program has become the city's hallmark. The program's tenth anniversary celebration in 2000 will involve nearly 2,000 volunteers. Program coordinators will recognize the 4,000 who have volunteered, with more than 1,500 volunteers providing 2,500 people hours in the year 1999 alone. More than 30,000 bulbs and 75,000 annuals have been added to the cityscape during the past ten years and forty-five new neighborhood gardens have been established. In all, nearly 200,000 Rochester residents participated in the Flower City Looking Good events during the 1999 season.

The small size of the city's park division has been an impetus for seeking volunteer help. Large-scale, citywide planting days mobilized individuals, corporate groups, and neighborhood associations. The city added *Rochester Blossoms!* as a citywide planting day for annuals in 1994 and then expanded the program in 1997 with a fall *Rochester Blossoms!* for the planting of spring bulbs. *Rochester Blossoms!* alone has provided the planting power to add thousands of bulbs and annuals to the cityscape since its inception. In just two years, the program has attracted 750 volunteers. To clean up area trails, special *Trail Days* also have mobilized dozens of volunteers to spruce up city park trails.

These efforts have united residents who desire more livable, attractive surroundings, and those who wish to raise the self-esteem, pride, and quality of life of fellow neighbors. These intangibles are difficult to measure in quantitative terms. "Flowers per square foot" describes the scope of a project, but not the pleasures that come from the planting, the strolling, and the fragrant breezes enjoyed by all.

Volunteers, bulbs, blossoms. Together these represent the transformation of Rochester from a city under ice to Flower City.

Avenue of the Arts
123 South Broad St.
Philadelphia, PA 19109
www.avenueofthearts.org

Contact: Ellen B. Solms,
Executive Director
215.731.9668

Philadelphia is developing its economy by building a downtown arts corridor.
Four miles along Broad Street, Philadelphia's historic center for theatre, are being revitalized through the Avenue of the Arts project. Rebuilding the arts and cultural facilities is designed as a catalyst for downtown revitalization. The liveliness of the arts district has attracted hoteliers, restaurateurs, and retailers, while helping transform surrounding neighborhoods into safer more livable communities.

The $330 million capital improvement project has returned the arts to downtown Philadelphia by producing 6,000 new performance venue seats, resulting in 1,600 new events annually. A nonprofit group manages marketing, fundraising, and streetscape improvements. Existing structures have been improved, renovated, and expanded to provide better space, while maintaining the historic character of the district. One joint venture managed the rehabilitation of five brownstones for use as office and

business incubator space, while another renovation project created the Freedom Theatre, the state's oldest African American theater with a renovated Italianate mansion as headquarters.

The Avenue of the Arts plan provided for scatter-site facilities that serve different arts and cultural groups, have a variety of uses, and draw diverse audiences. Regional and community-based troupes attract audiences of families, young professionals, children, and the elderly. The facilities include newly constructed buildings, as well as major renovations. New construction includes the Wilma Theater, a 300-seat theater incorporating rehearsal space, offices, technical support space, and a shared parking garage. One of the largest new projects is the Regional Performing Arts Center, a two-building complex consisting of the Academy of Music and a new facility to house a 2,500-seat concert hall and a 500- to 1,200-seat Adaptable Theater.

More than just a place to enjoy performances, the Avenue of the Arts includes the Philadelphia High School for the Creative and Performing Arts. Housed in the historic Ridgeway Library, with a new four-story addition, the renovated space will be a magnet high school for creative writing, dance, drama, visual arts, and instrumental and vocal music. Other Avenue of the Arts facilities preserve the diverse heritage of Philadelphia while promoting contemporary minority artists by providing gallery space and theater space for nonprofit groups.

The vitality of the Avenue of the Arts has made it a major tourist draw. Avenue artists also instruct Philadelphia's school children and their families in the joy and the power of the arts.

Bronzeville

Black Metropolis Conservation
Center & Tourism Council
44 East 48th Street
Chicago, IL 60615

Contact: Harold Lucas,
Director
773.548.2579

Chicago's Mecca for African-American business, culture, literature, and politics remakes itself as a draw for tourists.
Bronzeville, Chicago's historic African-American neighborhood, has become a major destination for those seeking a better understanding of Chicago's rich African-American heritage. Once the center of culture, literature, politics, and entrepreneurship in Chicago during its heyday in the twenties, Bronzeville was nicknamed *The Metropolis*. The steel industry from the 1920s to the 1950s brought a huge migration of blacks from the South. At the same time, black-owned businesses, banks, and the first black-owned insurance company flourished in Bronzeville, complemented by a thriving jazz- and blues-based cultural scene.

Influential Chicago African-Americans and residents of Bronzeville are now working together to restore the community. Historic structures and landscapes remain in the area, but the decline of industry coupled with discrimination and disinvestment have taken a toll and proven difficult to combat.

Community groups and residents are already preserving and restoring area structures. They have worked to create a major exhibition called "Douglas/Grand Boulevard: The Past and the Promise," that residents hope will improve appreciation for their neighborhood and boost contributions to its development. Through this and other *Keepers of Culture* projects, activists hope to create mutually respectful partnerships with neighborhood residents and community

groups that will lead to long-term, high-quality relationships.

Community commitment is bringing Bronzeville back. In addition, oral history projects help local residents become comfortable with interpreting community history and telling their own stories. By emphasizing oral history, these Chicagoans are renewing their neighborhood for the future.

Chattanooga Riverpark

River Valley Partners, Inc.
835 Georgia Ave., Ste 500
Chattanooga, TN 37402

Contact: Jim Bowen,
Vice-President
423.265.3700

The City of Chattanooga engaged the community in revitalizing the region's twenty-mile river corridor by giving citizens a role in its planning and design.
Chattanooga, Tennessee, officials include citizens in their community development planning. Thousands participated in building the Moccasin Bend Task Force to preserve and enhance the Chattanooga River beginning in 1982. Residents provided development recommendations for the creation of new parks, trails, attractions, and industry to replace and revive abandoned sites along the twenty-mile river corridor.

Planners rolled taskforce recommendations into the Tennessee Riverpark Master Plan, a twenty-year commitment to attract $750 million in new development along the river. As a downtown amenity, the corridor includes parks, housing, shops, offices, and attractions. The community participated in design *charettes*, planning sessions, and citywide visioning. Innovative partnerships among governments, corporations, foundations, and individuals proved instrumental in creating a thriving neighborhood. The Chattanooga Venture, a nonprofit orga-

nization, acquired a commitment portfolio from developers and city officials for downtown projects. The Venture helped raise $45 million for the Tennessee Aquarium and garnered funding for a new mass-transit system with environmentally friendly electric buses. Passengers can ride to all the new downtown attractions for free without contributing to pollution or traffic.

Millions visit the Tennessee Aquarium and merchants have opened hundreds of new stores and restaurants. The reopening of the nineteenth-century Walnut Street Bridge as a pedestrian parkway, connecting the Tennessee Riverwalk with the north shore, symbolizes the community renaissance. The bridge has attracted people to surrounding neighborhoods, increasing their vibrancy and economic activities. The bridge also has generated complementary activities, such as the furnishing of a carousel with animals carved by Chattanooga students.

Chattanooga's efforts have been highly praised. The *U.S. News and World Report* described the city as one offering valuable lessons on improving services, eliminating and combating blight, improving urban children's safety, and reversing downtown population declines. In the future, Chattanooga residents hope to attract more clean industry to its environmentally sound business core. To create viable, diverse urban neighborhoods, Chattanooga will continue to build consensus among planning and development partners and rely heavily upon its eager and involved community.

Regional Parks Master Plan Project
Community Design Center of Pittsburgh
211 Ninth St.
Pittsburgh, PA 15222

Contact: Richard St. John,
Executive Director
412.391.4144

Pittsburgh unites neighbors, business leaders, and government in developing a comprehensive plan for the city's extensive network of urban parks. With shrinking budgets to combat burgeoning inner-city decay, park maintenance and planning is often one of the first budget sacrifices. Such was the case in Pittsburgh. "Every year I put [a park planner] in my budget and it never gets funded," said Faith Gallo, Director of Parks and Recreation. However, recognizing that parks can be a focal point for community development and a fulcrum for change, the Pennsylvania State Department of Conservation and Natural Resources granted funds to Pittsburgh to prepare master plans for the renovation and maintenance of Pittsburgh's four regional parks: Frick, Schenley, Highland, and Riverview.

In an unprecedented effort, three groups of professionals will assist in developing a strategy to guide public and private investment in the maintenance, management, and improvement of the parks. After an inventory of park conditions (e.g., layout, maintenance, landscape features, zoning), local and national consultants will create the design guidelines for each park. The final ten-year plan will include alternative strategies to address park improvements and maintenance plans and to pay the estimated costs of the improvements. This extensive project is unique in that every effort will attempt a balance between the aesthetic, historic, environmental, and recreational uses of the parks. In addition, surrounding communities will be given multiple opportunities to offer suggestions.

At one of the first meetings to discuss the future of the parks, a group of landscape architects, land conservationists, and representatives of neighborhood groups recommended that a coalition of public and private organizations be established to create a vision and master plan for the parks. Step five of the resulting master plan is called the "Community Process." Community meetings and meetings with various constituent groups will be coordinated by management consultants, the project manager, and the Pittsburgh Parks Conservancy. Technical consultants will be required to attend these meetings. [Excerpted from the Pittsburgh Post Gazette, Sept. 9, 1997, B-1.]

Oriole Park at Camden Yards
Orioles Baseball
333 West Camden Street
Baltimore, MD 21201-2476
www.theorioles.com/

Contact: Roger Hayden,
Director of Ballpark Operations
410.685.9800

Capitalizing on the community's nostalgic yearning for the bygone years of baseball, Oriole Park at Camden Yards re-creates the baseball fields of the early years of the twentieth century.

Combining reuse and downtown revitalization measures create a unique and attractive space, drawing crowds to downtown Baltimore. Oriole Park at Camden Yards received a 1998 Partners for Livable Communities Investors in America Award. The park is credited with revolutionizing stadium design and it has inspired other cities to build their own version of old-fashioned, "retrostyle" ballparks. Its appeal stems from the historical details, real grass, and intimate seating that makes Oriole Park a true ballpark, rather than simply a generic stadium. The park's location near the Baltimore Convention Center and the

Inner Harbor shopping center promotes downtown pedestrian traffic and reinforces the growth of commerce in the three destinations.

Its unique design and harmonious relations with the city's existing landscape ensure it is more than a structure; it has become a source of civic pride. The presence of the Baltimore & Ohio Warehouse just beyond right field further enhances the district's historic environment. Additionally, a brick façade similar in color to the B & O warehouse refined the park's traditional appearance. This attention to historic detail adds a uniform design element to the downtown district. A street-fair plaza serves as a gathering place and includes retail, restaurants, food stands, and baseball memorabilia.

Camden Yards arises from the collaboration among several team members. Civic leadership, a team of architects, construction firms, real estate advisory members, food service providers, and financiers all worked to achieve this unique, attractive downtown amenity.

Twenty-First Century Tools

New Leaders Renew Our Communities

"We are obliged to open a new chapter in the struggle to revitalize our cities," said Trinity College President Evan S. Dobelle at the ground breaking for the new sixteen-acre Learning Corridor in Hartford, Connecticut. The work of an unusual town-and-gown alliance, the center aims to transform blighted inner-city blocks near the college into livable spaces for the communities on Hartford's south side.

Creating responsive new leadership requires a constituency's steady commitment to improvement.

Churches and other faith-based organizations across the nation have embraced the obligation Dobelle defines, prompting them to staff up, obtain public funds, provide community services, and undertake community revitalization. Local newspapers accept the obligation by choosing not merely to tell the story of corrosive urban problems, but also to urge readers to take corrective actions and show them how to do it. Community corporations meet the obligation by bringing money, power, coherent planning, and, most important, negotiating ability, to urban neighborhoods that have resisted, even fought, other efforts at improvement.

The college president, the minister from the community-based church, and the nonprofit alliances are termed *new leadership*. They are not new people approaching social problems for the first time. More often, they are seasoned individuals, groups, and organizations renewing the hunt for solutions to persistent problems of the urban and rural poor, and doing so in changing social, organizational, political, and regulatory environments.

An environment of communities with confusing definitions and conflicts over politics dictate the renewing and retooling of leadership. John Gardner, a student and analyst of leadership for more than twenty years, describes the difficulties in synthesizing plans among splintered interests:

"Leaders in this country today must cope with the fragmentation of the society into groups that have great difficulty in understanding one

another or agreeing on common goals.... All our leaders must spend part of their time dealing with polarization and building community."

The Evolution of New Leaders

The tasks of the new leadership—healing polarization and building community—are required now, in part, as a result of successful earlier reforms in our political structures and in our government's approaches to social-service delivery. Our cities have lost population and a disproportionate number of the families who remain need public assistance. Cities have met this need with increasingly professional social-service delivery, less dependent on the charity and caring of family and neighbors and more reliant on government.

The nation's intent in the Civil Rights Act of 1968 to ensure equal opportunity has helped minorities become educated and take midlevel jobs. In unintended and unpredicted ways, the act also has encouraged minorities to leave the cities for the suburbs. This out-migration, coupled with the earlier exodus of white families, has deprived urban communities of young and energetic leaders who would have formed the new generation of leaders.

(Above) *Trinity College students in Hartford, CT, serve as mentors, tutors, and coaches at the campus-based Boys & Girls Club.* (Left) *The historic chapel of Trinity College looms in the background as construction continues at the Learning Corridor, the centerpiece of a $175 million neighborhood revitalization effort spearheaded by Trinity.*

New communities, often defined by ethnicity or race, now share urban leadership, and the new leaders struggle to unite the diverse groups.

The old leadership system prompted dissatisfaction because elites—often defined by social class, hereditary, wealth, and race—could dominate communities, offering little opportunity for change. Decisions frequently reflected patronage, ward politics, and platforms shaped by bosses; interest groups sometimes made deals outside the public view. Unionized employees held sway over public services. Choices were limited and new approaches could be viewed as radical, irresponsible, and inherently opposed to the status quo and to mainstream interests.

Reform has shown that creating new leaders requires not just overcoming status-quo-leadership. Creating responsive new leadership requires a constituency's steady commitment to improvement.

In the nineties, a new cadre of leaders has emerged from the citizenry and from corporate, religious, and civic organizations. These groups demand diversity in leadership, service improvements, and results-oriented management. Effective demands have been made for:

- **Responsiveness.** Increased accountability at all levels, with emphasis on local accountability.

- **Diversity.** More diverse services, diverse representation, and more equitable participation in the services delivery.

- **Honesty.** More accountability at all levels of government as the most effective check on corrupt practices, patronage, and conflicts of interest.

- **Results.** Higher quality of services at all levels and in all aspects of public service, understood as requiring higher levels of professionalism.

- **Technical excellence.** Application of new results-oriented management.

- **Equity.** Public goods, resources, and infrastructure provided equitably, with strong commitments to meeting the needs of the poor, minorities, inner cities, and other marginalized communities.

As a result of these demands and incremental reforms many urban governance systems have moved (or at least are trying to move) toward:

- **Service with results.** More professional and disciplined public services with high-stakes consequences for failure and for even the appearance of any conflict of interest.

- **New politics.** Political leadership that is less committed to party, organization, or ideology and more accountable to broad constituencies of supporters.

- **Accountability.** Close scrutiny and monitoring of all aspects of public activity, backed by law and the courts.

- **Civil society partnerships.** Increasingly influential, well-established and professionally managed civil society organizations have emerged as quasi-governmental entities.

New demands have resulted in professional bureaucracies and regulatory and advisory bodies managing our public services. These professionals offer advantages and can effectively address valid concerns.

Enter new leaders determined to introduce flexibility. The large faith-based organizations intend to use both their private resources and public funds to employ professional staff and coordinate large numbers of volunteers. They display an ability to operate without a mandate from voters or even from the communities in which they work, and they are not limited by as many regulations as are bureaucracies. Established colleges and non-profit foundations, such as Trinity College and the Southside Alliance of which it is a member, intend to stimulate the coordination needed for solid planning for community revitalization. The institution's power, resources, and prestige enable it to bypass lines of authority and establish new relations to build structures.

The new leaders must be sensitive to regulatory necessity, establish solid community commitment to revitalization programs, and build communities as well as buildings. The way the new leaders relate to their communities and constituents, define the goals or mission, and exercise their considerable power, remains a large question,

the answer to which may determine the ultimate
success of the town-gown initiative and the
leadership by the college.

Several examples of the new leadership stand
out, mostly because of their capacity to forge a
common vision enabling stakeholders to work
together. Their successes point to a need for leaders
who collaborate effectively with communities and,
even more critical, for communities to learn to
work effectively with the new leaders.

The Town-Gown, Public-Private Alliance: What Works?

Stories are legion about the conflict between universities and other institutions and the communities
surrounding their campuses. The students take the
parking spaces, drive up rents, and disturb the peace,
while the administration buys up land, builds inap-
propriately massive structures, and pays no taxes.
At the same time, the university houses experts on
urban planning, sociology, and governance.

Obviously, Trinity College President Evan S.
Dobelle has a different vision of his college's role in
the town-and-gown dynamic. In the struggle to
revitalize the cities, he says, "Colleges and universities must do more than comment from the safety
of the sidelines. They must enter the battle and
they must lead."

True to his word, President Dobelle has led his
elite private college into projects and coalitions
determined to conquer the problems in its section
of Hartford, Connecticut, the deeply troubled Frog
Hollow/Barry Square neighborhoods.

In January 1996, the college announced a comprehensive $175 million neighborhood-revitaliza-
tion initiative. The initiative links local institutions
in a coalition designed to "create a safe, viable,
and vibrant neighborhood that is also a central
hub of educational, health, family-support, and
economic-development activities." The coalition—
the Southside Institutions Neighborhood
Alliance—broke ground in 1997 for the Learning
Corridor, a sixteen-acre development with new
schools, homes, and businesses. In 1999, Trinity
opened a club on campus for six- through twelve-
year-olds. Trinity students assist at the club,
operated by the Boys and Girls Clubs of Hartford,
through work-study programs, internships, and
volunteer opportunities.

THE REWARDS OF TOWN-GOWN ALLIANCES

A community of shared values. Trinity College could have chosen to continue as
an isolated academic community. Dobelle, however, has developed with the
College's trustees, alumni, and students a commitment to a more inclusive community—one that has even embraced youth from the surrounding neighborhoods.

Strength to collaborate. Trinity College formed and joined the Southside Institutions Neighborhood Alliance and, through this larger collaboration, managed to
influence the integrated development created by the local institutions, the city,
and the school system. Dobelle understood the Southside communities suffered
not just a shortage of housing, not just crime, not just a lack of access to education. Rather, problems stem from a complex, interconnected web of conditions.
Dobelle used the strength and prestige of the college to convene work sessions
with community residents and service providers and to remind nonprofit institutions of their "obligations" to the neighborhoods they occupy. The result has
been the innovative Learning Corridor—with its many funders and developers—
and the determination of the Alliance to design and implement projects to make
the communities stronger and healthier.

The Trinity College story could be read as one
of bricks and mortar, of a well-endowed private
institution finally using its money to clean up the
surrounding neighborhoods and making the environment safer for its students.

Public-Private Partnerships: What Works?

Company towns are defined, and often controlled,
by their biggest employers. The town aesthetic, its
buildings and street and highway grids, is determined by the needs of the oil company, the manufacturer, or the retail giant. Citizens pick up a
major part of the tab for the new sewer and road
systems as a hedge on current and future jobs.
Business failures, mergers, and the relocation of
corporations can leave the town, not only in debt,
but also with vacant buildings and unneeded
infrastructure.

Charlotte, North Carolina, has created a much
more collaborative version of the company town.
After bank mergers in 1998, Charlotte became the
headquarters of Bank of America and First Union,
and the second largest financial center in the
nation. The international and national strength of
Bank of America made it an improbable partner
in a major reshaping of the city. Yet, by all reports,
the developments have been spurred by intense
planning and an effective collaboration between
city officials and the city's powerful corporate

(Top) *Construction site of the Learning Corridor at Trinity College in Hartford, CT.* (Bottom) *The professional team of the Community Building Initiative of Charlotte, NC, works to improve racial relations in Charlotte and Mecklenburg County through dialogue and strategies for solutions to problems confronting the community.*

partners. Charlotte Mayor Patrick McCrory and other city officials, in collaboration with the chief executive officers of Charlotte's major corporations, guide what would otherwise be a jumble of projects: offices, condominiums, apartment buildings, town houses, green spaces, rebuilt neighborhoods, renovated historic houses, and overhauled public housing. The city has even built a sports stadium on a formerly contaminated industrial site.

Hugh L. McColl, Jr., chief executive of Bank of America, in a 1999 speech for the International Downtown Association, urged governments and corporations to share leadership decisions not only among themselves, but also among community

residents; define goals and focus on shared strengths, not shortcomings.

Philanthropies and Corporations in Concert: What Works?

Corporations have always been counted on more for the donations that provide goodwill for the corporation rather than for a coherent community revitalization plan. The foundation roughly followed the vision of its founder, building museums, library reading rooms, and other community programs. Even large donations had little impact on the community as a whole.

New leadership today in the corporate and philanthropic communities reflects new community thinking about social progress: Efforts must be long-term and strategic. Corporations and foundations are joining with public-sector agencies and institutions, like universities and labor unions, to launch major community programs. A realistic assessment of the financial resources needed for community development in Detroit led the Kresge Foundation to seek partners to leverage a $3 million investment. The Foundation finally secured $10.5 million to finance the Detroit Community Development Funders' Collaborative to help Community Development Corporations to launch affordable housing and commercial efforts.

Today, the philanthropic community has begun to use its skills at gathering, convening, packaging, and investing to support community projects that cover all aspects of a problem and, thus, has more hope of facilitating social improvement. For instance, the Ford Foundation joined with corporations and other funders to support the Adolfina Villanueva Child Development Center, a project including daycare, social services, speech therapy, and coordination with job training.

Corporations have realized it is rare to maintain viable downtowns without constructing viable neighborhoods. Cleveland Tomorrow, a broad collaboration of local corporations, was formed "to give something back to the communities where our employees live and where our service stations and convenience stores are located," says Steven Percy, CEO of Cleveland-based BP Oil, in a recent Ford Foundation report. The corporate partners of Cleveland Tomorrow have to-date leveraged over $122 million in direct investments.

The corporations realize business benefits by revitalizing inner-city neighborhoods because healthy neighborhoods improve the city and the region. Foundations recognize strategic giving increases their effective giving power.

Faith-based Organizations Assume New Leadership Roles

Inner-city churches, like traditional corporate leaders, also often acted outside the stage of their surrounding communities. Too frequently, the aging congregation members have moved to other communities, to return to their minister only on Sundays. Church neighbors experience the traffic jams caused by the double-parked cars, but acquire little wealth from the collection box or from the church enterprises. The pastors and elders minister to the immediate congregation and scarcely attempt to provide leadership in or to collaborate with their surrounding communities.

Faith-based organizations, churches, or coalitions of congregations or groups, often with ecumenical missions (including many inner-city churches), are rebuilding this church-community dynamic. Pastors, ministers, and governing boards have asked their congregations to expand their organizations' missions to include leadership in community revitalization, by overseeing construction of

STEPS TO CORPORATE-COMMUNITY PARTNERSHIP

Listen to each other. "In a rush to get things done, we have not always worked hard enough to make sure that all our citizens—newcomers and old-hands alike—have had an opportunity to have a say in how our city moves forward. No great idea will work—in the long run—if it doesn't take into account the needs of the whole community." The public/private environment should be marked by openness to all ideas and civic debate.

Define goals, have a plan. "Charlotte has a twenty-year plan—a draft plan—not having a plan guarantees fighting the same battles over and over again."

Leverage strength and avoid intergroup confrontation. "Respect each other's expertise. Business leaders, I am told, can be pushy and aggressive. Well, as much as we may not like it, we need to be patient with the political process of public debate. Public money is at stake, and elected officials have a sworn duty to use resources wisely." At the same time, Charlotte's public officials have also been willing to trust the investment and risk guidance of their corporate partners.

—Hugh McColl Jr., CEO, Bank of America,
 for the International Downtown Association

housing for low-income families or launching education programs. Some have hired professional staff, commenced social-service delivery projects, and coordinated large-scale volunteer ventures.

Governments rely more on community-based private providers for social service delivery, and now view faith-based organizations as efficient, effective, and compassionate in healing social problems such as addiction, unwanted pregnancies, homelessness, and poverty. Further, church leaders assert that their congregations, unlike public agencies, can instill the values, social

Dr. Francis Lawrence, president of Rutgers University, looks on as LEAP Academy students in Camden, NJ, practice on PSE&G-donated computers. PSE&G's New Millennium Fund provides educational technology for children and their families in New Jersey's inner cities.

MAXIMIZE CORPORATE AND FOUNDATION EFFECTIVENESS

Leverage strength and increase impact. The corporations focus on their strengths: strategic planning and financial packaging. The foundations use their ability to analyze, to convene both community and corporate groups, and to form partnerships to develop a coherent approach to social improvement.

Define goals. The partners involved in Cleveland Tomorrow, the Detroit Community Development Funders' Collaborative, and the Adolfina Villanueva Child Development Center were able to participate in more than one-off projects. The combination of the partners' skills and resources resulted in long-term, sustainable projects.

The Langenheim house on Liverpool Street in Manchester before it was restored by the Pittsburgh History and Landmarks Foundation. In addition to preserving historic landmarks, the Foundation develops downtown business centers in partnership with the City of Pittsburgh.

sanctions, and guidelines arguably missing in the lives of the urban poor.

Congress and states have earmarked ample funds for faith-based organizations. For example, in 1999, U.S. Department of Housing and Urban Development introduced the Super NOFA program, designed to "connect community and faith-based non-profit (sic) organizations with HUD funding." In the same year, Governor Christine Todd Whitman awarded New Jersey's first grants under the Faith-Based Community Development Initiative: $3.6 million in grants distributed among thirty-seven faith-based organizations to finance neighborhood revitalization and social-service programs.

The opportunities for and the invitation to faith-based organizations to provide new leadership in community revitalization are evident. To become effective, leaders in rebuilding our inner-city communities, churches, mosques, and synagogues must:

• Work to create a community contiguous to their congregation or membership—affirming values and developing unifying goals among diverse groups.

• Balance the traditional service and ministry to the poor with new obligations to include those served in their new community, involving all the actual participants in envisioning and guiding community revitalization.

• Moderate advocacy for religious absolutes to avoid intergroup confrontations and form effective coalitions with communities of dissimilar faiths but with a shared stake in the community welfare.

Faith-based organizations vary in their approach to spirituality and in the structure, motivation, professional preparation, management skills, and capacity to lead. Their advances in communities reflect their unique compositions and belief structures.

Faith-based Corporations as Leaders

The Allen African Methodist Episcopal Church, a 10,000-member congregation in Jamaica, Queens, boasts a successful parochial school; it has transformed neighborhoods, built housing for the elderly, and forged partnerships with government agencies to perform social services for the community. The church takes in nearly $6 million a year in collections and employs more than 800 people while administering millions of local, state, and federal dollars for social-service programs, such as teenage pregnancy prevention and daycare.

The Allen African Methodist Episcopal Church is a corporation headed by a charismatic leader, Reverend Floyd Flake. Similar megachurches, with numerous different denominations and congregations of every racial and ethnic mix, are found in most U.S. cities. The leadership structure encourages followers who form a large volunteer core and who have an opportunity to reexamine their mission weekly. The financial and membership strength provides a strong platform from which the church leaders can initiate and lead social-service and community-revitalization programs.

Reverend Flake built up a megachurch and effectively leads a complex corporation. He resigned from Congress in 1997 midway through his sixth term as a representative to work full time in Queens. Knowledgeable about government programs, Flake uses church money to leverage government dollars. For instance, on city-provided land, supported by low-interest loans and rent-back incentives, Flake built and sold 110 duplexes to first-time home buyers with incomes less than $35,000.

The Industrial Areas Foundation (IAF) has introduced the voting power of a congregation into a public discussion once dominated by spirituality and service. The IAF claims it fosters more than fifty church-based and interracial organizations stretching from East Brooklyn to the east side of Los Angeles.

The Washington, D.C.-based Washington Interfaith Network, an IAF organization, intends to influence political choice and guide the flow of public money. During the 1998 District mayoral elections, WIN demanded the candidates pledge to hire 900 foot- and bike-patrol officers, make $30 million available for after-school programs, allot $3 million for ten WIN after-school programs, commit to the construction of 1,000 additional low-income homes, and institute a Living Wage Ordinance.

The winning candidate pledged *yes* to each demand and now is working to make good on his promises. However, the demands were not necessarily from the whole community. For instance, public-housing professionals and potential host communities object to the economic segregation imposed by the construction of 1,000 low-income

CHALLENGES OF RELIGION-INSPIRED COMMUNITY DEVELOPMENT

To develop communities of shared values. Faith-based groups will have to work with both their members and the nonaligned poor. The Mid-South Foundation reports a great desire to do so on the part of some small black churches and a willingness to learn how to lead and serve a community larger than the congregation.

To find unifying goals or missions in the midst of diversity. By entering into public service, the faith-based organizations tacitly agree to work with all the groups that constitute their public. The IAF Robin-Hood approach—aggressively taking from the nonresponsive civil servants and giving more directly to the poor—could result in a more just distribution of public money. Their test of leadership, however, is whether their agitation advances from coercion to productive dialogue with other stakeholders. Is there room for intergroup collaboration or will these groups be yet another chapter in divisive political positioning?

To include followers in leadership tasks. Faith-based organizations often have strong charismatic leaders—the traditional pastor shepherding the flock. Reverend Flake shares the challenges of other charismatic and influential leaders who head large corporations. He must ensure that communications and ownership of development originate from all segments of the communities he leads.

homes in a single settlement. It is yet to be seen if this organization's demands will be met or will be seen as coercion and as an unsound means of developing a social agenda.

Other members of the Interfaith Network claim success. Ernesto Cortés, Jr., IAF's Southwest region supervisor and organizer of the San Antonio-based Communities Organized for Public Service (COPS), reported in the May 1996 edition of the *Boston Review* that COPS provides "an alternative strategy and an alternative public space" and has "brought over $800 million of streets, parks, housing, sidewalks, libraries, clinics, streetlights, drainage, and other infrastructure to the poor neighborhoods of the inner city." COPS "agitated" for the $800 million from federal and local public sources, using its "faith/power/politics" muscle on behalf of the poor.

Faith-based organizations—their emergence as direct-service providers receiving public monies for community betterment—are new phenomena. Their ability to lead long-lasting urban revitalization depends on their responsiveness to their followers and to their ability to build equitable relationships with other leaders.

THE POWER OF MEDIA LEADERSHIP

Explaining key to a community of shared values. Instead of castigating the public for its failure to participate, the *Journal Star* in Peoria, IL, uncovered the reasons for the decline in civic leadership and reported its findings. Armed with the explanations, individuals and groups were better prepared to take action.

Sharing leadership tasks. *Star* editor Brimeyer reports that a delegation of businessmen and other civic leaders asked him to apply for the Pew funds and develop a project to focus the city and region on the leadership crisis. Average readership rose during the series, and public meetings were extremely well-attended. In many ways, followers were pushing Brimeyer to lead.

Building coalitions leverages strengths. The *Star* established the basis for action and enabled the Illinois Central College to respond to citizen requests for training.

Focusing a mass audience. The *Springfield (MO) News-Leader* forced recognition of a serious problem by its sustained emphasis and by committing most of its resources to the story.

The Media as Leader

The public blames the media for its alienation and indifference to their communities and their politics. The media's generation of negative stories and its fixation on scandals, critics assert, persuade the public it has no control and, thus, no reason to be involved. In response, newspaper and TV editors claim that standards of objectivity require them to report facts, limit analysis, and refrain from openly advocating actions except on the editorial page. In short, the media often chooses not to lead, but to tell the news.

Numerous local media across the country are rejecting the extremes of both objectivity and public involvement, and are assuming leadership by exercising *civic journalism*. The Pew Center for Civic Journalism helped create the notion and now finances community-media civic alliances. The Pew website [www.pewcenter.org] succinctly states the philosophy:

"Journalism has an obligation to public life, an obligation that goes beyond just telling the news or unloading lots of facts. The way we do our journalism affects the way public life goes. Journalism can help empower a community or it can help disable it."

The *Journal Star* in Peoria, Illinois, has taken a leadership role, first by explaining the news, then emphasizing the needs and obligations of maintaining governance structures, and finally by providing a platform for collaboration among those individuals and organizations that could meet those needs.

Star editor Jack Brimeyer could not ignore the dwindling number of civic leaders when, in 1995, no candidates filed to run for mayor. Not only were elected offices vacant, but also, civic associations and nonprofits reported a deficit of volunteers and willing board members. Brimeyer ran a series titled "Leadership Challenge: Building a New Generation of Leaders." Rather than simply report the decline of civic culture, the *Star* openly proffered a strategy to improve the quality and quantity of leadership and civic involvement in Peoria. With support from the Pew Center for Civic Journalism, the paper's management conducted focus groups and civic meetings and identified five obstacles to leadership: access, training, knowledge, time, and rewards.

One finding commanded attention: Eighty-five percent of citizens surveyed said they would become involved "if someone encouraged them and showed them the ropes." Illinois Central College Center for Non-Profit Excellence, which trains nonprofit administrators to conduct meetings, work with the media, delegate, build consensus, and develop budgets, created a Neighborhood College to teach leadership skills to neighborhood activists.

The Neighborhood College began training Peorian leaders who are not necessarily Junior League members or bank presidents. In the end, eight candidates ran for mayor following the Leadership Challenge series, and the city elected a retired businessman. The nonpartisan composition of this community-wide collaboration allowed the *Star* to enter the civic sphere and retain the independence vital to its position as opinion and news leader.

Local media have enormous power to encourage, suggest, and focus the attention of the community, just as they have tremendous power to oppose. The *Springfield News-Leader*, in Springfield, Missouri, led by giving the same emphasis to the growing juvenile crime crisis as it would to a major disaster. Editor Randy Hammer saw the problem developing slowly, not dramatically, insidiously becoming business-as-usual. Hammer decided to assign the story to all his reporters and give it the space and emphasis usually reserved for the state basketball play-offs. Hammer sent thirty-seven reporters and photographers to cover youths, for one day, during the hours of three to seven p.m. when the biggest increase in crime was occurring.

Springfield News-Leader readers got a jolt the next day when thirty stories with bylines from twenty reporters and thirteen special correspondents, ranging in age from nine to seventeen, provided painful details about teen activities during the period of lowest adult supervision. Hammer followed up the "When Kids are Kids" exposé with "The Good Community" series that ran for twenty-eight days straight and featured a citizen editorial board; community ombudsman; collaboration with local TV, radio stations, and the local college paper; and the "Good Community Fair." The campaign erased community complacency and kick-started programs and volunteerism for teens.

Media reaches, and can unite, an urban center's fragmented communities. Media has a tremendous ability to draw these communities closer through shared information and understanding.

JOHN GARDNER'S TASKS OF LEADERSHIP:

- **Envisioning goals.** Setting goals that define the group or galvanize it around a solution or unify an internally divided organization into a group.

- **Affirming values.** Articulating shared norms, expectations, and purposes.

- **The regeneration of values.** "Rediscovering the living elements in its own tradition and adapting them to present realities."

- **Motivating.** Tapping shared motives "that serve the purposes of collective action in pursuit of shared goals."

- **Managing.** "Leadership and management is not the same thing, but they overlap." Leaders plan and set priorities; organize and build institutions; keep the system functioning; set agendas and make decisions; and exercise political judgment.

- **Achieving workable unity.** Dealing with polarization and building communities.

- **Trust.** Inspiring trust in themselves.

- **Explaining.** Explaining what and why followers are being asked to do something.

- **Serving as a symbol.** Symbolizing collective identity and continuity.

- **Representing the group.** "Carrying on dealings with external systems."

- **Renewing.** "Reinterpreting values that have been encrusted with hypocrisy, corroded by cynicism or simply abandoned;" finding new ways for the group to work around and through outmoded procedures and habits of thought.

* John W. Gardner, former Secretary of Health, Education and Welfare, founding chair of Common Cause, cofounder of The Independent Sector and former director of Shell Oil Company, the New York Telephone Company, American Airlines, and Time, Inc., is the author of *On Leadership, Excellence, Self-Renewal, No Easy Victories, the Recovery of Confidence, In Common Cause and Morale.*

NEW LEADERSHIP CRITERIA

In the fragmented environment of urban America, the new leadership must create vigorous relationships between leaders and their followers. This often means engagement with a nebulous public made up of groups and stakeholders that appear to have little in common. The new leadership must be creative enough to:

- Design and implement an agenda informed and supported by the community;
- Identify unifying goals and missions;
- Build leadership structures that promote shared decision making; and
- Strengthen coalitions to avoid intergroup confrontations.

The successful leaders also will sustain and provide for the continuation of their organizations by preparing new leadership cadres.

1. Share power with stakeholders to increase sustainability.

Increasingly, urban leaders make a priority of capturing and channeling the intelligence, creativity, and energy of their communities. When stakeholders explore new ideas and programs together, they find new ways to use community resources and power to solve persistent problems. Power sharing often requires leaders to transmit skills, such as goal setting, and engage in strategic planning and brainstorming to enable stakeholders to set meaningful agendas.

The leaders of Rochester, New York and Chattanooga, Tennessee engage citizens in tackling their persistent problems. Municipal officials could have employed a gaggle of specialists who would have provided technically credible recommendations. Instead, they looked to their communities. Chattanooga, for example, asked more than 1,700 residents to sketch their vision of their "new" city. Rochester moved further in its Neighbors Building Neighborhoods program by incorporating community visions into the city's comprehensive plan. Leaders in both cities report enduring participation in the resulting development plans, a marked decrease in cynicism, and a quickening of citizen involvement.

The Greater Kansas City Community Foundation engages the region, three counties on the Missouri side and two in Kansas, in philanthropy, not only by receiving aid, but also by programming and providing it. Foundation President Janice Kreamer defines the Foundation's role as a "convener of citizens and organizations around

local pressing issues . . . problem solvers to address critical community needs."

The Foundation and its affiliated trusts, a major donor with combined assets of more than $600 million from hundreds of individuals, families, businesses, and community organizations, created 500 charitable funds and planned their uses. Community volunteers participate in the Board of Directors and must build consensus with other board members to determine which projects the philanthropy will fund.

"We believe that the well-being of each citizen is connected to that of every other and that the vitality of a community is determined by the quality of those relationships," Kreamer says, as she explains the Foundation's provision of small individual donor accounts and the convening of annual donors' meetings.

2. Make public participation real, fun and useful.

Leaders, while insisting on power sharing by stakeholders, must work out how to encourage public participation in planning, development, and implementation. Each potential mechanism for participation has a purpose as well as benefits and limitations. Public hearings and other gatherings allow policymakers to obtain information and listen to public opinion. The public comes together to exchange ideas and opinions with other citizens, and policymakers use the information obtained to mold policy. However, articulate populations accustomed to public speaking can dominate these forums. Battling community groups can transform a civil gathering into a hostile confrontation, both unpleasant and unrewarding for noncombatants.

Increasingly, leaders not willing to accept mere symbolic participation facilitate brainstorming sessions and focus groups to ensure all parts of the community are heard. At the recent Washington, D.C. Citizens' Summit, funded both by the District government and a consortium of local foundations—Wolfensohn Family Foundation, Eugene and Agnes E. Meyer Foundation, The Fannie Mae Foundation, The Annie E. Casey Foundation, and The George Washington University Center for Excellence in Municipal Management—organizers used electronic polling and instantaneous reporting of small groups' discussions to hear all participants. Dramatic big-screen projection of report-out sessions, a continental breakfast and lunches served by tuxedo-clad waiters, and the opportunity to talk about topics dear to their communities kept nearly 3,000 residents participating in the District's planning process for more than six hours on a Saturday.

The Charlotte-Mecklenburg public schools began using focus groups in the early nineties in an effort to ensure more broad-based participation in school policymaking. The focus groups, mostly paid for by local foundations, enable school officials to gather information from its stormy public hearings over court-mandated changes in busing and attendance zones, as well as from representative parents talking in quieter settings.

Whether participants of the D.C. Summit or of the Charlotte-Mecklenburg focus groups feel that their involvement is real and useful depends on how their information is treated. One Summit participant decided the city's commitment to the Summit goals would determine its success.

3. Continue communication with public participants.

At the D.C. Citizen Summit, eighty-five percent of the participants indicated through electronic polling that they, not city bureaucrats, were the most responsible for the progress of the District. Sixty-three percent asked to be included in future planning exercises. The mayor has at least two thousand citizens who now expect they will be told about options and decision points and will be involved in making those decisions.

4. Depersonalize leadership.

Participation, in order to be more than just a feel-good exercise, must result in ownership and support of a process or result. The "Citizens' Summit" is more valuable than a "Mayor's Summit" if the goal is to engage citizens in planning for their neighborhoods. Successful collaborations and partnerships adopt the goals and objectives of the team, not only those of the partnership or collaborative's most powerful member.

5. Develop strategic options grounded in economic realities.

Leaders must make clear to their public the trade-offs and choices required to obtain the money and resources needed to implement their vision. Frequently, this means organizing partnerships, coalitions, and alliances to obtain the financing. It often means debt financing and all the risk inherent in debt. For example, the Ford Foundation's Program-related investments (PRIs) are usually loans, although they may also be loan guarantees or equity investments. Although organizations in low-income communities can obtain needed capital to finance important projects, the participating community must know that PRIs are recoverable, debts to be paid.

Ambitious projects frequently are needed to make the progress envisioned. Before the new benefits are enjoyed, the participating community may incur significant costs, taxes, and lost services. The community may require help from consultants and other employees to organize collaboration between foundations or locate credit, leverage additional financing, and accumulate assets.

6. Renew leadership.

Leadership evolves and must be renewed, requiring each generation to identify, train, and develop new leaders. Leaders come from surprising places. The deacon of a small church in a desperately poor southern town can be the motivating force needed to open a day care center or bring in workforce training. The incredibly busy CEO of a multinational corporation may be just the right person to lead a city-wide discussion of what growth is desirable.

Many new leadership organizations recruit candidates and provide leadership training. The Interfaith Network, for example, has developed a structure in which members can take on increasingly responsible positions within the organization as they receive training. The Neighborhood College, established by Illinois Central College, provides training for self-identified neighborhood leaders.

As the new leadership matures, the enduring organizations will:

- Honor, reward, and support their leaders, not for their personal characteristics or charisma, but for their efforts to implement the collective agenda.
- Provide formal processes and institutions for the renewal and/or retirement of leaders and for selection and transition to new leadership.
- Nurture a network of civic trustees—residents that form the backbone of civic organizations, government agencies, business and professional associations, volunteer groups, and cultural organizations.

New leadership today in the corporate and philanthropic communities reflects the new community thinking about social progress: Efforts must be long-term and strategic.

Janice Kreamer: Nurturing Donor-Leaders in Kansas City

Janice Kreamer, executive director of the Greater Kansas City Community Foundation, has created one of the leading community foundations in America based on a simple principle: Rather than simply accept and direct donations to programs donors designate, the Foundation also leads some donors in understanding and solving community problems. Kreamer believes stimulating donor participation and leadership will ultimately increase charitable giving in the five-county Kansas City region.

have participated in charitable giving—is an important objective of the Greater Kansas City enterprise. For Kreamer, it is not enough for people to donate to the Foundation. More important is the transformation of donors from passive, reactive players to engaged participants, involved and committed to community causes and issues.

Six years ago, the Foundation dramatically altered its role in the community. The leadership recognized an obligation to harvest what Kreamer viewed as an enormous venture capital pool. The Foundation decided that if donors simply gave money and allowed the Foundation to carry on with its work, in solo, the Foundation would not maximize the effectiveness of the venture-capital pool. Now, the Foundation does not simply make giving easy by being flexible and effective; it also

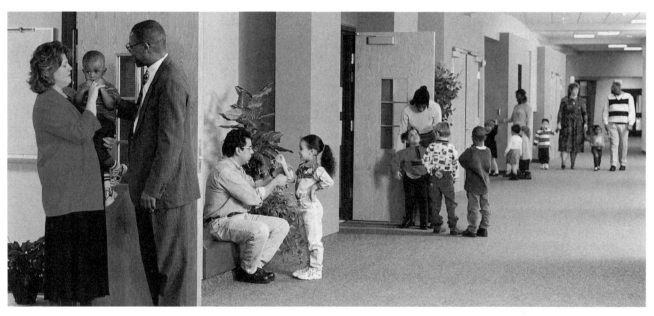

The Francis Child Development Institute is a major program of Penn Valley Community College. The program works to improve the quality of childcare in Kansas City and receives support from both the private and public community, including the Greater Kansas City Community Foundation.

The strategy paid off last year when the foundation ranked first among community foundations for gifts received and third for grants distributed. Yet, Kansas City is only the thirty-second largest market in the country. With assets of more than $600 million, Greater Kansas City Community Foundation is among the fastest growing of 550 community foundations. In 1998, the Foundation awarded more than $50 million in grants to 1,350 organizations.

But the real story, according to Kreamer, is not the amount of money raised and granted; it is the number of people becoming involved in the community. Involving new donors—who may never

creates a dynamic relationship between the donor and the community. The Foundation uses staff and board expertise to identify the needs of the Kansas City region and connect donors to new ideas and trends they may not have considered.

Kreamer envisions a continuum of giving that expands the initiatives donors care about into a wide-ranging set of community solutions. For example, a donor may give to a traditional agency like the YMCA or the Boys and Girls Club. The Foundation will make the donor aware of how much idle time children have on their hands, both before and after school and during the summer vacation, expanding the donor's awareness of children's broad needs for programs. With the new knowledge, the donor may decide to open schools or finance new alternatives for children who return to empty homes after school and watch television. These activities not only ensure a safe environment for children; they also contribute to youths' future development.

Although the Foundation remains committed to donor-designated giving, it also exercises its own leadership based on its knowledge of the community. Kreamer is quick to point out that leading versus simply adapting to donors' needs is not an either-or situation. The community leadership role involves only the targeted use of unrestricted dollars that, despite representing only a small fraction of the donor-designated dollars, can make a significant difference in the community. The Foundation leadership has proven to be a catalyst to help solve some of the city's community-development logjams. Kreamer is especially proud of the Foundation's "ability to proactively identify issues, apply grant dollars with staff and board leadership, and form collaborations and coalitions to move community change forward."

The Foundation has adopted a regional-affiliate strategy that divides its giving and granting among counties in the extensive Kansas City region. Each affiliate has committed its own funds and selected its own board of directors to expand charitable giving by reaching out to friends and contacts. The Foundation conceives joint projects with the affiliates, although it respects their independence and tries to avoid dominating the debate about programs.

The Greater Kansas City Community Foundation also seeks constructive relations with the local Heart of America United Way. Staff and board leadership of both organizations work to create an effective division of labor rather than duplicating activities or competing for turf. The partners engage in constructive dialogue and strategizing. For example, Kreamer's foundation will help finance the United Way's needs assessment in 2000. The Foundation will use the document to help inform its own donors about community needs. Kreamer believes this shared product will help market United Way to the Foundation donors and at the same time avoid duplication of effort. Together the development staffs of both organizations also work to build the United Way's endowment, and the Foundation shares its expertise in

planned and deferred giving with United Way. Ultimately, it takes senior staff and board leadership to avoid needless and detrimental competition. The experience in Kansas City may be a model for the rest of the nation where the combined strength of community foundations and the local United Way might work magic in improving quality of life.

Kreamer and the Greater Kansas City Community Foundation ascribe success to a clear definition of purpose: Every community needs a foundation to build bridges, take risks, plan for the long-term, foster collaborations, and cultivate a base of donor-inspired leaders. Kreamer believes these leaders will become a force for creating and stabilizing the community's social venture-capital infrastructure.

Janice Kreamer, executive director of the Greater Kansas City Community Foundation (second from the right), leads donors in understanding and solving community problems and has increased charitable giving in the five-county Kansas City region.

Spreading the Gospel of Community Self-Help

LEADERSHIP
PROFILE

Reverend Floyd Flake preaches a message of economic independence and communal responsibility, reflecting a growing pragmatism among African American religious leaders. From the pulpit of the Allen African Methodist Episcopal (A.M.E.) Church in the St. Albans neighborhood of Queens, New York, Flake embodies the values and work ethic of his congregation, one of the nation's largest black middle-class communities. The congregation, which built the new $23 million church, tithed more than $5 million for church enterprises, which translates into nearly $1,000 per adult.

During his stint as a U.S. representative from 1986 to 1998, Flake, a Democrat, championed initiatives to revitalize urban commercial and residential communities. He authored and brokered bipartisan support for the Bank Enterprise Act of 1993.

That provision of the Community Development Financial Institutions Act includes incentives for financial institutions to make market-oriented investments in destabilized urban and rural economies. The law has resulted in increased capital flows to distressed communities.

Another plank in Flake's political platform, however, raises controversy among African-American leaders, civil libertarians, and teachers' unions: He favors government vouchers for private schools—a pet project of Congressional Republicans. Flake founded the 500-student Christian School at his church to address the inadequate education and low expectations that characterize many black inner-city schools.

Flake knows from personal experience the importance of education. His parents instilled the work ethic and encouraged a philosophy of self-improvement among their thirteen children that reflects the ideology of Booker T. Washington. He earned an undergraduate degree from Ohio's

Wilberforce University and a doctorate of ministry degree from the United Theological Seminary in Dayton, Ohio.

Since his arrival in Queens in 1976, Flake has helped transform Allen Church into a community-development powerhouse. The church created a 300-unit senior citizen housing project, renovated a dilapidated block of storefronts into a clean and thriving strip mall, and purchased a fleet of luxury buses. Allen Church now has an annual budget of $25 million, and church-owned enterprises employ 825 people, making it the second largest African-American employer in New York City behind the TLC Beatrice Corporation.

Allen Church works with the city's Community Development Agency, reflecting Flake's talent to form productive partnerships and coalitions. Project Student Community Action Learning Experience (SCALE) places Allen Christian School students in after-school community-service positions to cultivate their communal responsibility.

SCALE includes on-the-job training and job-readiness programs, equipping participants with skills and building their work ethic.

Flake's support for issues like school vouchers usually associated with conservative Republicans has not endeared him to his colleagues in the Congressional Black Caucus. He talked about balancing liberal social policy and conservative fiscal policy in an interview with the *Village Voice*:

"I can look at...communities as fields of opportunity, balancing a liberal voting record with conservative approaches to community development. I can see a real chance for building new models for urban change, of marrying the best elements of historic liberalism with conservative economic policy."
(*Village Voice*, February 17, 1998.)

To which, his congregation at Allen A.M.E. would probably respond: *Amen.*

(Above) *Reverend Floyd Flake, Pastor of the Allen African Methodist Episcopal Church in Jamaica, NY, preaches a message of economic independence and community responsibility.* (Opposite) *The Allen Christian School focuses on teaching basic education in a disciplined environment.* (Left) *The Allen Senior Citizens Complex provides housing and services for over 340 elderly and handicapped residents.*

Pittsburgh History and Landmarks Foundation

One Station Street, Suite 450
Pittsburgh, PA 15219-1134
www.phlf.org

Contact: Arthur D. Ziegler, Jr.,
President
412.471.5808

While preserving historic landmarks, the Pittsburgh History and Landmarks Foundation has restored and developed multiple downtown business centers.
Most cities support a historical society but few can claim possession of a historical foundation, particularly one as active as the Pittsburgh History and Landmarks Foundation. Established in 1964, the Foundation originally intended to save a Victorian neighborhood of 1,500 houses from alteration and destruction. In the last twenty-five years, the Foundation's mission has expanded to include some of the biggest downtown renewal projects in the history of Pittsburgh. The Foundation aims to alert residents to the value of historical architecture, to help organize public and private funding for preservation projects, and to intervene with city agencies to promote building preservation and renovation. The Foundation's accomplishments are amazing.

The Foundation proposed turning a deteriorating forty-acre railway complex into a mixed-use center to include dining, hotels, shopping, entertainment, and a river walk along the Monongahela. Not only would the development alleviate an eyesore, potentially it would also generate considerable income for the surrounding neighborhood. Yet the Foundation determined that the city should rehabilitate and retrofit the buildings, rather than demolish them and build anew.

In the beginning, investors were hard to find. No one expressed a belief that the project would work. Financiers were reluctant to invest in a mixed-use center. A cornerstone element—a hotel—

appeared particularly implausible because a river cut off the complex from the main part of the city. When the Foundation managed to secure funding from a separate family foundation, members met objections from the city-planning department. City planners saw no need for eight-foot-wide sidewalks, and viewed the antique low-level light fixtures as a security risk. The Foundation persisted in its aim to preserve the old buildings and fixtures while creating a pedestrian-friendly plaza. Other conflicts followed concerning shrubbery and signs, illustrating a deep ideological difference between the Foundation and the city planners.

Today, Station Square is the most-visited tourist attraction in Pittsburgh. The Square's Sheraton Hotel enjoys the highest occupancy rates in the city. An outdoor courtyard houses concerts, and a thriving tour-boat industry shuttles passengers across the river. The sidewalks are eight feet wide and historical elements such as industrial artifacts abound. The Foundation used no state, county, or city money in the development of Station Square, the largest downtown renewal project in the history of Pittsburgh. The Pittsburgh History and Landmarks Foundation's leadership provides an example of a nontraditional player acting as a development leader in a neighborhood or a city.

The Foundation now collaborates with the city on several development and renewal projects. A private Preservation Loan Fund has been established, providing money for architectural surveys, feasibility studies, and construction. The Foundation also provides educational programs for adults and children; members and non-members take advantage of the Foundation's walking tours, lectures, and events.

Urban Initiative
Public Service Electric & Gas

80 Park Plaza
Newark, NJ 07102-4194

Contact: Marion O'Neill,
Public Affairs Executive
973.430.7842

The Urban Initiative of the Public Service Electric & Gas Company (PSE&G) aims to revitalize the burned-out wards of its hometown, Newark by forming partnerships with other industries to build a telecommunications infrastructure and provide job training, child care, and other basic services. With its new program, the "Power of Commitment," PSE&G promotes the state's urban economic development and, in the process, has become a true community leader.

By serving as an intermediary between private companies and the public, PSE&G has focused on improving:

- **Quality of Life:** providing for safety, basic family needs, financial skills, training, child-care and after-school programs;
- **Transportation:** increasing access to services and amenities;
- **Environment:** air and water quality, environmental education;
- **Housing:** increasing the amount of low- and moderate-income housing; and
- **Education:** boosting job skills, job readiness, technology and infrastructure.

PSE&G has worked in one community at a time, beginning with its corporate headquarters, Newark. The company initiated partnerships among local residents, merchants, corporations, local and county governments, and social, civic and cultural organizations. In the South Ward district of Newark, PSE&G and its community partners attract new businesses and build the human-resource training capacity of the city's nonprofits. In partnership with AT&T, Microsoft, and the New Jersey Institute of Technology, PSE&G is building a technology infrastructure consisting of an extensive cable/telecommunications system, and training South Ward residents how to use it.

To address quality of life in the South Ward, PSE&G invited twenty nonprofit leaders to the Community Partners for Youth Program. At-risk youth and families now receive services such as childcare, GED classes, training in crisis-intervention and leadership development. The availability of affordable housing has increased, thanks to PSE&G's work with the Metropolitan Ecumenical Ministries, Episcopal Community Development Inc., and Muslim, Inc. PSE&G is also developing community-policing programs with the Newark Police Department and the Rutgers School of Criminal Justice.

PSE&G has measured its success by tracking the number of jobs and new businesses created, and surveying focus group members for their critical analysis. Since working in Newark, the company has expanded its Urban Initiative to six additional New Jersey cities. During a recent White House ceremony, President Bill Clinton recognized the Urban Initiative for its outstanding achievement in community service.

According to PSE&G's Al Koeppe, senior vice president, external affairs and corporate services, "The Urban Initiative starts from a simple premise–an enduring change must come from within the people who live in a community and understand its needs best. We listened and learned that if we had any chance of making a fundamental and lasting difference, we needed to approach the community model comprehensively–through economic and community development, education, and social services."

Brisbane Call Centre
Brisbane City Enterprises
Brisbane, Australia

Contact: Alan Hale,
Chief Executive Officer
bma@bce.au

Brisbane City Enterprises (BCE), a wholly owned subsidiary of the city government, created, and now manages a twenty-four hour, 365-day clearinghouse of information and services dubbed the Call Centre. By contracting with a private firm, the city has created a seamless service network for citizens.

City residents can call one number to access a real human being at Call Centre, rather than navigating the phone trees and electronic answering services endemic to most government bureaucracies. The city trains its 150 operators for eight weeks, learning much more than how to rout calls. Few callers are ever referred for further action. Instead, the operators themselves can answer almost any question—what to do about a downed power line, for example, or how to complete a tax form. If, in the odd case, further action is required, callers are given an estimated completion time.

Call Centre is a product of city manager Robert Carter and Jim Sorley of the Labor Party. The two formed a leadership team in an effort to achieve more efficient, customer-oriented government. The team first had to reorganize information and request-handling procedures throughout all city departments. They also had to design and standardize information forms. The result is a successful collaboration with the private firm of BCE. Based upon the Brisbane results, BCE now markets their product to other cities around the world.

Community Building Initiative
1043 East Morehead Street, Suite 204
Charlotte, NC 28204

Contact: Dianne English,
Director
704.333.2595

The Community Building Task Force works to unite divided races through mediation and dialogue. After a white police officer shot a black motorist in 1996, racial tensions ran high in Charlotte. Civic leaders recognized the community's need to discuss racial polarization. The Foundation for the Carolinas served as a neutral convener of a task force on race and ethnicity. The Foundation created The Community Building Task Force with its forty-five members representing the full diversity of Charlotte and of Mecklenburg County. Mecklenburg Ministries, an interfaith organization that advocates for compassion and justice, guided the development of the dialogue.

The Task Force developed and conducted fifteen community focus groups. Leaders also developed an inventory of the groups that work on race and justice issues. Efforts culminated with a Community Conference in December 1997 with more than 600 citizen participants. Recently, as part of Phase II, the Task Force has been renamed an "Initiative" in order to encourage more people to participate. The Initiative aims to:

• Organize action teams around issues identified at the 1997 conference;
• Encourage a broad-based dialogue and create public awareness activities within the community; and
• Promote collaboration with existing community organizations, institutions, and programs to work for community change.

Many communities facing racial tension focus either on racial dialogue or high-level problem-solving approaches. The Initiative intends to combine dialogue with research and education to produce new strategies for solutions. The intent is to influence individuals, groups, and institutions. Six teams each address planning and identify issues and leadership.

In addition to fostering dialogue, the Initiative published findings of research in three working documents on education, economics, and public safety. Leaders used the papers for building public awareness within civic departments and schools, and in the general public. Citizen volunteers donated more than 2,700 hours in developing solutions to problems that took time to solve because of their scope and complexity.

The Community Building Initiative incorporates lessons and addresses challenges as they emerge. Volunteers also understand that to be effective, Initiative teams have to make and maintain connections with community institutions and key community stakeholders. The Initiative incorporates institutional and organizational involvement and community participation to ensure the Task Force work will continue to engage the community in collaboration for racial harmony.

Asset-Based Community Development Institute

Institute for Policy Research,
Northwestern University
2040 Sheridan Rd
Evanston, IL 60208-4100

Contact: John Kretzmann,
John L. McKnight,
Codirectors
847.491.8711

The Asset-Based Community Development Institute (ABCD) compiles resources for community builders involved in the process of capacity-based initiatives, and helps them to identify, nurture, and mobilize neighborhood assets.

The ABCD Institute was established in 1995 by the Community Development Program at Northwestern's Institute for Policy Research to expand and implement the research of its co-directors, John Kretzmann and John L McKnight on capacity-building community development. By utilizing and disseminating the research of leaders, the ABCD Institute helps communities capitalize on proven capacity-building techniques.

The tremendous popularity of McKnight and Kretzmann's 1993 guidebook, *Building Communities from the Inside Out,* led to the creation of the center, which helps community organizations map their community resources. Assets include the unique capacities of residents; the availability of quality public schools, colleges, and universities; and distinctive historic or cultural institutions. The ABCD Institute receives continual feedback from diverse communities and provides information on successful strategies, innovations, and policy reforms.

Thirty ABCD Institute faculty members answer requests from community organizations, provide information for speeches and workshops, and as consultants to different groups, explain and illustrate asset-based community development as a useful strategy for neighborhood revitalization. These thirty researchers formerly worked in foundations, community groups, churches, universities, consulting groups, and health organizations in the United States and Canada. The Institute also has established an arsenal of tools to provide communities with technical assistance. In addition to a manual, the Institute creates videotapes of training procedures and workbooks about community economic development. ABCD also organizes electronic discussion groups where community builders across the nation can exchange strategies.

Decentralized Planning Model

City of Fort Wayne
One Main Street
Room 900
Fort Wayne, IN 46802
www.cityoffortwayne.org

Contact: Office of the Mayor,
219.427.1111

Community-Oriented Government (COG) creates citizen-leaders by placing them in direct contact with municipal employees and breaking down bureaucratic barriers to improve the quality of life in Fort Wayne's neighborhoods. In early 1998, neighborhood crime worried Fort Wayne neighborhood association president Lin Wilson. She arranged a meeting with several police officers, and, within two weeks, police made more than 150 arrests (for everything from speeding to drug trafficking) in her neighborhood. Troublemakers were put on notice: Crime would not be tolerated. Illegal activity began to drop off.

COG maintains government should operate with direct input from the citizens it serves. COG encourages residents to take concerns to one of 227 organized neighborhood associations. Working through these neighborhood groups over the last three years, residents have identified problems, such as graffiti, abandoned vehicles, and weed growth—and worked one-on-one with city government employees to solve their problems.

Four area partnerships address problems affecting multiple neighborhoods. The partnerships involve leaders who meet monthly to discuss, prioritize, and address problems within their quadrant of the city. The partnerships bring unsolved problems to the Community Services Council, a group of leaders from government, faith-based institutions, social service agencies, businesses, schools, and neighborhoods.

The COG helped Oxford neighborhood residents clear empty, overgrown lots. The neighborhood code enforcement officials could not notify owners to mow the lots. Instead of paying contractors to mow, the city paid Oxford neighborhood residents. The new program worked so well that other neighborhoods took part. Together they mowed 846 lots from 1996 to 1997. Through COG, residents are empowered to improve the quality of life in their neighborhoods.

BankBoston
Community Banking Group
100 Federal Street
Boston, MA 02110

Contact: Gail Snowden,
Managing Director
617.434.5105

BankBoston provides specialized urban banking expertise and resources to inner-city communities, a market that has traditionally been shunned by other lenders.

BankBoston chose to approach the inner city as an emerging market. The financial center has concluded community development is sustainable, corporate commitment can be profitable, and offering capital, credit, and technical assistance to entrepreneurs can create jobs, opportunity, and wealth that will transform the inner city and help it enter the economic mainstream.

BankBoston began its urban banking efforts in 1990 with the creation of First Community Bank (FCB). The bank has given low- to moderate-income individuals and small businesses throughout New England far greater access to banking services. Entire communities have been revitalized, and shareholders have seen a profitable return on their investment.

FCB has risen from seven under-performing branches in under-served, impoverished Boston neighborhoods to a profitable network of forty-two branches with $1.6 billion in deposits.

FCB introduced extended branch hours, developed consumer education programs, and hired residents who speak different languages and understood varied cultures. FCB also hired community development officers to work within the community, forging strong ties with customers and leading workshops on basic banking, money management, and credit issues.

FCB has tailored its services to multicultural customers, respecting the distinct customs and languages that are at the heart of the community. In addition to FCB, the Community Banking Group created the BankBoston Development Company (BBDC).

Formed in 1997, the BBDC became the first urban investment bank in the nation to be created by a commercial bank. It invests in and provides equity capital to businesses and nonprofits that serve low- to moderate-income and disadvantaged communities.

In BBDC's first fifteen months, it has approved $66 million in urban investments. In 1999, President Bill Clinton awarded CEO Chad Gifford the Ron Brown Award for Corporate Leadership. It is the only Presidential Award to honor companies for outstanding achievements in employee and community relations.

Historic East Baltimore Community Action Coalition
Johns Hopkins Medical Center
808 North Chester St.
Baltimore, MD 21205

Contact: Michael Seipp,
Executive Director
410.614.4216

The Johns Hopkins Medical School created a partnership with the local community to help leverage financing for new businesses, after-school enrichment, housing, and other programs. The

managers of Johns Hopkins had watched the surrounding neighborhood undergo a severe decline.

Recognizing university and community relations had been strained and the university needed to contribute to neighborhood improvements, Hopkins committed itself to developing a working partnership with the neighborhood.

This work led to the creation of a new entity, the Historic East Baltimore Community Action Coalition (HEBCAC), a nonprofit community-development corporation with a board composed of Hopkins, neighborhood, and city government representatives.

HEBCAC has become an important instrument for planning and implementing neighborhood improvements. Hopkins has developed a community-based primary health care plan to improve the quality of health care delivery services. The university also has adopted five area elementary schools and established after-school tutorial and computer programs.

A $38 million federal loan was secured for a major housing development project and rehabilitation of existing homes, with the help of the university. Hopkins has also developed a plan to provide sustainable businesses, jobs, and job-training programs for residents of East Baltimore. This activity has led to business expansions and the creation of a $1 million equity-investment fund targeted for businesses in East Baltimore.

Hopkins has committed to purchasing from companies in distressed areas within Baltimore: In 1996 and 1997, Hopkins' purchases averaged about $34 million or twenty-three percent of its total Maryland purchases.

Hopkins has been a major funder of the planning needed to create a new community development bank, and has invested $6 million, a sum that will be matched by governmental funds.

Hopkins has launched a modest employer-assisted housing program to encourage employees to purchase homes in the neighborhood that surrounds the medical center.

The economic investments made by Johns Hopkins should boost the standard of living in the community, and reestablish a sense of goodwill between the university and the neighborhood.

Indianapolis Church Park Initiative
Indianapolis Parks Department
(INDY Parks)
City and County Building
200 E. Washington, Suite 2301
Indianapolis, IN 46204

Contact: Joseph L. B. Wynns,
Director, INDY Parks
317.327.7275

The Indianapolis Parks and Recreation Department (INDY Parks) has established a unique partnership with residents reconnecting communities to parks, increasing church revenues, saving the city maintenance costs, and freeing funds for park maintenance.

In 1995, INDY Parks determined it could no longer economically maintain parks of five acres or less because large maintenance equipment could not be used. The department worked with faith organizations to build a business opportunity for congregants.

The urban park ministry placed the clergy in charge of community park maintenance. Youth and homeless people get paid to do most of the work.

Now the city provides $60,000 a year for the partnership program and publishes requests for bids to community churches outlining the scope of services required. Each contract is for general maintenance and grass mowing, and includes baseline standards for turf care, litter, surfaces, benches, and shelters. After accepting a bid, the city trains congregants in maintenance and management.

Grants range from $500 to $5,000 per year depending on the size and scope of

the maintenance work. Churches that already maintain property are ideal candidates for the program, because they have made investments in equipment and maintenance personnel.

The local union, which voluntarily forfeited its contract to maintain the small parks, supported the initiative and shaped the contracts and reviewed the bids every year. The city's fully unionized parks department maintains the larger parks.

The program has saved the city money on mowing equipment, fuel, gasoline, and the disposal of clippings and trash, freeing funds for the larger parks. Both smaller and larger parks are in considerably better shape and many have new playground equipment, walks, and pavements. Youth outreach programs in local parks have increased.

Churches are given substantial authority over the parks, including program planning and site supervision. They pay nothing for use of services that normally cost a fee. In one case, a church has generated enough revenue from these programs to start a summer day camp in their park.

FAITHS Initiative
The San Francisco Foundation
225 Bush Street, 5th floor
San Francisco, CA 94104

Contact: Dwayne S. Marsh,
Director
415.733.8500

FAITHS organizes strategy sessions and forums that focus on specific community issues such as community building, welfare reform, corporate-community relations, tax policies, state budgeting, the media, and race relations. San Francisco Bay has always been a racially and ethnically diverse region. But growing suburbanization, the concentration of industry and jobs in Silicon Valley, and economic and political disparities have done much

to deepen social and racial inequalities.

In November of 1993, the San Francisco Foundation convened a meeting of fifteen pastors, interfaith leaders, and directors of faith-based organizations to discuss ways of revitalizing their neighborhoods. Participants soon identified that it was not enough to work within their own communities; they needed to create alliances across communities to better build partnerships with foundations, donors, and social justice activists.

The FAITHS Initiative's small staff is housed at the San Francisco Foundation and offers technical assistance as well as follow-up. It also serves as the hub of the over 300 congregations, religious organizations, nonprofit allies, and foundations. This network is important because the resources available to faith-based institutions are direct reflections of the resources of their communities, and religious leaders are often unfamiliar with the opportunities that lie outside of their neighborhoods.

Through FAITHS events, the representatives of communities most in need of financial resources, volunteers, and connections to powerful people have an opportunity to benefit from the "community capital" of wealthier congregations.

A leadership group and two planning teams meet quarterly to give direction to FAITHS' activities. In keeping with its primary goal of improving race relations, FAITHS has helped antiracism educators to collaborate with religious institutions. The Initiative has also begun to raise money for a small grant-funding pool. Proposals for new projects are continuously solicited from community leaders.

The challenge for FAITHS is to strike a balance, on the one hand, between having enough internal capacity and leverage with funders to attract community leaders and provide their institutions with tangible resources, and on the other, to ensure that the participating groups gain stature through the process.

Center for Excellence in Municipal Management

George Washington University
2033 K Street, N.W.
Suite 240
Washington, DC 20052

Contact: Herbert Tillery,
Executive Director
202.994.5390

A public-private partnership, led by a major university, pools expertise and resources to develop and support research projects, management efforts, and leadership training in the Nation's capital. All cities need leadership and management capacity within the ranks of municipal government if they are to survive and thrive. The George Washington University Center for Excellence in Municipal Management was created in May 1997, in partnership with the District of Columbia and the Fannie Mae Foundation, to address these needs within the District of Columbia government. It is the Center's mission to translate the city's commitment to excellence in public service into actions that help create a more effective, efficient, and responsive government.

The Center and its partners from the public, nonprofit, and academic sectors work toward their mission through three major activities:

- Rigorous high-quality executive leadership and management education;
- Expert management advisory services to the District government; and
- Research on state-of-the-art leadership and public management policies and practices.

The Center's Program for Excellence in Municipal Management (PEMM) for D.C. government managers has produced over 135 graduates and has an additional 101 presently going through training. PEMM begins with an intensive weeklong residential basic leadership course and follows up with monthly courses focusing on topics such as leadership values and ethics, project management, budgeting, and strategic planning. Upon completion of the thirteen-month program, PEMM participants receive designation as a Certified Public Manager. In addition to PEMM, the Center also runs the Leadership Management Institute for the D.C. Public Schools that also has a residential basic leadership course, budgeting, strategic planning, and human resource management.

Harlem Community Partnerships

Abyssinian Development Corporation
131 West 138th Street
New York, NY 10030-2303

Contact: Darren Walker,
Chief Operating Officer
212.368.4471 ext. 113

The buzz of activity and investment in Harlem these days demonstrates the power of "new leaders" to effect community revitalization. Two major contributors to what some are calling Harlem's Second Renaissance are Pathmark Stores, Inc. and the Abyssinian Development Corporation (ADC), a subsidiary of the Abyssinian Baptist Church.

In the spring of 1986, Reverend Calvin O. Butts, III, pastor of Abyssinian Baptist Church, challenged his parishioners to join forces with him to reverse the urban decay that made Harlem a national symbol of disinvestment, abandonment, high unemployment, crime, and homelessness. In response, the ADC emerged in 1989 with a mission of comprehensive neighborhood revitalization through real estate and economic development. Its record of success includes a renovated building for homeless families, a 100-unit complex for senior citizens, and a number of affordable rental properties. ADC has grown to a staff of fifty and built successful partnerships with social service agencies and funders.

ADC teamed up with Pathmark to open the first large grocery store in Harlem on East 125th Street—Harlem's main commercial corridor. Grand opening of the 50,000-square-foot store occurred on April 30, 1999. Providing around-the-clock service, seven days a week, the store offers everything residents need, including a pharmacy and a bank. Pathmark employs over 250 associates, more than seventy-five percent of whom reside within Harlem. Moreover, construction of the $16 million project created 150 construction jobs, making it the first major development in Harlem in over a generation.

Far from being a model of urban decay, Harlem is set to be a shining example of community revitalization, as well as evidence of what can be accomplished when private industry and communities work together.

Best Practices

8 | New Financial Partnerships Revitalize Regions:
Old Money, New Thinking, Untapped New Sources

A decade ago, New York City faced a potentially crippling predicament: Although it had one of the purest water supplies of any municipality in the United States, the city faced an Environmental Protection Agency (EPA) order to filter that water to remove potential contaminants. In 1990, the agency ordered all public supplies of surface water in the nation to be filtered. Nevertheless, for a city of more than eight million people, the required treatment plant would cost $7 billion to build and incur annual operating expenses of hundreds of millions of dollars.

At the same time, the upstate communities of the rural Catskills—where streams and mountain lakes provide ninety percent of New York City's water—faced problems of their own. Their fragile economies relied too heavily on financial decisions made by the owners of country homes, weekend tourists, and the owners of timberland, many of whom lived in the city. An aging infrastructure in these cities required substantial investment to keep sewer lines and septic systems from deteriorating.

The solution for both city and community was disarmingly simple and mutually beneficial: Rather than build a $7 billion filtration plant, New York City agreed to spend $1.4 billion to protect the Catskills' watershed by buying and conserving undeveloped land, paying for sewer and septic upgrades, and helping farmers and loggers adopt better management practices to keep contaminants from entering streams and lakes. To obtain backing from skeptical rural communities, which had long resented their status as economic colonies of the urban juggernaut, the city sweetened the pot by establishing a $60 million regional economic development fund called Catskills Fund for the Future. The EPA embraced the idea that keeping the water pure in the first place would protect public health as effectively as filtering it later.

This innovative partnership illustrates the important role that creative financing can play in resolving problems in America's cities and towns. Political willpower and leadership remain vital to twenty-first century communities. But, to transform aging urban, suburban, and even rural districts into places of economic vitality and social richness, the public and private sectors must find ways to pay for new systems. They may invest in transportation systems and public services, or finance building renovation and new-business incubation.

Like New York City and the Catskills towns, successful communities across the country are demonstrating innovative methods of financing development, avoiding problems associated with traditional private and public financing mechanisms. The Federal Urban Renewal Program of the 1950s and 1960s, for example, often resulted in the division or destruction of ethnic neighbor-

The Price of Past Programs

Half a century of expensive social programs directed by the federal government has left the American public with an intense distrust of grandiose tax-financed schemes. Evidence of public censure includes the California tax revolt and the widespread condemnation of the *culture of dependency* created by federal antipoverty programs. Nine other states subsequently adopted supermajority requirements for tax increases, and twenty-seven states now limit some government taxation and expenditure, according to the National Taxpayers Union. The public also expresses a lingering bitterness about Urban Renewal projects that produced sterile cityscapes under the guise of slum clearance. To many, widely publicized incidents of drug-related crime and violence in public housing projects such as Chicago's notorious Cabrini Green, embody everything wrong with the modern inner city and with Washington's poorly conceived plans to restore it.

The private sector also has failed to sustain financing for the quality developments critical to maintaining the health of urban neighborhoods, and corporate trends may put up more obstacles to financing future revitalization. Bank mergers in the 1990s have created huge multipurpose nationwide financial service companies, resulting in the disappearance of the small community-based lending institutions that historically provided loans for

(Above) *The Burlington Community Land Trust in Burlington, Vermont. Community land trusts are an important mechanism for acquiring land for commercial space as well as affordable housing and parks.*
(Left) *A drawing of Kansas City's Union Station, which will house Science City, restaurants, shops, a theater, and intermodal transportation facilities. The renovation of the Station is funded in part by a bistate tax in Kansas and Missouri.*

hoods and left the public disillusioned by government involvement in community and neighborhood development. Public antipathy toward costly government programs gave rise to a tax revolt in California in 1978 that spread to other states during the next twenty years. As a result, public officials in the twenty-first century will find it more difficult than did their predecessors to invest taxpayer money in traditional revitalization plans and subsidies.

Communities instead must focus on alternate financial mechanisms, including private investment, new public funds, and nonprofit support. Regions must equalize investment and opportunities for growth among wealthy and distressed communities. Existing federal, state, or local government funding programs must be used in tandem with private capital to leverage maximum benefits from limited pools of dollars.

Before and after photos of The Park at Lakewood, an affordable apartment community in Atlanta, Georgia that includes an on-site computer learning center for residents. The distressed property was acquired and redeveloped by a community development corporation of Bank of America that provided development capital as well as construction financing and investment in low-income housing tax credits.

modest businesses, home-improvement projects, and small speculative developments. The booming stock market has encouraged an investment shift to mutual and pension funds.

When the Community Reinvestment Act (CRA) became law in 1977, to encourage lenders to invest in low- and moderate-income neighborhoods, banks, and savings and loans were responsible for eighty percent of mortgage loans. That number has now fallen to forty-two percent, with fifty-eight percent provided by mortgage companies, sometimes owned by banks, but not covered by the CRA requirements. Similarly, in 1977, banks held nearly seventy percent of the long-term savings subject to CRA rules. Today, banks hold only about thirty percent of those savings, and in five years, that amount could fall to ten percent or less, according to the Center for Neighborhood Technology in Chicago.

Fortunately, community and business leaders hoping to revive moribund urban areas can still take advantage of a wide range of financial strategies. Some solutions are familiar; others represent new ways of using old sources of money, while still others represent emerging community investment trends.

Public-Spirited Private Investment

The Business Improvement District (BID)—a voluntary business association that taxes each member to pay for urban improvements—relies on business self-interest in attracting consumers to the commercial districts. BIDs represent the antithesis of traditional government-imposed, tax-supported urban revitalization programs.

Although the details vary from state to state, generally, local governments and property owners who control more than fifty percent of the land within a district must approve the BID. The public agency levies the fee, collects the money, and returns it to the BID, whose members elect a professional manager or board of directors empowered to make budgeting decisions. BID funding typically provides supplemental support for programs often regarded as public responsibilities—security, landscaping, street signs, sanitation, and maintenance—as well as for business marketing and promotion.

In New York, for example, a BID campaign to improve safety, lighting, and sanitation helped

reinvent Times Square, transforming it from a neighborhood notorious for sleaze and crime to a vibrant urban crossroads. In Washington, D.C., police say crime in the downtown BID dropped fifty-four percent during the year after the privately funded security patrols began.

The 1,200 North American BIDs invest billions in a new kind of urban renewal project, according to the American Planning Association (APA). In San Diego, for example, BIDs have raised more than $1.3 billion during the past two decades to pay for amenities, such as median landscaping, and community events, such as street festivals.

BIDs often finance projects to make suburban shopping malls effective competitors for the consumer dollars that once supported downtown business districts: effective security and maintenance, coordinated advertising and promotional campaigns, and convenient parking and transit connections.

Sometimes BIDs go well beyond hiring trash pickers and security guards. In Washington, D.C., the district pays one full-time staff member to conduct outreach to homeless people. The BID also has opened a daytime drop-in center in a local church where the homeless can eat, shower, wash clothes, and meet representatives of various government and nonprofit agencies offering job training and detoxification programs.

The cost of such activities to the BID members themselves varies widely, depending on the reach of district plans and the kind of businesses that join the BID. Typically, commercial BID members pay ten to fifteen cents per square foot, according to the APA. The total annual assessment usually equals five to six percent of the yearly property tax bill.

In Philadelphia, according to the City Center District, the highest annual 1996 assessment was $306,082; the lowest $8. A typical office building paid $102,774, a typical hotel paid $27,759, and an average residential property paid $117. In downtown Denver, the BID added two cents to the four-cent-a-square foot BID fee for property owners to finance sidewalk cleaning and streetscape improvements in the blocks around a pedestrian-transit mall. Area rents are about $25 a square foot.

A few industrial and residential areas also have established BIDs. Some consolidate security services and business recruitment in light industrial areas. At the Stockyards Industrial Park in

Chicago, for example, the BID financed a twenty-four-hour security force that helped reinvent a rundown complex of stockyards and packing plants. A tremendous reduction in break-ins, illegal dumping, and vandalism has led to the creation of a warehouse, trucking, and food-packaging center.

Only a handful of residential BIDs exist. In the sprawling Charles Village BID in Baltimore, residents and businesses pay for community security, sanitation, and marketing.

Although business BID members applaud BIDs, this financial tool also has its shortcomings.

Some activists and good-government groups criticize BIDs as not subject to the checks and balances inherent in government development programs. Because members privately invest millions of dollars into what are essentially public spaces—sidewalks, streets, and plazas—they circumvent traditional disclosure rules designed to foster accountability.

This intrusion of private activity in the public sphere can have troubling consequences. In Los Angeles, the American Civil Liberties Union filed a class-action lawsuit in November 1999 against four BIDs and their hired security companies, accusing private guards of harassing and assaulting homeless people. The BIDs' representatives deny wrongdoing, but the suit demonstrates the prickly problems of privately regulating behavior in public spaces.

Critics also charge that BIDs displace representative local governments. Such criticism has heightened as BIDs have expanded their traditional roles of sweeping sidewalks and installing lights to issuing bonds and planning neighborhoods. Despite the undeniable success of the Times Square campaign, for example, activists criticize some of the city's forty BIDs as autocratic shadow governments, granting concentrated political power to nonelected officials. Detractors also insist BIDs deepen the divide between a city's rich and poor, with wealthy business owners able to buy better security and public services than can their less-fortunate neighbors.

The BIDs are tools only for areas that maintain some minimal vitality. Truly depressed areas cannot muster the resources needed to achieve significant improvements.

BIDs also may encounter difficulty when their role as business booster conflicts with their responsibility to improve unsatisfactory social and economic conditions. It can be tempting for BIDs to present a cheery but false report of accomplishments in the interest of reassuring shoppers, but at the risk of neglecting problems, such as homelessness or the lack of appropriate shopping and recreational opportunities.

Avoiding the many pitfalls requires energetic and adroit leadership. To be successful, BIDs must follow several fundamental rules:

- **Start with a solid organizational plan.** Identify the problems to be addressed, and outline precisely how specific BID projects will contribute to a solution. Every business owner should understand exactly what the BID hopes to accomplish and how progress toward that goal will be measured. The goal should be realistic given the amount of money to be raised.
- **Define and address root causes.** If shoppers avoid the downtown because they believe it is dangerous, spending money on a new parking lot will not accomplish anything. Likewise, if the strategy is to secure money, hiring a private security force should not be a high priority.
- **Do not allow the largest or wealthiest property owners to dominate the BID.** If smaller business owners feel they are being taxed to promote projects that do not benefit them in

(Above) *View of Cleveland's Playhouse Square Business Improvement District.* (Below) *Cleveland's Business Improvement Districts (BIDs) rely on business self-interest to attract consumers to commercial districts.*

BALTIMORE: EMPOWERMENT ZONE FEDERAL TAX INITIATIVES

Baltimore's award of an Empowerment Zone means $100 million in Social Service Block Grants, financial and in-kind commitments by businesses, institutions, and city and state governments, and three important federal tax initiatives for Baltimore businesses. The federal tax initiatives created to assist businesses are: (a) wage-tax credits, (b) increased Section 179 expensing, and (c) tax-exempt *Enterprise Zone Facility Bonds*. Zone employers receive a twenty percent tax credit against income tax liability for the first $15,000 of qualified wages per employee. For 1994-2001, the credit is $3,000 per employee per year. After 2001, the credit decreases each year.

Source: Shapiro & Olander, Baltimore

Aerial View of the Inner Harbor in Baltimore, Maryland. Located in close proximity to the Harbor is Allied Signal Baltimore Works, constructed on the site of a cleaned-up brownfield. Federal funds are available for the redevelopment of brownfields.

proportion to their contributions, they will rebel and undercut the BID's effectiveness.

- **Engage the public in BID planning.** BIDs invest private money in public spaces, and it is important for people who live, work, and shop in the district to understand and influence it. Property owners must recognize the general public may not share their concerns, and ultimately the public—by choosing to visit or stay away—will determine whether the BID succeeds.
- **Hire skilled management to run day-to-day activities.** This can be difficult in small communities with modest resources and small pools of home-grown talent, but many hire a consulting firm to provide staffing for the first year or two. This helps assure that the BID and its directors get off to a fast start.

- **Adopt diverse services to attract a broad support base.** Poll the business owners for their priorities and needs; outline a service regime to assist both the large and the smaller owners.
- **Be sensitive to the local political environment.** In New York, reverberations continue from a showdown between Mayor Rudolph Giuliani and Dan Biederman, who directed three Manhattan BIDs and earned a salary greater than the mayor's. The mayor's office accused Biederman of amassing too much power, revoked the power to issue bonds, and, in 1998, withheld their budgets until Biederman had resigned. Politicians are accountable to the voters for providing public services, even those funded by business interests, and they must retain some measure of control over the BID's activities. BID directors challenge that prerogative at their peril.
- **Resist the temptation to use BIDs for political purposes.** Because local government generally has a role in approving the boundaries of a BID, approving the budget, and levying the tax, city councils often tinker with the assessments for particular properties to reward supporters or score political points. Succumbing to this temptation will quickly undercut support for the BID and may even reduce its revenue until it no longer can pay its staff or finance its projects.

For all the criticism and pitfalls, BIDs remain a popular and effective way to attract consumers and boost financial returns, handily winning renewal in the great majority of cities with BIDs. They prompt the communication and cooperation necessary among business owners to build communities. And they require the beneficiaries to bear all or nearly all the costs of narrowly targeted improvement programs.

New Uses for Old Money

Federal support for urban revitalization did not end with the Urban Renewal and public housing programs of the 1950s and 1960s. Billions of dollars continue to flow each year from federal coffers into urban programs, but the programs have changed in administration and purpose. The balance of authority between local and federal agents has also evolved. The federal government has replaced the old top-down prescriptive model with a bottom-up, locally directed process designed to help communities solve their own problems. Creative municipal governments can steer federal money, scattered among dozens of different programs, to maximize project effectiveness.

The $217 billion Transportation Equity Act for the 21st Century (TEA-21) passed in 1998, for example, can finance innovative programs. The funding bill encourages creative community approaches to land-use planning and related transportation issues, inviting beneficial experimentation. San Diego, for example, uses TEA-21 funding for a pilot program intended to manage traffic on Interstate 15—a major north-south commuter route—by charging tolls that vary with the density of highway occupancy. Electronic sensors linked to toll booths allow motorists to pay less by driving at less congested times. Market forces help modify motorist behavior and increase the capacity of existing pavement. Similar experiments in congestion pricing are being funded by TEA-21 money in Houston and Fort Myers, Florida.

TEA-21 money is also paying for innovative approaches to regional planning. The program authorizes $122 million for the Transportation and Community and System Preservation Pilot Program, a terrible name for a promising program intended to link transportation planning and land-use regulation through broad regional partnerships. The goal is to minimize the effects of new developments on transportation systems. The first round of pilot projects authorized in 1998 include an Idaho program coordinating the master plans of seven cities and two counties.

The federal government provides substantial tax credits and other incentives intended to attract private investment to urban neighborhoods and rural communities with high unemployment, widespread poverty, and other signs of economic distress. The Empowerment Zone/Enterprise Community (EZ/EC) Initiative approved in 1993, builds on twenty-year-old state and local government programs to influence private decisions about where to locate job-producing business activities. Governments extend relief from some land-use regulations, such as restrictive zoning, and abate inventory, bank, and gross income taxes to businesses that locate in deprived commercial districts.

An enterprise zone established in the old industrial heart of Evansville, Indiana—where a Whirlpool plant shutdown eliminated 3,200 jobs—is credited with attracting investments that created 5,000 positions. The new companies occupy two million square feet of vacant industrial and commercial space and have prompted construction of another one million square feet. Clothing retailer T.J. Maxx, lured by promised relief from the state's hefty inventory tax, chose the Evansville zone as a major distribution center, employing more than 1,700 people.

The federal program combines the regulatory and tax relief available under older state programs with direct grants to designated rural and urban Empowerment Zones (EZ) and Enterprise Communities (EC). To qualify, local leaders must submit competitive grant applications documenting their community's poverty and outlining a ten-year plan to remedy economic problems through targeted programs using federal funds. Under the first round of grants from 1994 to 1997, the government granted $40 million to rural and $100 million to urban EZs. U.S. Department of Housing and Urban Development (HUD) granted urban and rural ECs $3 million from Social Services Block Grants.

Enterprise zones—whether established under the federal program or by state and local authorities—have proved an important economic-development tool. They create partnerships between the public and private sectors, provide for local decision-making, and address one of the root causes of poverty by attracting jobs. They work best, however, when coupled with other programs intended to address social problems and community decay. Tax incentives and regulatory relief can attract capital into an area, but communities cannot sustain development without reducing crime, homelessness, and other characteristics of blighted areas. The city cannot solve all the problems of a depleted neighborhood by bringing in federal money; it must also provide police and other neighborhood services to protect the landowners.

The Brownfields Initiative offers another source of funding by providing money to help communities clean up and develop contaminated industrial sites. During the forties and fifties, companies typically established these sites for waste disposal in poor neighborhoods. The now-abandoned

A large old tree in front of the historic Pauline James Home, renovated by the Evansville Urban Enterprise Association in Evansville, Indiana, site of a state sponsored Enterprise Zone. The historic home is used as a meeting facility for nonprofit groups.

TOP TEN COMMUNITY FOUNDATIONS

Name/(state)	Total Giving
New York Community Trust (NY)	$144,912,318
Greater Kansas City Community Foundation and Affiliated Trusts (MO)	66,788,615
San Francisco Foundation (CA)	45,298,867
The Cleveland Foundation (OH)	41,379,161
California Community Foundation (CA)	40,867,398
Columbus Foundation and Affiliated Organizations (OH)	32,928,123
Foundation for the Carolinas (NC)	32,052,775
Chicago Community Trust and Affiliates (IL)	31,934,730
The Boston Foundation (MA)	29,957,746
Marin Community Foundation (CA)	26,576,952

Source: The Foundation Center

TOP CORPORATE FOUNDATIONS, BY LEVEL OF GIVING

Name/(state)	Total Giving
The Ford Foundation (NY)	$439,323,000
Lilly Endowment Inc. (IN)	425,188,708
W. K. Kellogg Foundation (MI)	260,837,874
The David and Lucile Packard Foundation (CA)	257,227,198
The Robert Wood Johnson Foundation (NJ)	241,543,631
The Pew Charitable Trusts (PA)	161,411,658
John D. and Catherine T. MacArthur Foundation (IL)	156,976,932
The New York Community Trust (NY)	144,912,318
The Andrew W. Mellon Foundation (NY)	142,232,000
The Danforth Foundation (MO)	105,450,727

Source: The Foundation Center

sites can become valuable resources: Urban neighborhoods can benefit from the development of affordable housing or job-creating commercial activities. Often, the fields represent the only sizable parcels of available urban land.

In just over two years, the Dallas Brownfields Program leveraged more than $109 million in private investment and $1.9 million in federal funds to pay for brownfields redevelopment with assistance and financing from the EPA, HUD, and the Economic Development Administration. According to the EPA, the program has helped reclaim more than 1,200 acres of brownfields and anticipates the creation of more than 1,700 jobs.

In May 1999, the Clinton administration offered $30 million in grants to help communities clean up and redevelop brownfields, the first of several annual distributions expected under an ambitious EPA program intended eventually to distribute $700 million to more than 300 communities. Communities must apply for the grants, which are issued on a competitive basis after screening by a committee comprised of the EPA and other federal agencies involved in the program.

Other public sector programs aim to stimulate traditional investment by lending institutions in troubled urban areas. The CRA has long been an important mechanism to ensure that banks include the low-income sectors of their markets when lending money for business activities and home purchases. The consolidation of the U.S. banking industry from an estimated 15,000 banks in 1977 to roughly 8,500 in 1999 has given federal regulators more leverage to force balanced credit opportunities as a condition of approval for mergers and acquisitions. Local community groups can also use the CRA to leverage money for urban programs from private lenders. By carefully analyzing bank reports to HUD, community groups persuaded the lending institutions to finance business microloan funds in New York's Washington Heights and Inwood neighborhoods, and developed limited-equity housing cooperatives in Washington, D.C., for example.

Public agencies also can nudge financial institutions to help secure loans for young businesses that fail to meet traditional investment criteria, such as a minimum collateral level or low debt-to-equity ratio, or that have experienced rapid—but short-lived—growth. Some governments provide default insurance, matching a percentage of the down payment on each loan with public funds that cushion the bank against losses. Michigan, Minnesota, Massachusetts, and other states have created capital access programs (CAPs), leveraging nearly $24 in loans for each $1 in public investment.

Prosperity Builds Foundations

The same burgeoning stock values that have attracted huge investments in mutual funds and financial markets and increased the power of financial-services corporations to compete with banks have yielded tremendous benefits to private foundations, making them potent players in the field of community economic development.

Between 1975 and 1995, foundation assets grew from $30 billion to $275 billion, and their expenditures rose from $1.9 billion to $12.3 billion. The availability of so much money, particularly as federal, state, and local budgets have grown more constricted, has made private foundations attractive sources of support for strapped communities.

In Baltimore, the Enterprise Foundation finances antipoverty efforts in the Sandtown-Winchester neighborhood. The Foundation also is active in at least fifteen other cities, including Charlotte, Denver, Rochester, Cleveland, and Miami, and has raised or leveraged more than $3 billion since 1982 to create 100,000 affordable homes and place more than 30,000 people in jobs. In the South Bronx, seventeen foundations and corporate funders provide venture capital and other support for community development. The McKnight Foundation in Minneapolis spends $20 million on welfare-to-work programs in Minnesota.

The Packard Foundation, with 1999 assets of $13.5 billion, provided $200 million in community grants in 1997 and $348 million in 1998. Although national and even international in scope, Packard has focused on cities in northern California. The MacArthur Foundation hands out more than $170 million annually to child and youth development projects, mental health organizations, programs increasing access to economic opportunity, and research and policy analysis.

The Enterprise Foundation provides at its Web site, www.enterprisefoundation.org, a comprehensive guide to applying for foundation grants. The Foundation also provides abundant information

(Above) *Bryant Park, a public park in New York City, maintained by the Bryant Park Restoration Corporation, a privately funded group that receives funds from property assessments and on-site concessions.*

on available grants, government programs, and foundations that provide funds for community development projects:

- **Unrestricted.** The money can be used for operating costs often unavailable through other grants.
- **Restricted.** Only for specific purposes defined by the grant or the funder.
- **Program or project grants.** To support a specific program, usually with measurable outcomes. Community projects can be adapted to program regulations, but this requires a comprehensive understanding of grant requirements.
- **Seed money.** For new, experimental, or innovative projects (pilot or demonstration programs). Depending on initial outcome, funding may be renewable. Seed funding is attractive; it enables an organization to experiment and prove the viability of a project to attract or leverage additional funding.
- **Capital grants.** Earmarked for capital projects to meet future service demands, such as the

(Above and Opposite) *The Crested Butte Land Trust in Colorado has saved or helped save 1,000 acres of natural resources and open space from development. The success of the Trust is primarily due to its reliance on multiple public and private funding sources.*

purchase, construction, or renovation of a physical facility; and land acquisition or major equipment purchases.

- **Endowment.** Grant to provide for an organization's future security. Endowment funds are invested to provide annual income, usually a percentage of income earned.
- **Challenge (matching) grant.** Restricted or unrestricted grants may be made in the form of a challenge to the organization to raise an equal or specified amount from other sources. The grant is made contingent upon the match being raised.

Some communities will seek foundation funding, and the Enterprise Foundation provides a helpful map to this kind of financial support:

- **Community Foundations.** These organizations collect funds from donors who target specific communities or geographic regions and often can play a leadership role by consolidating funding from several sources, connecting donors to the programs they fund, and engaging multiple community organizations.
- **Independent Foundations.** Also known as private foundations, they are usually funded or endowed by a single source, such as an

individual or family, from wealth that has been inherited or accumulated through business activity. They may be large and serve multiple purposes, exist to promote a single goal, and/or be a family operation. Their support may be limited to special purposes designated by the founder; larger ones may hire a staff and publish guidelines.

- **Operating Foundations.** Established by a nonprofit to fund its own programs. External grants are seldom awarded.
- **Company Foundations.** Funded by a profit-making entity for the purpose of charitable giving. Not all companies and corporations establish foundations; contributions may be made directly by the company, even if it also has a foundation. Often they contribute to programs related to their businesses; for example, many pharmaceutical companies donate to medical research institutions. They also may focus giving in the cities that house headquarters or branches.

Foundation funding carries risks: The organizations are accountable to boards, not to voters, and their goals do not always coincide with those of community leaders. Cities that seek and accept foundation funding for community development

must ensure that projects are integrated into a comprehensive urban-revitalization strategy to make sure that such investments reinforce—rather than impede—overall public-policy goals. Still, the independence that makes foundations politically risky partners also frees them to be bold and innovative, making them potentially valuable allies as communities seek improvements.

Creative partnerships may also find new uses for such old standbys as sales taxes. The state legislatures of Kansas and Missouri enacted a Metropolitan Culture District Compact in 1996 that allowed counties to authorize a Metropolitan Culture District, form a commission to govern it, and levy a retail sales tax to support such activities as museums, arts programs, concert halls, and other enriching additions to the urban scene. Voters in Johnson County, Kansas, and neighboring Jackson, Clay, and Platte counties in Missouri, subsequently adopted a one-eighth-cent sales tax to support restoration of historic Union Station in Kansas City. The renovated station, a 1914 landmark that remains the nation's second-largest terminal, now houses retail shops, restaurants, and Science City, an ambitious interactive attraction that is part theater, part museum and learning center, and part theme park.

It was the first such public financing to cross

state lines. Precinct figures showed that while older neighborhoods opposed the tax, it passed handily in newer suburbs inhabited by young families who clearly were swayed by the promise of enhanced educational opportunities for their children.

"We made a concerted effort to sell the Science City educational aspect of this like a school bond issue," campaign cochairman Steve Rose told the local newspaper after the election. "I think it was the educational component that brought in the newer subdivisions."

Creating New Sources of Capital

So far, this discussion has focused on variations in traditional sources of money for urban revitalization and economic development. In recent years, innovative financial managers have experimented with squeezing mileage out of municipal revenue streams by privatizing public services or turning revenue flows into investment capital. These promising strategies deserve greater attention as communities greet the challenges of the twenty-first century.

During the past decade, a handful of organizations built a secondary market for community-development loans made by traditional lenders as part of their regulatory mandate to extend credit

Before and after photos of the Avery Hill project in Laconia, New Hampshire. The Laconia Area Community Land Trust (LACLT), a local nonprofit, successfully revitalized the deteriorated neighborhood by working with neighborhood residents and the City of Laconia. LACLT put together a financing package of $1.6 million dollars from nine sources to complete the renovation.

to low-income neighborhoods. Lending by nonprofit community-development organizations, city and state revolving loan funds, and public and quasi public redevelopment agencies also can be sold on the secondary market.

The well-developed secondary market for traditional single-family home mortgages shows the potential benefits that sector offers. More than two-thirds of mortgages in the United States are resold to firms that bundle and use them as security for such instruments as bonds and mortgage-backed securities. The system enables lenders to recycle their funds quickly, allowing them to offer mortgages at reasonable costs, and provides private investors robust returns with relatively little risk. Cities, nonprofits, and revolving loan funds hold an estimated $4 billion in loan assets. They make

potential targets for loan recycling.

The Community Reinvestment Fund (CRF) in Minnesota has pioneered the use of the secondary market to boost economic development. CRF has purchased hundreds of small-business, economic-development, and housing loans to secure community reinvestment bonds. Banks, life insurance companies, and pension funds purchase the loans. In New York, the Local Initiatives Managed Assets Corporation acquires housing loans from private and public agencies and sells them to banks and pension funds. Nationwide, Neighborhood Housing Services of America purchases single-family affordable housing and rehabilitation loans through a network of local affiliates. Since its establishment in 1974, Neighborhood Housing has purchased loans worth more than $200 million and sold the investments primarily to insurance companies and financial institutions. Multiple funding sources provided seed money. The organization tapped foundation grants, Community Development Block Grants, the federal HOME program, local tax increment financing, private capital, rural development grants through the U.S. Department of Agriculture, Economic Development Administration grants, and other state or local funding sources.

Community Land Trusts (CLTs) are another emerging mechanism for financing affordable housing, commercial space, and parks. Similar to the conservation trusts that acquire agricultural land and open space to keep it from being developed, CLTs combine funding from government grants, foundation loans and grants, pension fund investments, and mortgages and construction loans from banks to purchase urban property. The CLT constructs housing or some other structure serving the community's needs (as defined by community members who direct the trust) on vacant land. Organizations can demolish empty residential or commercial buildings. In both cases, the trust continues its ownership of the land. This removes the land costs from the building purchase price, making it more affordable. Most CLTs impose limited equity policies and formulas that restrict the resale value of housing, extending home ownership to low-income families.

Municipalities also can turn revenue flows into capital. Many cities issue revenue bonds that rely on anticipated future income generated by the project finances—a new municipal garage to be paid for with parking fees. Other proposals are more daring. Scott Bernstein, director of the Center for Neighborhood Technology in Chicago, proposes using revenue from monthly transit passes to back securities.

Municipal governments also find other ways to harness private-sector forces for the public good. They may sell naming or advertising rights to municipal structures and other public property. New Jersey's Garden State Arts Center, owned by the New Jersey Highway Authority, in 1996 became the P.N.C. Bank Arts Center. In New York City, the mayor's office asks private corporations to clean up rubble-strewn vacant lots and turn them into neighborhood parks and playgrounds in return for the right to erect commercial advertising. Public school systems also have found a potentially lucrative source of money for textbooks and audio-visual devices by marketing exclusive rights to sell soft drinks on campus to the highest-bidding company, or by putting ads in hallways and restrooms. In Colorado Springs, Colorado, school buses carry the logos of Burger King. A school near an airport in Texas sells rooftop-advertising space.

Concerns about the ethics of turning students into captive audiences for commercial pitches have prompted backlashes against advertising in the public schools. Voters complain less about raising money for the municipal treasury by selling space on government buildings. Opposition generally is muted by the prodigious potential payoff. In 1996, the New Jersey Sports and Exposition Authority reached a deal with Continental Airlines to rename the Brendan T. Byrne Arena in the Meadowlands. The arena, home to the New Jersey Devils and the Nets, was dubbed Continental Airlines Arena, and Continental also bought the right to name parking lot sections after airline destinations. The twelve-year deal brought $29 million.

Cities need not sell themselves to reap financial rewards from the private sector. By privatizing public services, or by requiring public agencies to bid against private contractors for the right to operate government programs, some cities have realized substantial savings and freed general funds for other purposes.

Phoenix pioneered public-private competition in the 1970s by letting private companies bid for trash hauling contracts. The strategy reduced costs so effectively the city extended the practice to other public works departments.

Indianapolis requires many of its agencies,

including sewage treatment plants and airport managers, to compete against private bidders. City agencies do not always decide to bid; when they do, they squeeze average savings of twenty-five percent from their budgets. Such competition, the city estimates, saved $200 million in seven years. From 1992 to 1995, the city payroll dropped forty percent. To assuage employees, the city required that union workers who lost their jobs because of competition be hired by the private contractor, placed in another city job, or retrained and placed in another private-sector job. That assurance has so far turned out to be unnecessary; no union workers have lost their jobs as a result of privatization.

Requiring public agencies to bid against private contractors only works well when the service can be easily segregated from other municipal functions and operated as a self-supporting enterprise. The purported cost savings may turn out to be illusory if the reduced budget for an agency that wins such a contract hides a shift of overhead and other costs to other city agencies.

Cities Will Use Creative Financing in the Future

Traditional approaches to urban revitalization, particularly the top-down programs of the nation's ambitious antipoverty and Urban Renewal efforts in the 1950s and 1960s left the public and many elected officials disillusioned. Resistance to such undertakings, shrinking state and local budgets, and growing taxpayer demands that beneficiaries of publicly financed programs assume the cost of those programs dictate a new financial approach.

Innovative initiatives abound. Communities repackage existing sources of revenue, capture new ones, and forge partnerships with the private sector and with other communities to address the root causes of urban decay. The changing nature of the national economy, while presenting new hurdles for traditional sources of investment capital—banks and the municipal bond market—also presents new opportunities to attract financing from flush foundations and investment-fund managers.

In the twenty-first century, financing plans to improve and defend the vitality of American communities will require cooperation and creativity. Such qualities have served the nation well throughout its history. They will play a critical role in its future.

Neighborhood Matching Fund

Seattle Department of Neighborhoods
700 Third Avenue, Suite 400
Seattle, WA 98104-1849
www.wa.us/don/home.html

Contact: Jim Diers,
Director
206.684.0464

The Neighborhood Matching Fund provides money—$4.5 million in 2000—to Seattle neighborhood groups and organizations for neighborhood-initiated improvement, organizing or planning projects. To receive support, a proposed project must demonstrate a public benefit and must involve neighborhood members in the identification, planning, and execution stages. Once a project is approved, cash from the Neighborhood Matching Fund will match community-donated labor, materials, professional services, or cash.

Since 1988, residents have completed more than 1,000 Neighborhood Matching Fund projects. They also have built and installed playgrounds, begun community gardens, planted trees, started community schools, created intergenerational history projects, and worked on neighborhood planning efforts.

The Neighborhood Matching Fund includes five grant programs, each with its own guidelines and application methods:

1. **The Semi-Annual Fund** is for projects requiring grants of $10,000 to $100,000 that take up to one year to complete.

2. **The Small and Simple Projects Fund** is for projects seeking awards of $10,000 or less that can be completed within six months.

3. **The Neighborhood Membership Recruitment and Leadership Development Fund** awards $750 to build neighborhood organizations.

4. **The Involving All Neighbors Fund** awards between $500 and $2,000 to projects that promote the inclusion and participation of neighbors with developmental disabilities in the civic life of Seattle neighborhoods.

5. **The Tree Fund** provides free trees to neighborhoods. Groups can apply to obtain ten to forty trees for planting along residential planting strips or in parks. Trees are purchased wholesale by the city and delivered to neighborhood sites.

Purchasing Development Rights

Grand Traverse Regional Land
Conservancy
624 Third Street
Traverse City, MI 49684-2226

Contact: Glen Chown,
Executive Director
231.929.7911

Upper Michigan Peninsula townships have generated millions of dollars to preserve scenic land with a property-tax increase dedicated to land purchases.
The Grand Traverse Regional Land Conservancy centered in Traverse City, Michigan, works with the American Farmland Trust and area landowners to preserve their shared landscape heritage. By buying up farmland, open space, and scenic views, they curb development and safeguard the regional landscape.

Peninsula township voters have been extremely active in preservation measures. In 1994, they voted to approve an increase in their property taxes to purchase conservation easements on unique farmland. They bucked a trend by raising their taxes to defend a cherished way of life. These are far-sighted voters among the vanguard of a national movement to preserve farmland threatened by the economic pressures of real estate development.

The Purchasing Development Rights project works through a voter-mandated funding structure to purchase high-priority properties—properties valued for agriculture, proximity to historic and development sites, or scenic view. The first round of the program exceeded expectations.

Conservancy members have preserved more than 3,500 acres. Townships leveraged millions of matching funds from state and federal grants, as well as from private foundations. Farmers sell their development rights, and are paid the difference between the land's worth if subdivided and developed and its value as agricultural land. The land becomes part of a public trust, forever protected from large-scale, commercial development, though some land may be used for nature trails.

The tax has helped the townships protect prime fruit-farming regions from development and preserve the bucolic environment. The Land Conservancy acquired Fruithaven, ranked as one of Michigan's most valuable orchards, for example and offered 300 of 555 acres to small farmers who agreed to maintain the trees. The remaining acres will be open to the community as a nature preserve.

By agreeing to never subdivide the land, the Conservancy recoups some state money. Bank loans will be repaid from private donations. Donations and state contributions allow the Land Conservancy to move on to other properties.

The Grand Traverse Regional Land Conservancy has served as a model for several communities and has stimulated international interest in agricultural land preservation. The conservancy recently provided a special information session for Japanese officials interested in growth management and tourism. The Grand Traverse Regional Land Conservancy's Purchasing Development Rights program has demonstrated people's commitment to their environment and natural heritage and has proven a useful model for national and international organizations.

Better America Bonds

U.S. Environmental Protection Agency
Washington, DC
www.epa.gov/epapages/babs/index

Contact: Vicky Simarino,
Special Assistant to the Administrator
202.564.4700

The U.S. Environmental Protection Agency (EPA) issues tax-free bonds to help communities finance growth without expanding into the suburbs or into rural acreage. With the new emphasis on *Smart Growth*, American communities are seeking ways to grow and preserve the spaces they treasure as well as create parks, clean up brownfields, revitalize older neighborhoods, and improve water quality.

The *Better America Bonds* provide financing for sound growth management. These bonds generated $9.5 billion in bond authority to preserve open space, protect water quality, and clean up brownfields. Communities pay no interest on the bond, with the principle due fifteen years after the bond issue. Bondholders receive tax credits from the federal government equivalent to the amount of interest they would have received from the communities, keeping funds in circulation for economic development. Compared to traditional tax-exempt bonds, this tax-credit bond provides a considerable community subsidy. For example, assuming annual payments of five percent into a sinking fund, the issuer of a million-dollar bond saves more than $700,000 over fifteen years by issuing a *Better America Bond*. Bonding authority is given directly to the communities after a competitive bidding process. To be eligible, state, local, and tribal governments submit proposals to the EPA for review in consultation with other federal agencies. To emphasize regional stewardship and collaboration, the EPA expresses a preference for proposals that reflect joint planning among cities, suburbs, and rural areas.

To qualify for *Better America Bonds*, projects must meet one of three primary goals—preserving and enhancing open space, protecting water quality, and cleaning up brownfields. For example, the EPA identified the Illinois River Watershed/ Fox River, Illinois as a strong candidate for protection. The Fox River flows through several historic towns where the population has grown thirty percent in the last twenty years. In addition to the strain on the drinking water supply, the Fox is subject to sewage and runoff from Chicago's sprawling suburbs. By purchasing land along the river or by requiring controls on runoff pollution, *Better America Bonds* could finance projects to protect the water quality of Fox River, safeguarding the drinking water and health of thousands of Illinois residents.

The language of *Better America Bonds* legislation is brief. State and local authorities make the decisions about how best to create livable communities. The EPA simply provides the tool.

BiState Cultural Tax

Mid-America Regional Council
Ninth and Broadway,
Kansas City, MO. 64105

Contact: Molly McGovern,
Administrator
816-474-4240

Kansas City collects a tax from two states to pay for its renovation of Union Station, a tourist draw for the region. The Kansas City Consensus began a bi-state initiative to establish an asset tax for Kansas City's Historic Union station. The Mid-America Regional Council and several area arts organizations in the five-county, two-state region endorsed the station project. A five-county task force debated financing options and four of the five counties decided to charge a one-eighth-penny tax

on assets until the city raises $118 million, or roughly half the project's funding. Local foundations and businesses augmented the tax revenue by donating $82 million. Andy Scott, the executive director of the Union Station Assistance Corporation says the tax helped unite the region.

"Citizens in both Kansas and Missouri have long wanted to do something together," he said. "This gave them that opportunity."

Kansas City will use the funds to restore its historic train station and build a museum called Science City. The site preparation required extensive demolition and repairs, as well as the clearing of ten million pounds of debris and thirty-five miles of pipes. The renovation will help Union Station once again become the centerpiece of Kansas City.

The museum is expected to attract at least a million visitors a year, generating $8 million annually for the metropolitan economy. Property values in the downtown have risen and dilapidated buildings are being converted into art galleries and lofts.

No other bistate tax has ever passed. The unique funding tool evolved from a public-private partnership led by the Mid-American Regional Council. The tax brought together competing interests to build a stronger, more unified metropolitan community.

Livability at the Ballot Box

Center for Urban and
Metropolitan Policy
The Brookings Institution
1775 Massachusetts Ave., N.W.
Washington, DC 20036

Contact: Phyllis Myers,
President
State Resources Strategies
202.797.5402

**A national survey called *Livability at the
Ballot Box* suggests a majority of Americans want their states and local governments to finance growth management
and land conservation; though they
prefer to use existing financial resources,
some would agree to tax increases.**
Myers and the Brookings Institution
examined state and local conservation
and *Smart Growth* ballot issue results
during the November 1998 elections.
Myers, a conservation consultant, also
surveyed 240 state and local measures
related to conservation, parklands, and
smarter growth. The survey found:

- voters approved seventy-two percent
  of the 240 measures;
- the approved ballot measures will
  trigger more than $7.5 million in
  additional state and local conservation spending; and
- conservation ballot measures elicited
  strong constituency and grassroots
  engagement.

The goals, financing techniques, and
strategies of successful measures differed
from region to region. Myers' paper dis-
cusses the variation in regional success
rates. The paper also summarizes lessons
learned from the defeats and assesses
"what growing grassroots support for
land conservation and more livable communities means for policymakers and
practitioners."

Voters who consistently reject new tax
proposals agreed to set aside revenue
from existing tax sources. They were also
willing to finance environmental

programs with bonds repaid from general
revenue. Other statewide finance
measures involved renewals of popular
conservation programs. Myers noted that
though voter initiatives were remarkable
in their number, these 240 initiatives do
not represent the entire picture. Lawmakers also are creating environmental and
Smart Growth tools that do not require
direct voter approval: conservation easements, local option taxes for conservation and open space, endorsements for
agriculture, partnerships with nonprofits,
and developer impact fees.

Myers' research provides keys to effective programs for local communities. It is
a guide and inspiration for these grass-
roots organizations seeking useable
strategies for reaching conservation goals.

Central Park Conservancy

14 East 60th Street
New York, NY 10022

Contact: Richard Lepowski,
Director of Communications
212.310.6600

**The Central Park Conservancy, a private
nonprofit organization, manages Central
Park in contract with the City of New
York.** Founded in 1980, the Conservancy
has raised more than $193 million to
transform Central Park into a model
urban park. In addition to drafting a
management and restoration plan for the
park, the Conservancy has funded major
capital improvements, created programs
for volunteers and visitors, set standards
of excellence in park care, and provided
several endowments for long-term management and upkeep. In short, the Conservancy maintains the lawns, restores
the benches and landmarks, and
commands recreational and educational
programming in the park.

While these may seem simple tasks, the
Conservancy also provides eighty-five
percent of the $20 million in funds

needed to operate the park. The Conservancy pays the salaries of three of every
four Central Park employees and has
built an outstanding staff of park management professionals. In addition, the
Conservancy relies on volunteers to
ensure that twenty million yearly visitors
enjoy the park.

Conservancy crews maintain landscaping; upkeep ball fields and playgrounds;
remove graffiti; conserve monuments,
bridges, and buildings; and care for the
ponds, streams and woodlands of the
park by controlling erosion, maintaining
the drainage system, and protecting the
more than 150 acres of streams and lakes
from pollution, siltation, and algae.

To finance this work and the restoration of more than three-quarters of the
park, the Conservancy and the City have
raised millions of dollars. In 1993, a Conservancy trustee offered a $17 million
challenge grant the City matched within
three years for a total of $51 million. The
Conservancy raised an additional $26.2
million, to pay its operating budget and
finance an endowment for the ongoing
care of the restored landscapes.

Under its contract with the City, the
Conservancy receives an annual fee for
services. In return, the Conservancy must
raise and each year must spend a
minimum of $5 million in private funds.
The annual fee from the City depends on
the Conservancy's expenditures and on
revenues generated by concessions. Of
every $1 the Conservancy raises, $.83
goes toward direct spending on horticulture, operations, maintenance, education,
recreation, and public programs. The
Conservancy is accountable to the City of
New York, while the City retains control
and policy responsibility.

A model for public/private partnerships, through thorough and aggressive
fund-raising and careful budgeting, the
Conservancy has returned the park to its
status as the nation's finest urban park.

Scientific and Cultural Facilities District
899 Logan Street, Suite 500
Denver, CO 80203
www.artstozoo.org/scfd

Contact: Ellen Dumm
Public Information Officer
303.860.0588

A small sales tax increase in a six-county district finances Denver center-city arts, cultural, and scientific organizations. In 1988 arts organizations across the United States suffered from dwindling government funding. The Scientific and Cultural Facilities District (SCFD) annually generates roughly $24 million for more than 200 arts, cultural, and scientific organizations.

A nine-member board of directors—a representative from each county and three governor's appointees—reviews applications and distributes grants. The SCFD limits its administrative costs to three-quarters of one percent of the total tax revenues collected. A mandatory review and reporting structure ensures accountability, as do the publicly defined administrative procedures and public meetings. First tier funds support four major institutions: the Denver Natural History Museum, Denver Zoo, Denver Art Museum, and Denver Botanical Gardens. The second tier comprises organizations with annual budgets exceeding $750,000, including the symphony, ballet, and children's museum. Tier III funds are allocated to the six counties for distribution to smaller local organizations such as theatres, historical societies, orchestras, nature conservatories, and arts centers.

Denver's cultural organizations have used this new funding source to return resources to the community. During the celebration of the tenth year of the SCFD, recipient organizations expressed their thanks to the citizens of Adams, Arapahoe, Boulder, Denver, Douglass, and Jefferson counties by offering free performances, exhibits, and workshops.

The organizations financed by SCFD "provided more than 1.1 million art and science opportunities for 330,000 area school children; offered more than two million free admissions and 750,000 reduced-rate admissions to area cultural and science venues; and provided more than 1,000 programs for the elderly, minorities, people with disabilities, and children," according to district publications. The cultural institutions also expanded programs to hard-to-serve populations.

The tax does not drain area resources. The recipient organizations generate more than $520 million in economic activity, attract tourists, and employ 4,000 people. Together, under the SCFD, these arts and science organizations gain more revenue than each could collect. In 1994, voters renewed the SCFD for an additional ten years and it has served as a model for Pittsburgh, Salt Lake City, and Fresno, California.

Somerset Shared Services Neighborhood Groups
Somerset Alliance for the Future, Inc.
166 West Main Street
Somerset, NJ 08776

Contact: Stephen Dragos,
President
908.704.1010

The Somerset Shared Services Neighborhood Groups (SSSNG) aims to negotiate shared services agreements across jurisdictions—among towns, schools, and counties—to reduce the cost of government and to enhance government service. It started small, but grew into a tremendous community. SSSNG came out of an earlier initiative, called the Somerset Alliance, that consolidated three municipal police forces into one.

The Alliance attracted 200 individuals to more than a dozen committees and task forces to talk about sharing services. The Somerset Alliance also conducted two baseline studies of twenty-one municipalities and eighteen school districts to understand services that were being shared, define those that could be shared, and recommend methods for sharing. Based on the meetings, the Alliance created the SSSNG, with a coordinating council of county and municipal officials, to help prioritize activities and administer the project.

The group uncovered creative funding mechanisms, such as funding the consolidation project with municipal and county dues and New Jersey Department of Community Affairs grants. It also leveraged local corporate and foundation support to hire consultants who facilitated sharing services across municipalities. SSSNG has also been successful in clarifying the major issues for sharing among the communities, namely joint purchasing, school-to-town sharing, shared inspectors, personnel and labor negotiations, and computers and document imaging. The most valuable outcome of SSSNG has been the networking and information exchange made possible between people in all levels of government. With the help of talented consultants and private sector volunteers, the SSSNG has determined the best course for future service sharing and has renewed Somerset residents' confidence in one another and their government.

9 | Going To Scale

Partners for Livable Communities asked a group of distinguished community-development leaders for help writing a blueprint for urban policy in the next century: To what degree does the best practice model address intractable urban issues such as early learning, crime reduction, economic development, and inner-city revival? Problems like urban sprawl, pollution, and inadequate schools top many civic agendas. The challenge is to make a successful program in one place work in more places. Can the nation go to scale by transferring models to other cities?

Top-down and cookie-cutter approaches do not work, according to community development experts, youth-service policymakers, and program leaders in communities. Too often, problems that appear to be similar actually differ. Not all urban areas share histories and demographics.

A solution for teaching English to Mexican immigrant children in Dalton, Georgia, for example, may not achieve results in New York City, where the majority of the Hispanic populations come from different geographical and cultural backgrounds.

Some communities experience difficulties replicating programs because they cannot access information and technology, according to William Dietel, the former president of the Rockefeller Brothers Foundation. Although many communities want to solve "intransigent" problems, Dietel says, "the ignorance of leadership about reform efforts tried elsewhere is especially discouraging."

Often the civil servants and unions who benefit from the status quo will block any attempt at reform or change, even if new programs prove effective in another city, said Peter Harkness, editor and publisher of *Governing* magazine. Seemingly minor reforms, such as retooling government-procurement systems, can generate remarkable improvements because they are less likely to attract opposition by powerful forces, Harkness says.

Cities could do well to learn from corporate practice, according to Harkness and Dietel. Harkness believes many companies hired by local governments learn to adapt to disparate individual populations and cultures. The federal government could lead the way by incorporating *Smart Growth* principles in its own work, adds Representative Earl Blumenauer (D-Oregon). As the largest landowner, landlord, and employer, the federal government enjoys a unique capacity to encourage livable solutions. It can "establish policies consistent with the plans, needs, and environmental concerns of local communities and require other federal agencies to abide by those policies," Blumenauer says. "[This] could have a tremendous impact on issues of urban form, land use patterns, and transportation choices in that community."

Christopher Gates, president of the National Civic League, asserts the quality of a community's "civic infrastructure—the complex interaction of people and groups through which decisions are made and problems resolved" determines the success of any reform. Going to scale does not work by adopting specific programs, he concludes. Nevertheless, information and experience can be translated from one community to another by "sharing the lessons that have been learned in the process of establishing the model."

Like Gates, most leaders cautioned against trying to create copycat programs, but they did reveal the principles they believe necessary for building and replicating successful reforms.

Success at going to scale, according to Paul Brophy, requires a bold vision. Replicating programs, adds Brophy, a national community development consultant, also requires "persistent leadership, a rational and participatory decision-making process, and excellent technical talent."

The United Way of America replicates local-affiliate programs in their own communities, in other cities, and in concert with other agencies with mixed success, according to Betty Beene, the organization's president and chief executive officer.

Although solutions are local, Beene concludes, "efforts to go to scale across systems and across the country can be enhanced by engaging other national/local networks." Successful programs unite citizens, private enterprises, nonprofit organizations, and public agencies in leadership. "Systemic change," she says, "cannot occur unless [these sectors] are equal owners of the change process."

Mary Lee Widener, president of Neighborhood Housing Services of America, adds that home owners must command a leadership role in community development partnerships. They hold the key to sustainability because they are the first to be affected by neighborhood reforms; ultimately, they will live with the consequences.

Program leaders should seek staff willing to share leadership roles with the people served, says Marion Pines, director of the Sar Levitan Center for Social Policy Studies. Pines urges program leaders to nurture staff by providing them training and opportunities to develop professionally. "When I was creating programs for the City of Baltimore," Pine says, "I put my senior staff in Outward Bound to learn survival skills and team building and [how] to make decisions under stress."

Youth development programs, like any, work best with the backing of community institutions, Pines says. Weiming Lu adds that maintaining community support requires an attitude of service and a willingness to share credit with community players. Lu, president of Lowertown Redevelopment Corporation in St. Paul, Minnesota, also urges community developers to make long-term commitments and to seek assistance from established leaders in banks, government, and other institutions. "It takes time and effort to create a sustainable project," Lu says. "It isn't a quick solution, quick fix, or whatever."

The views of the community leaders follow.

Marion Pines
Director
The Sar Levitan Center for Social Policy Studies
Johns Hopkins University
Baltimore, Maryland

I am hesitant to talk about replication of successful program models that steer at-risk youths into jobs, education, and training programs. It is very difficult. If I must talk about replication, I would rather talk about replicating program principles, rather than programs.

If you try to replicate models, the best guarantee of success is the quality of the staff. You must find people who are committed to young people, who believe in their success, who believe they are not just losers.

If I'm looking to recruit staff, I would look for people who share similar backgrounds and experiences with the students—those who young people can identify with, who can readily walk the walk, talk the talk. I look for some commitment to the idea of young people themselves making decisions. Would [the prospective staff member] be threatened by the concept?

If we want young people to grow up to be leaders, they need experience in leadership. It's hard if we develop the whole model and say: "Look what we developed for you."

If you are recruiting for a manager, you are looking for understanding and experience; understanding what it means to manage a system that has twenty providers, understanding what you look for in picking a provider, and understanding the needed experience level.

Once you select a staff, every organization requires diversity training—training in being sensitive to people's differences. One of the things you want to look for is not only staff recruitment, but also is staff training. For example, the National Youth Employment Coalition New Leaders Academy brings in people from all over the country for four or five days of intensive training to grow the next generation of leaders.

You have to have a commitment to training. When I was creating programs for the City of Baltimore, I put my senior staff in Outward Bound to learn survival skills and team building and how to make decisions under stress. Unfortunately, people are insulated in their jobs and never get a chance to grow and learn. This is true of teachers; they remain in the classrooms, rarely exposed to new ideas or new techniques outside of the work world. We haven't built training into our culture enough; we expect staff to do a good job but we don't invest enough.

The newest federal initiative for youth is the Department of Labor, Youth Opportunity Grants program. The government will be awarding $5 million to $12 million per city to about thirty cities on a competitive basis. Federal officials will interview a variety of people in a community to see how much the whole community is buying into the idea of comprehensive system building for at-risk youth.

We need a broad partnership system—incorporating juvenile justice professionals, the community colleges, faith communities, and Workforce Investment Act Councils and community-based organizations. We want to see if they are all at the table and if they are all reading out of the same hymnal.

WHAT WORKS:
Youth SERVICE Principles

- Ensure a continuity of contact with caring adults committed to their labor market success;
- Emphasize the centrality of work and connections to employers;
- Provide opportunities and encouragement for postsecondary education;
- Provide a variety of options for improving educational and skill competencies;
- Offer "hands-on" experiential training in areas of labor market growth and community rebuilding;
- Guarantee ongoing support through the first jobs, coupled with sustained efforts to improve skills;
- Set up incentives to improve and provide recognition of achievements;
- Afford opportunities for leadership development, self-governance and decision making; and
- Link young people with sources of external support.

—FROM THE SAR LEVITAN CENTER FOR SOCIAL POLICY STUDIES

WHAT WORKS:
Youth SYSTEM Principles

- Seek to achieve an expanded school-to-work model for out-of-school youth;
- Build on what exists; use multiple resources;
- Utilize a community collaborative for leadership;
- Adopt a system of home rooms or community anchors for youths to access services;
- Find and utilize an effective intermediary to work with both youth and the employer community; and
- Coordinate and integrate with other systems whenever possible.

—FROM THE SAR LEVITAN CENTER FOR SOCIAL POLICY STUDIES

Peter Harkness

Editor and Publisher

Governing

Washington, D.C.

I have found when you try to change behavior on a mass level, it doesn't work. If you've been able to lower the teenage pregnancy rate in city X through a specific program, for example, don't think that program is going to work in city Y. It will depend on the politics in city Y; whether the religious right is strong, for example. Take for example, some great schools in Harlem. When you look behind the scenes, an incredible amount of resources are invested in those schools.

There is a reason why successful programs are not replicated—the reason is the cost and the cost isn't just money. The forces arrayed against replication or reforms of any kind are enormous. Administrations are against reform; unions are against reform; so many powerful groups are against reform. Real reform in schools, for example, will take more of a revolution than we are ready to stomach.

In Atlanta, [Governor] Roy Barnes had central authority take over planning for the entire state of Georgia. He was elected over a very strong opponent and the first thing he did was create the Georgia Regional Transit Authority, known in the state as "Give Roy the Total Authority." He's a dictator of an entire region. Sometimes that needs to happen—to take power away from the counties and give it to a czar. Barnes had to get authority from the legislature; they not only gave him authority, there are amendments tacked on to give him more power. Top business people in the state are getting on the telephone and giving him votes.

Now people say if it happened in Georgia, one of the most conservative states in the country, you can do it anywhere. I don't think you can. In Chicago, I don't think you'd have a snowball's chance in hell. You couldn't do that in Pittsburgh. Northeastern cities are more dynamic.

The kind of replication that works the best is something simple, achievable—not the kind of thing that will stir up a lot of opposition. That's why reform in the areas of technology—how you do business—and changes in the way you finance projects [can be successful].

When the state started purchasing on-line rather than by a paper system, it drove down costs and opened the government to a lot of vendors. It's that sort of practical thing that doesn't require people to really change their habits that seems to work best.

Strong political support for reform—in some places you have it and in some places, you don't. Where you don't have it, it's going to make things difficult. If you have strong leadership from the top, it's more likely to succeed. If you don't, forget it.

I think, oddly enough, some of the people who do this best are private sector companies who do government work around the country. They've worked in lots of different communities and have learned how to go in and figure out the politics of a place, the culture of a place, and what it is that makes this place tick—to figure out how best to make a place work.

You are going to see a lot of this in welfare-to-work, in child-support enforcement, in parking systems around the country. A lot is being outsourced; companies like Lockheed Martin are becoming conversant [in government administration]. They are really clever about figuring out

> The power of the people who resist changing things is much greater than the power of the people who want to change them. There's not much advantage in being the one who goes out on the limb for systemic reform; not many people who have done it have fared very well.

> Business-like, day-to-day, nitty-gritty stuff governments have to do; that is where reform is likely—such as changing the whole way procurement works in the state of Oregon. — PETER HARKNESS

what will work in one place and what won't. Their profits are on the line; the private sector is very pragmatic; contractors may do the best kind of replication you can find.

Some companies over do it or don't do it well. Technical-consulting firms will try to sell to state X what they've sold to state Y and don't get away with it. You've got to be careful that what you are trying to replicate isn't something that's very special; because an awful lot of thought went into it.

Neal Peirce
Syndicated Columnist
Washington, D.C.

Most important innovations only move to scale when a community stakeholder[s] challenge old ways with informed, determined, and tenacious pressure. Otherwise, lethargy, complacency, and professional rigidity will win out every time. The secret is not just in getting the word out on innovations that work, though that's a vital step in the process. Community organizing, by stakeholders willing to challenge existing ways, has to come into play.

All the people pushing for some kind of change or improvement —[for example,] those that are starting charter schools and putting pressure on state legislatures to permit charter schools or on school boards to authorize them—are only making their way through determined and continued pressure on the system. [Our] very rigid education system is not prone to change unless it is forced.

Take the new *Smart Growth* movement: Gradually it is forcing policymakers to take notice, and even forcing developers to stop thinking [solely in terms of] standard suburban products and saying those products fill all needs. The *Smart Growth* movement is gaining support as people are [becoming] dissatisfied with the way we are growing and are insisting on new ways to develop. [People are] moving the *Smart Growth* movement to significant scale.

William Dietel
Former President
Rockefeller Brothers Fund
New York City

Going to scale is a complicated matter, we all know, and while there is no single or simple solution, surely the need to communicate more effectively and efficiently the successful efforts of successful communities is a priority. Despite the growing use of telecommunications, we are a long way from fully exploiting modern technology. As the number of communities ready and eager to tackle the most intransigent issues grows, the ignorance of leadership about reform efforts tried elsewhere is especially discouraging.

Communities with a commitment to substantive change need the assistance of the corporate world and its telecommunications capacity. Without such a partnership not only will reform be slow in coming, but also it will be expensive in financial and human terms. —WILLIAM DIETEL

Betty Beene
President and Chief Executive Officer
United Way of America
Alexandria, Virginia

As I reflect on community building efforts in which United Way has been involved, it appears successful efforts often begin in one or more neighborhoods and expand based on knowledge gained from the experiences of the original target areas. Housing development efforts and community mobilizations around early childhood development come to mind. Our experience with housing involved a multiyear partnership with the Ford Foundation in which selected United Ways, and their community partners, helped develop and support neighborhood-based community development corporations. Our work with early childhood education resides in the network of more than 300 communities with a Success By 6® (SB6) early child development initiative.

With SB6, Bridges to Success (United Way community school model), America's Promise, and the 5 Goals 4 Kids Coalition to Prevent Youth Violence, we share knowledge and methods among United Ways to help many different communities address the challenges and opportunities faced by children and youth. We have also found that efforts to go to scale across systems and across the country can be enhanced by engaging other national/local networks, such as the National Collaboration for Youth, which is comprised of national organizations with local affiliates. Each national organization can mobilize its own network and encourage local connections between its affiliates and those of other national network partners.

Going to Scale: Requirements

- Genuine partnership between the public, private,
  and nonprofit sectors.
- Integration of the strategies and work of agencies

Getting federal agencies working in concert on the same strategy can be a challenge. In our experience with efforts to reduce youth violence, the commitment to change cuts across federal agencies, but strategies and programs are fragmented.

Yet, ultimately, change does not occur in the United States because the federal government wills it. Ours is a public/private system and I believe going-to-scale change can occur only when the government and the for-profit and not-for-profit sectors work together. Systemic change occurs when public, private, and nonprofit sectors are equal owners of the change process.

Arthur P. Ziegler, Jr.
President
Pittsburgh History and Landmarks Foundation
Pittsburgh, Pennsylvania

Taking a program that works well in one community to other communities can be well intentioned but misguided. The replication of programs, lock-stock-and-barrel, creates one of the biggest problems in community development. The notion that a central authority wields all the knowledge and can impose its rules on communities informs many HUD grant programs. Jim Rouse's festival market ideas—replicated in Boston, New York, Baltimore, and Miami—stem from this belief in replication; it also forms the root of the mid-twentieth century urban renewal programs resulting in economic, architectural, and human disasters. Today we sell a standardized answer to revitalizing

> I suggest we first know our own place and understand it from the grassroots,
> always working from the bottom up, not only socially, but also by working with
> living patterns and shopping patterns. —ARTHUR P. ZIEGLER, JR.

communities. Small towns follow suit with new brick sidewalks, trees, and streetlights. But new shops fail to follow because the new city lacked the conditions necessary for success.

Not that we don't want one community to take lessons from another—but in each place we need to start with conditions of that place, learn from the people, the architecture, the history, the economic life, the transportation systems, the cultural values, and the racial relationships. We should bring to bear our studies of what is working in other places with similar circumstances; to take those operating principles that are successful in one place and try to adapt those principles.

Had Mr. Rouse replicated the working principles of his festival markets rather than the standardized formats and applied those uniquely in each city, he would have enjoyed a great deal more success, and many cities would have saved considerable subsidy money.

We should gauge young people's feelings, talk to customers, and visit with the elderly. We must

New stadiums, Nordstrom's, Hard Rock Cafes, and up-to-date stadium-style movie theatres provide examples of communities' desires to replicate programs from other cities. The Hard Rock Cafe was interesting when located in one or two cities. One wanted to visit it because of its uniqueness. But when it appears everywhere, it might as well be nowhere. —ARTHUR P. ZIEGLER, JR.

study programs at work in other cities for their strengths and weaknesses, and solicit the best and most sensitive professional help, whether it is from architects or economists or publicists.

We marry the national and local professionals. From the knowledge acquired from combining people and ideas, an understanding will emerge to define the right local project. The operating principles of projects in many other locales will operate in this one as well, but only as an adaptation for this particular environment, not the imposition of a Platonic model meant to work everywhere.

One of the most successful forms of neighborhood revitalization has been the historic preservation movement that is always adapting to the local scene primarily because it is not dependent on any national sources of money that require the implementation of a standardized model. The preservationists remain financially short-handed, but acquire strength from their unique flexibility. They create successful projects through adaptation of good ideas and sound goals—not from trying to repeat projects that worked successfully somewhere in the world.

John P. Mascotte

Former Chairman
Local Initiatives Support Corporation
(LISC)
Kansas City, Missouri

Intermediaries [with] a little challenge cash and out-of-town-expert credibility are important. Those intermediaries have to be tightly focused and willing to be patient with their own egos. LISC has really committed to facilitating community development activity and has not been particularly eager to stand in the spotlight on its own. If the intermediary, rather than the local group, is going to get credit [for a program], I think that's doomed to failure.

In the LISC projects I have been involved with across the country, nothing substitutes for what I call [the] highly vulnerable risk capital you need up front. Because of LISC's patient funding from [the] Ford [Foundation] and ultimately from others, [we have had an] ability to hire good people and to have them stay at projects until they solve problems.

A corollary to having adequate capital is flexibility. I think even the most well-intentioned federal program has . . . so much oversight [that it] slow[s] down and . . . [its] capacity to move freely [is restricted]. What would really help LISC's work [is the ability to] commit to [providing] a quarter million dollars at the front end and say, "if you guys locally will raise a quarter of a million dollars, we'll match that. Let's get this thing started."

We continue to underestimate the amount of money it cost[s] to get [projects] successfully launched. A subsidiary LISC started a few years ago, called the Retail Initiative, is focused on doing grocery stores. It took us three to four years to get the first one done, and now we have ten or eleven. LISC was fifteen or sixteen years old before we started that initiative, and we still underestimated the cost by at least fifty to sixty-five percent. We also underestimated the amount of time it would take us to get done by more than two years.

New initiatives take an enormous amount of time. You uncover problems that you honestly didn't know existed in the first place, and you have this enormous level of what I call heavy-hearted skepticism. It is not that people don't wish you well; it's just that they say, "it is a shame, but we know that just won't work."

The necessity of overcoming [skepticism figures] in issues as complex as lending to minorities at the home mortgage level and to facilitating bridge loans to close redevelopment projects. [It also presents obstacles in] working with tax credits to prove you really can use the low-income housing tax credit in an economically effective and socially desirable way. All those [projects] have their skeptics until they are done. You have to convince the community they have the capacity—in terms of leadership, money, and guts—to do something. [Communities] can be encouraged with some technical assistance and initial money—and a hand-off to the local leadership. Once the projects are done, they become the poster children for how you can do it in other places.

Congressman Earl Blumenauer
Third Congressional District
Portland, Oregon

Interstate highways that cut cities—sterile redevelopments where neighborhoods once stood—and ever-growing circles of sprawl around towns and cities: We are still dealing with the legacy of sixties-style urban renewal that too often damaged more than it renewed. Built from the top down, these failed experiments reflect their bias toward cookie-cutter solutions and their lack of citizen input into planning. Their most positive outcome is the growth of dedicated, community-based groups working to make their cities livable again.

The federal government can encourage people and communities to make better decisions. It can spend resources to encourage more livable solutions: offering local jurisdictions more federal dollars for building transit rather than roads, for example. The federal government also can adopt uniform and fair rules of the game, as it has recently—equalizing tax benefits for transit commuters and car commuters.

Most important, the federal government can lead by example. As the nation's largest landowner, landlord, and employer, the federal government is pervasive and could be a powerful model for the behavior we seek from individuals, businesses, and institutions. The General Services Administration (GSA) is the steward for federal buildings, responsible for a million square feet or more in sixty commu-

nities and a national inventory of over 300 million square feet. Allowing GSA to establish policies consistent with the plans, needs, and environmental concerns of local communities, and requiring other federal agencies to abide by those policies, could have a tremendous impact on issues of urban form, land use patterns, and transportation choices in that community.

Tempting as the idea of taking the movement national may be, staying local is really what we are all about. — EARL BLUMENAUER

Ideally, the federal government would be a positive influence on decisions made at the local level, but would not make those decisions, allowing the people with the best understanding of local conditions, causes, and solutions to chart their own courses. We can learn from the successes of others; their techniques and tactics may spark good new ideas about how we can approach local and regional problems. But ultimately, the best solutions are homegrown, based on people's understanding of their own communities and their sense of where they want to go.

Suzanne Morse
Executive Director
Pew Partnership for Civic Change
Charlottesville, Virginia

The tendency is for communities to want to do the quick fixes. We all want that. But when communities go back in and tinker with the most important elements of programs, they tend to have more success. In Rapid City, South Dakota, their issue was a very high high-school dropout rate among Native Americans. When they began to address the issue, they found out it wasn't just about dropouts. It was the system and the whole way it related to Native American people: The community discovered violence, a lack of academic achievement, and a whole range of other things. They began to get a handle on the drop-out rate in a systematic way. That's being able to look beyond the simple.

Replicability has to do with the way to frame the problem in a different way. Cookie-cutter approaches don't work. One city is never quite the same as another. In North Carolina, [officials] thought the issue was unemployment for a large number of counties. They found it was not so much unemployment as it was packaging the assets they had. They reframed their issue, not as unemployment, but as creating that region of North Carolina as the center for handmade crafts. [Communities in western North Carolina created HandMade in America Inc., a craft production and sales company that now delivers crafts throughout the country.]

Principles of Reform and Replication

• Seek out root causes and learn how to frame—or define the problem to focus on those root causes.
• Identify your assets and resources.
• Lead with your strengths.

Their model, most people would say, is about crafts. But their model is learning about their regional assets and framing their issues so they can adapt multiple local components to model programs.

One of the pitfalls of the cooking-cutter approach is that people tend to think, "If we don't have [the right] building and we don't have fifteen trained youth workers, we can't do this model."

You have hidden treasures, hidden aspects of the community, hidden people with whom you've never worked. You don't think of youth workers, for example, being critical to the job-training issue; you don't think of artists being critical to community development. But in some communities these unusual suspects are vital.

It's not that easy framing an issue. The second thing is being able to have a better sense of what you have at the table and then, thirdly, being able to lead with those strengths and fill the holes to adapt a program in some unique ways to make this model applicable to your communities.

Paul Brophy
Principal
Brophy & Reilly, LLC
Columbia, Maryland

Jim Rouse's modus operandi was to build an image of the possible and vault the obstacles to a better future: Going to scale in our community programs starts with a bold vision. Once a vision takes hold, it develops its own life: It draws people to the idea something better is possible. But vision is not enough. Success at going to scale requires:

• vision;
• persistent leadership;
• a rational and participatory decision-making process;
• and excellent technical talent.

Only with these ingredients can the human and financial resources be garnered to produce effective new futures for our communities.

Christopher Gates
President
National Civic League
Denver, Colorado

For the past 105 years, the premise that successful community-based programs serve as models to be replicated has guided the National Civic League (NCL). We recognize and celebrate model programs in hopes these innovative efforts will go to scale. For example, for more than fifty years, NCL's All-America City Award has highlighted exemplary community-based problem-solving efforts. Yet, we find models often don't directly transfer from one community to another.

Providing hands-on technical assistance for the past fifteen years, we have found a community's civic infrastructure can determine the success of replication. Civic infrastructure describes the complex interaction of people and groups who make decisions and solve problems.

The days where government, or for that matter, any sector of a community, can act alone are long gone; cross-sector collaboration is key to successfully establishing community-based programs.

At one time, community players like the mayor, the city manager, the large local employer, and the wealthy family in town for generations could sit down in the room and make a decision or cut a deal. Now politically, racially, geographically, ethnically, and economically diverse stakeholder groups need their voices heard and their concerns valued.

Going to scale, in the end, might not so much be about directly mapping one community's project onto another community, but instead about helping each other navigate the changing problem-solving sea. —CHRISTOPHER GATES

Involving diverse perspectives may initially complicate program development and add length to decision making. Nevertheless, engaging diverse players can help speed the program implementation. Project outcomes and policies are, in effect, pre-sold to interest groups and the general citizenry who help decide policy options. Community stakeholders are not inclined to block implementation of a project that reflects their own interests and efforts.

NCL has found communities who ground model program adoption on the democratic ideals of participation are more likely to successfully replicate effective programs. We also understand these practices represent a new way of doing business: Inclusion of multiple sectors and diverse voices runs contrary to traditional, top-down exclusionary approaches to community government.

As we enter the next century, the need to go to scale is becoming more apparent. A host of social problems the federal government once attempted to solve have been thrown into the laps of local communities. The more we share ideas, plans, and problem-solving tools—the more we replicate each other's successes, the better we make each community in our nation a Livable Community.

The help we can give each other may be more replicable than are the specific programs. Communities may better replicate a problem-solving process than adopt specific programs. Sometimes the value of the model isn't in direct replication; it is in sharing the lessons that have been learned in the process of establishing the model.

George Knight
President
Neighborhood Reinvestment Corporation
Washington, D.C.

1. Going to scale means shifting from personality-driven to system-driven efforts. The low-income housing tax credit (LIHTC) has prompted the building of thousands of units with assistance from many hundreds of different actors. The financial system guided the activity—although the details of where, how, and how much were driven by individual personalities.

2. Going to scale assumes a commonality of problems to be solved. The NeighborWorks Campaign for Home Ownership grew from twenty organizations providing home ownership for 1,600 families in 1993 to over 110 organizations providing it to 7,000 families in 1998. Similar problems—lack of access to down payments, rehabilitation loans, and financial information—prompted the program's expansion.

3. Going to scale is possible only when the flow of critical resources is assured with a minimum of uncertainty year in and year out. In the early days of the LIHTC, uncertainty about the credit's permanence made its use costly. The NeighborWorks Campaign for Home Ownership spread rapidly, however, because Neighborhood Reinvestment committed to a five-year effort of grants to local revolving loan funds.

Mary Lee Widener

President
Neighborhood Housing Services of America
Oakland, California

I am as certain today, after working twenty-five years in community development, as I was a quarter century ago: The right stuff for going to scale is a true partnership of business, local government, and residents of the community in need of development. Each partner is essential.

Community development attempts to help a distressed community become an emerging market, attractive to business and residents. The importance of partnerships of business and local government is well accepted. Even today, however, we find resistance to including residents as equal partners, often for fear of time delays, increasing cost, or lack of professionalism. The more enlightened community developer knows that, ultimately, residents, especially home owners, make the best partners in a community development effort.

A NeighborWorks organization in the Fruitvale community of Oakland, California, the Unity Council provides an example of a national initiative that has gone to scale. It is a solid partnership of residents, businesses, and local government. The Council recently broke ground on a $100 million Fruitvale BART Transit Village project, has created and manages over 430 units of affordable housing, provides child-care services for 445 low- and moderate-income families, and leads an uplifting of the entire community. The Unity Council's work is resident-based with highly respected home owners providing strong leadership in partnership with business and local government.

The home owners' stake in the community gives them partnership rights in neighborhood housing development. Their community strength brings value to the partnership. Ultimately, as consumers, borrowers, or taxpayers, they will retire the long-term debt associated with the development.

When the business and local government partners move on to other priorities, resident partners remain as caretakers to sustain the work of the partnership.

—MARY LEE WIDENER

Obviously, extraordinary leadership and financial resources are essential in any successful community building initiative. I am convinced all lasting community development efforts begin with residents as equal partners.

Weiming Lu

President
Lowertown Redevelopment Corporation
St. Paul, Minnesota

I have worked as a consultant to cities helping them create urban villages like Lowertown [St. Paul, Minnesota] for many years. Ten or twelve years ago, I helped the [Lyndhurst] Foundation create a new corporation in Chattanooga. They devoted $20 million to Riverpark and to downtown development. More recently, the Rhode Island Foundation set up a kind of funding that would be helpful to them in the rejuvenation of downtown Providence. We shared our experiences with groups involved in the reconstruction of South Central Los Angeles—Seattle—at the Hartford, Connecticut, riverfront. I am helping businessmen in Yokahama, Japan, save their business district and am serving as a planning adviser to the City of Beijing.

The two main problems with replicating programs are territorial disputes and misuse of funds. Each case is a little different; some use private funding; some are public kinds of initiatives; the third is foundations. I don't think there is any magic formula; we can share experience, but each city has to figure out its own solution. We can help cities kick around ideas…get something they need. We suggest an attitude, maybe—how we would approach these things. In the end, it's the community; it's the building that counts. In the end, the leader will change, but the community will remain and will evolve.

- **Bring something to the table.** For example, we were invited by the private foundation to help an inner-city neighborhood on the other side of the city. We bring in resources and expertise, know-how, and connections with city hall. That's the way we are successful in getting resources from the state and local government as well. You always have to have something to trade; it could be your connection with the mayor, your credential within the community. We have established a kind of credential within the community and even developers feel if they can get our help they will have a better chance of getting their plan approved by the community.

- **Leadership is critical.** I don't think you can do it alone. The political infrastructure is either there or not. Because of mergers and consolidations in the financial sector, we are losing the bankers; they are moving across the Mississippi River, even to the West Coast. Banks represent the kind of leadership that typically the community can rely on. It is very difficult to keep politicians involved and also the political setup is such that always people are looking for the next elections—every two years, every four years.

- **Shared credit is critical.** When we were lucky enough to get a presidential award for design excellence, the White House called me, "Who would you like to invite to get the awards?" I named these different public-private entities; seven or eight, a small representation of the forty-to-fifty I normally work with. We gave all five awards to other people; we have kept none for ourselves. The award to us is the community—artists find a home here, high-tech entrepreneurs find a home here.

- **You have to look at the long-term.** Communities need to look much further than two years or four years. You do need the kind of leadership that is committed to the community. It takes time and effort to create a sustainable project. It isn't a quick solution, quick fix or whatever. Quick fixes don't last very long. My former chairman, the mayor, served office for fourteen years, the longest term in St. Paul history. That makes a difference. I don't change jobs—I have job offers all the time. I'm more committed to the community than sitting on the musical chairs; I think the persistent effort, and the willingness not to be totally fixed in your vision strengthens the community; we are continuing to re-envision; continue to build Lowertown.

You must have interdisciplinary expertise. Development is so complicated. You go from the envisioning process, the design, and the plan to the financing—then how to put it together. We have to help market the area. Design, finance, and marketing—all are very complicated. You also have to have political skill to build bridges. You must use the resources in an intelligent way. Resources are very short—you cannot waste them. For every dollar we put in, we leverage thirteen to twenty.

Index of Best Practices

Resource Reading

American Public Transit Association. *Access to Opportunity: Linking Inner-City Workers to Suburban Jobs.* Washington, D.C.: 1994.

Atkins, Patricia. *The Emerging Regional Governance Network.* Washington, D.C.: National Association of Regional Councils/National Academy of Public Administration, 1999.

Atlas, John. *Saving Affordable Housing: What Community Groups Can Do and What Government Should Do.* Washington, D.C.: National Housing Institute, 1997.

Beaumont, Constance, editor. *Challenging Sprawl: Organizational Response to a National Problem.* Washington, D.C.: National Trust for Historic Preservation, 1999.

Benner, Chris and Walsh, Phil. *Urban Parks: Campaigns and Strategies.* Washington, D.C.: Partners for Livable Communities, 1997.

Benner, Christopher. *Business Improvement Districts: Taxation with Representation.* Washington, D.C.: Partners for Livable Communities, 1997.

Berens, Gayle and Garvin, Alexander. *Urban Parks and Open Space.* Washington, D.C.: Urban Land Institute, 1997.

Bianchini, Franco. *Importance of Culture for Urban Economic Development in Great Britain.* London: Comedia Consultancy, 1991.

Bianchini, Franco and Parkinson, Michael, editors. *Cultural Policy and Urban Regeneration: The West European Experience.* Manchester, UK: Manchester University Press, 1993.

Bond, Evagene H., editor. *La Comunidad: Design, Development, and Self-Determination in Hispanic Communities,* Washington, D.C.: Partners for Livable Places, 1985.

Booth, Kathy. *Culture Builds Communities: A Guide to Partnership Building and Putting Culture to Work on Social Issues.* Washington, D.C.: Partners for Livable Communities, 1995.

Booth, Kathy. *Institutions as Fulcrums of Change: A Creative Reimagination of Every Community's Resources.* Washington, D.C.: Partners for Livable Communities, 1996.

Bosselman, Fred P.; Peterson, Craig A.; and McCarthy, Claire. *Managing Tourism Growth, Issues and Applications.* Washington, D.C.: Island Press, 1998.

Bowes, David. *Creating the Globally Competitive Community.* Washington, D.C.: Partners for Livable Communities and the Manufacturing Institute, 1997.

Brandes, Roberta. *Cities Back from the Edge: New Life for Downtown.* New York, NY: John Wiley & Sons, Inc., 1998.

Carnegie Corporation. *Great Transitions: Preparing Adolescents for a New Century.* Washington, D.C.: 1995.

Carnegie Council on Adolescent Development. *A Matter of Time: Risk and Opportunity in the Nonschool Hours.* New York, NY: 1993.

Chicago Department of Cultural Affairs. *Gallery 37 Model: A Resource Manual for Designing an Arts-Based Youth Employment Program.* Chicago, IL: 1998.

Cisneros, Henry, editor. *Interwoven Destinies.* New York, NY: W.W. Norton & Company, 1993.

Cisneros, Henry. *Preserving Everyone's History.* Washington, D.C.: The Urban Institute, 1996.

Cisneros, Henry. *The University and the Urban Challenge.* Washington, D.C.: U.S. Department of Housing and Urban Development, 1996.

Clay, Grady. *Real Places.* Chicago, IL: University of Chicago Press, 1994.

Comedia Consultancy. *Borrowed Time? The Future of Public Libraries in the UK.* London: 1993.

Committee for Economic Development. *Rebuilding the Inner-City Communities: A New Approach to the Nation's Urban Crisis.* Washington, D.C.: 1995.

Corbett, Anne and Cuff, Penny. *Arts in the Living Downtown: The Next Step,* Washington, D.C.: Washington D.C.: Partners for Livable Communities, 1998.

Council of Europe Publishing. *Culture and Neighbourhoods.* 1995.

Cruikshank, Jeffrey. *Going Public: A Field Guide To Developments In Art In Public Places.* Washington, D.C.: National Endowment for the Arts, 1990.

Daniels, Tom. *When City and County Collide: Managing Growth in the Metropolitan Fringe.* Washington, D.C.: Island Press, 1999.

Dixon, John. *Economics of Protected Areas.* Washington, D.C.: Island Press, 1990.

Dorn, Charles N., editor. *Developing Communities Through Cultural Heritage and Ecological Tourism.* Washington, D.C.: Florida State University Center for Arts Administration, 1995.

Downs, Susan Whitelaw. *Neighborhood-Based Family Support*. Detroit, MI: Wayne State University, May 1994.

Duckworth, Robert; Simmons, John; and McNulty, Robert. *The Entrepreneurial American City*. Washington, D.C.: Partners for Livable Places, 1985.

Envirobook Publishing. *Placemaking in Australia*. Sydney, NSW: 1995.

Ewing, Reid. *Best Development Practices*. Chicago, IL: Planners Press, American Planning Association, 1996.

Fulton, Bill. *Steps Towards Regional Solutions: The Rochester Forum*. Washington, D.C.: Partners for Livable Communities, 1998.

Fulton, William. *New Urbanism: Hope or Hype for American Communities?* Cambridge, MA: Lincoln Institute of Land Policy, 1996.

Furdell, Phyllis. *Paths to Economic Opportunity: Case Studies of Local Development Strategies to Reduce Poverty*. Washington, D.C.: National League of Cities, 1995.

Gardner, John. *On Leadership*. New York, NY: Free Press, 1990.

Garvin, Alexander. *American City: What Works, What Doesn't*. New York, NY: McGraw-Hill, 1996.

Grogan, David; Mercer, Colin; and Engwricht, David. *Cultural Planning Handbook: An an Essential Australian Guide*. Queensland, Australia: Arts Queensland, 1995.

Hayden, Dolores. *Power of Place: Urban Landscapes as Public History*. Cambridge, MA: MIT Press, 1995.

Heath, Shirley Brice and Smyth, Laura. *ArtShow: Youth and Community Development, A Resource Guide*. Washington, D.C.: Partners for Livable Communities, 1999.

Hudnut III, William. *Cities on the Rebound: A Vision for Urban America*. Washington, D.C.: The Urban Land Institute, 1998.

Johns Hopkins Institute for Policy Studies. *A Generation of Challenge: Pathways to Success for Urban Youth*. Baltimore, MD: Johns Hopkins University, June 1997.

Landry, Charles. *Creative City*. London: Comedia Consultancy, 1994.

Landry, Charles and Bianchini, Franco. *The Creative City*. London: Demos, 1995.

Lipske, Mike. *Artists' Housing: Creating Live/Work Space That Lasts*. Washington, D.C.: Publishing Center for Cultural Resources, 1988.

Longo, Gianni. *A Guide to Great American Public Places*. New York, NY: Urban Initiatives, 1996.

Lowenstein, Evan. *The Maryland Smart Growth Initiative: A Report*. Washington, D.C.: Partners for Livable Communities, 1999.

Makower, Joel. *Beyond the Bottom Line: Putting Social Responsibility to Work for Your Business and the World*. New York, NY: Simon & Schuster, 1994.

McNulty, Robert H. and Page, Clint, editors. *State of the American Community*. Washington, D.C.: Partners for Livable Communities, 1994.

McNulty, Robert H.; Penne, R. Leo; and Jacobsen, Dorothy. *The Return of the Livable City: Learning from America's Best*. Washington, D.C.: Acropolis Press, 1986.

McNulty, Robert H.; Penne, R. Leo; and.Jacobson, Dorothy. *The Economics of Amenity: Community Futures and Quality of Life:* Washington, D.C.: Partners for Livable Places, 1985.

McNulty, Robert. "The Role of Nonprofit Organizations in Renewing Community." *National Civic Review*, vol. 85, no. 4 (winter 1996).

McNulty, Robert. *Amenities and Your Community Futures*. Washington, D.C.: Partners for Livable Communities, 1997.

McNulty, Robert. *Community Empowerment Manual*. Washington, D.C.: Partners for Livable Communities, 1999.

McNulty, Robert. *Cultural Tourism in America*. Washington, D.C.: Partners for Livable Communities, 1997.

McNulty, Robert. *Tourism and Cultural Conservation: Insuring Uniqueness of Place* Washington, D.C.: Partners for Livable Communities, 1997.

McNulty, Robert; Jones, Patricia; and Green, Laura. *Culture and Communities: The Arts in the Life of American Cities*. Washington, D.C.: Partners for Livable Places, 1992.

Murfee, Elizabeth. *The Value of the Arts*. Washington, D.C.: President's Committee on the Arts and Humanities, 1993.

National Association of Regional Councils. *A Report on Results of the First National Regional Summit*. Washington, D.C.: 1998.

National League of Cities. *Building Learning Communities: Workforce Development and the Future of Local Economies.* Washington, D.C.: 1995.

National Trust for Historic Preservation. *Getting Started: How to Succeed in Heritage Tourism.* Washington, D.C.: 1993.

Office of Juvenile Justice and Delinquency Prevention, U.S. Department of Justice, *Gang Suppression and Intervention: Community Models.* Washington, D.C.: 1994.

Partners for Livable Communities and Corporation for Enterprise Development. *The Community Reinvestment Scorecard: Identifying Resources, Building Partnerships and Scoring Progress.* Washington, D.C.: 1994.

Partners for Livable Communities and Karlsberger Planning. *Wild Kingdoms in the City: Conference Proceedings,* Washington, D.C.: 1992.

Partners for Livable Communities. "Cooperating for Change: Steps to Strategic Action." Washington, D.C.: *Governing Magazine,* (February 1997).

Partners for Livable Communities. *"Crossing the Line: Conference Proceedings and Workbook on Regional Strategies."* Washington, D.C.: 2000.

Partners for Livable Communities. *Rebuilding American Communities: Reinvestment by Design: A Collection of Best Practices.* Washington, D.C.: 1995.

Partners for Livable Communities. *Town-Gown Dynamics: Best Practices.* Washington, D.C.: 1997.

Partners for Livable Places. *Retrofitting Suburbia: Making it Livable for Aging in Place: Best Practices.* Washington, D.C.: 1996.

Partners for Livable Places. *The Better Community Catalog: A Source book of Ideas, People, and Strategies.* Washington, D.C.: Acropolis Books Ltd., 1989.

Penne, R. Leo and Shanahan, James. *Sourcebook: Economic Impact of the Arts.* Washington, D.C.: National Conference of State Legislatures, 1987.

People for Places and Spaces. *Local Government Culture Development Evaluation and Benchmarking.* Sydney, NSW: 1997.

Pines, Marion. *Family Investment Strategies: Improving the Lives of Children and Communities.* Washington, D.C.: Partners for Livable Communities, 1994.

Pines, Marion. *Putting Families First: Managing Resources to Restore Communities.* Washington, D.C.: Partners for Livable Communities, 1994.

Pittman, Karen. *Bridging the Gap: A Rationale for Enhancing the Role of Community Organizations in Promoting Youth Development.* Washington, D.C.: Academy for Educational Development, 1991.

Pugh, Margaret. *Barriers to Work: The Spatial Divide Between Jobs and Welfare Recipients in Metropolitan Areas.* Washington, D.C.: Brookings Institution Center on Urban and Metropolitan Policy, 1998.

Randall, Paula. *Art Works!: Prevention Programs for Youth & Communities.* Washington, D.C.: National Endowment for the Arts, 1997.

Royer, Charles, narrator. *Back from the Brink: Saving America's Cities by Design* (video). Washington, D.C.: American Architectural Foundation, American Institute of Architects, 1996.

Royer, Charles, narrator. *Becoming Good Neighbors: Enriching America's Communities by Design* (video). Washington, D.C.: American Architectural Foundation, American Institute of Architects, 1999.

Rusk, David. *Inside Game Outside Game: Winning Strategies for Saving Urban America.* Washington, D.C.: Brookings Institution Press, 1999.

Scheie, David M. *Better Together: Religious Institutions as Partners in Community-Based Development.* Minneapolis, MN: Rainbow Research, 1994.

Schweke, William, *Bidding for Business: Are Cities and States Selling Themselves Short?* Washington, D.C.: Corporation for Enterprise Development, 1994.

Sherman, Lawrence. *Preventing Crime: What Works, What Doesn't, What's Promising.* College Park, MD: University of Maryland, 1997.

Smolcic, Elizabeth and Mansfield, Carol. *Black Heritage Tourism: Education or Exploitation?.* Washington, D.C.: Partners for Livable Places, 1989.

Snedcoff, Harold. *Cultural Facilities and Mixed-Use Development.* Washington, D.C.: The Urban Land Institute, 1985.

Social Compact Between Financial Services Institutions and America's Neighborhoods. *Case Studies of Partnership Achievement for America's Neighborhoods.* Washington, D.C.: 1993.

Sperr, Portia Hamilton. *Museums in the Life of the City.* Philadelphia, PA: The Philadelphia Initiative for Cultural Pluralism, 1992.

Spitzer, Theodore Morrow. *Public Markets and Community Revitalization*. Washington, D.C.: Urban Land Institute, 1995.

Stokes, Samuel. *Saving America's Countryside: A Guide to Rural Conservation*. Baltimore, MD: Johns Hopkins University Press, 1997.

Sucher, David. *City Comforts: How to Build an Urban Village*. Seattle, WA: City Comforts Press, 1995.

Transit Cooperation Research Program. *The Role of Transit in Creating Livable Metropolitan Communities*. New York, NY: National Academy Press, 1997.

U.S. Department of Housing and Urban Development. *Beyond Shelter: Building Communities of Opportunity*. Washington, D.C.: 1996.

U.S. Department of Housing and Urban Development. *Cityscape: Issues in Urban Environmental Policy*. Washington, D.C.: 1996.

U.S. Department of Housing and Urban Development. *Cityscape: Bridging Regional Growth and Community Empowerment*. Washington, D.C.: 1996.

U.S. Department of Housing and Urban Development. *University-Community Partnerships: Current Practices*. Washington, D.C.: 1999.

U.S. Department of Justice. *Safe Kids - Safe Streets*. Washington, D.C.: 1996.

U.S. Department of Transportation. *Building Livable Communities through Transportation*. Washington, D.C.: 1996.

Urban Land Institute. *Smart Growth: Economy, Community, Environment*. Washington, D.C.: 1998.

Van der Ryn, Sim. *Ecological Design*. Washington, D.C.: Island Press, 1996.

Walsh, Phil. "Classification of Regional Benchmarking." Washington, D.C.: *The Regionalist*, vol. 2, no.2 (April 1997).

Walsh, Phil, and Davis, Sara. *Partners' Community Indicators*. Washington, D.C.: Partners for Livable Communities, 1996.

Williams, Susanna. *Arts and Culture as Assets for Community Building: A Community Handbook*. Washington, D.C.: Partners for Livable Communities, 1997.

Wireman, Peggy. *Partnerships for Prosperity: Museums and Economic Development*. Washington, D.C.: American Association of Museums, 1997.

Partners for Livable Communities
Community Futures and Quality of Life

In 1995, Partners began Community Futures and Quality of Life, a four-year collaboration with twenty laboratory jurisdictions around the country to define the role livability plays in our cities' futures, and to promote inclusion of livability strategies on each community's social, regional, and economic agenda. The working relationship established with these cities, counties, and state provided the foundation for understanding local problems and defining livability strategies to address those problems.

While some communities view livability in terms of institutions—libraries, parks, schools, museums—and think of them as "luxuries," others have discovered that adopting a livability strategy can assist with issues such as workforce preparedness, at-risk youth, and racial conflict. For example, a museum becomes a necessity when it offers after-school programs to improve the job skills or academic achievement of at-risk young people.

The work in the twenty jurisdictions involved a broad range of issues that covered both programs for people and enhancement of physical places; there were large projects as well as small projects—each jurisdiction adopted a program that was unique to their needs. The common thread of all of these places was a dynamic and innovative leadership with a desire to improve the local quality of life for all citizens.

The participating jurisdictions benefited from Partners' on-site technical assistance; practical information on model projects; workshops, conferences and publications; and networking opportunities with their peers. In turn, Partners discovered a great deal from working with innovative leaders around the country. We salute these individuals, who came from every sector of the community, for their spirit and motivation and thank them for the opportunity to learn.

COMMUNITY FUTURES AND QUALITY OF LIFE PARTICIPANTS

Arlington County, VA	Ft. Wayne, IN	Philadelphia, PA
Atlanta, GA	Kansas City, MO	Pittsburgh, PA
Baltimore, MD	State of Maryland	Richmond, VA
Chattanooga, TN	Shelby County, TN	Rochester, NY
Cincinnati, OH	Minneapolis, MN	San Diego, CA
Cleveland, OH	Orlando, FL	St. Louis, MO
Denver, CO	Camden, NJ	

COMMUNITY FUTURES AND QUALITY OF LIFE SPONSORS

Arlington County, VA	Denver Foundation
Bank of America Foundation	Fannie Mae Foundation
Buhl Foundation	First Union Foundation
City of Chattanooga, TN	Greater Kansas City Community Foundation
City and County of Denver	Gund Foundation
City of Ft. Wayne, IN	McCune Foundation
City of Orlando, FL	City of Minneapolis, Department of Planning
City of San Diego, CA	The Pittsburgh Foundation
City of Cleveland, Department of Planning	Pittsburgh History and Landmarks Foundation
Cleveland Foundation	Shelby County, TN
Cleveland Neighborhood Development Corporation	William Penn Foundation

Partners for Livable Communities
National Center for Community Action

Partners' National Center for Community Action is a comprehensive clearinghouse of solutions to community problems that includes best practices, organizations, individuals, reading materials and other information needed to develop livable communities. It is a resource for decision makers at all levels—city officials, private sector leaders, neighborhood and civic activists—who seek to foster agendas for community success and opportunity.

The Center can provide:
- Best Practices and Case Studies.
- Resource lists.
- Contact information for experts in every discipline of livability around the world.
- Toolkits.

The Center collects information and resources on the following issues:

Leadership and the New Civics
- Developing community visions agendas, strategies, goals, and plans.
- Fostering regional dialogue, visioning, and collaboration.
- Building civic capacity.
- Increasing public participation.
- Goal setting and measuring progress.

People and Human Development
- Strategies for education, public health, children and families, and the elderly.
- Examples of new community programs created by museums, libraries, and other institutions.
- Efforts to improve community safety.
- Programs to build multicultural understanding.

Place and the Physical Environment
- Using cultural and heritage assets to build economic strength and community involvement.
- Strategies for preserving open space.
- Balancing growth and environmental concerns.
- Protecting important natural and man-made assets.
- Planning sustainable development, and effective and efficient transportation and infrastructure.

Jobs and Economic Development
- Job creation and retention strategies.
- Growing neighborhood enterprises.
- Job training skills.
- Harnessing economics of amenity.
- Development strategies for small towns and rural communities.

Finance
- Innovative strategies for funding local efforts to improve the quality of life.
- Fostering public-private partnerships.
- Capitalizing on private philanthropic and corporate support.
- Creating entrepreneurial programs.

International Initiatives
American communities are not the only ones where problems are being solved. Through Partners' international network, the National Center for Community Action also collects and disseminates examples of community and regional solutions to the problems of leadership, finance, people, place, and jobs from abroad.

Contact Information
Partners for Livable Communities
1429 21st Street, N.W.
Washington, D.C.
202.887.5990
202.466.4845-fax
partners@livable.com
www.livable.com

Photo Credits

The following individuals, organizations and jurisdictions generously loaned images to illustrate this report.